Visual Cues

Visual Cues

Practical Data Visualization

Peter R. Keller   Mary M. Keller

Library of Congress Cataloging-in-Publication Data

Keller, Peter (Peter R.)
    Visual Cues / Peter and Mary Keller.
        p. cm.
    Includes bibliographical references and index.
    ISBN 0-8186-3102-3
    1. Science—Methodology—Handbooks, manuals, etc. 2. Engineering—Methodology—
Handbooks, manuals, etc. 3. Visualization—Techniques—Handbooks, manuals, etc.
    4. Computer graphics—Handbooks, manuals, etc. I. Keller, Mary.
Q175.K29 1992   92-23865
502.85'66—dc20   CIP

Copublished by

IEEE Computer Society Press
10662 Los Vaqueros Circle
PO Box 3014
Los Alamitos, CA 90720-1264

IEEE Press
445 Hoes Lane
PO Box 1331
Piscataway, NJ 08855-1331

IEEE Computer Society Press Order Number 3100-04   IEEE Press Order Number PC0286-5
Library of Congress Number 92-23865
ISBN 0-8186-3101-5 (microfiche)
ISBN 0-8186-3102-3 (case)

Additional copies can be ordered from

IEEE Computer Society
  Press
10662 Los Vaqueros Circle
PO Box 3014
Los Alamitos, CA 90720-
  1264

IEEE Computer Society
13, avenue de l'Aquilon
B-1200 Brussels
BELGIUM

IEEE Computer Society
Ooshima Building
2-19-1 Minami-Aoyama
Minato-ku, Tokyo 107
JAPAN

IEEE Press
445 Hoes Lane
PO Box 1331
Piscataway, NJ 08855-
  1331

This book was acquired, developed, and produced by
Manning Publications Co., 3 Lewis Street, Greenwich, CT 06830
Copy Editor: David Lynch
Cover Design: Krzysztof Lenk
Book Design: Paul Kahn
Printed in Hong Kong

Contents

Preface vii

Acknowledgments viii

Introduction 1

    Purpose 2

    Audience 2

    Structure 3

    Vocabulary 3

    Background 4

Section I   **Effective Visualization 5**

Visualizing Data: Focusing on an Approach 6

    Identifying the Visualization Goal 7

    Removing Mental Roadblocks 7

    Deciding Between Data or Phenomena 10

    Constructing Ideal Images 12

    Conclusion 13

Output Media: Communicating the Visualization 14

    Types of Output Media 14

    Image Components Affected by Medium 14

    Selecting an Output Medium 18

    Conclusion 19

Design: Selecting and Arranging Image Components 20

    Image Components 20

    Design Principles 23

    Conclusions 24

Color: Managing a Complex Component 26

    Selecting Color 26

    Formulating Color 29

    Color-Output Media 31

Conclusions   33

Additional References   33

Section II   **Illustrated Techniques   35**

Organization of Examples   35

Presentation of Examples   36

Using the Examples   37

Computer Science Resources   38

The Process of Visualization   39

Illustrated Examples   43

   1 Comparisons and Relationships   43

   2 Multivariate   52

   3 Time   65

   4 Process   74

   5 Animation   82

   6 Motion   94

   7 2-D Data   105

   8 Surface and Slice   115

   9 Volume   126

   10 Models   136

   11 Multiform Visualization   147

   12 Artistic Cues   159

   13 Black and White Examples   169

Appendixes   Appendix A: Choosing Visualization Techniques   183

Appendix B: Taxonomy of Visualization Goals   187

Appendix C: Major Visualization Goal of Image   200

Appendix D: Number of Variables   202

Appendix E: Discipline and Application   204

Appendix F: Hardware and Software   207

Appendix G: Contributors   210

Glossary   213

Index   224

Preface

Our longstanding interest in visualization and our many years of helping others use visualization has led to this book. We share our experience to demonstrate how the available visual tools can help you meaningfully depict your data. Other publications have described visualization use in specific disciplines, or have concentrated on analyzing how an algorithm produces an image. Those approaches appeal particularly to experts in those respective fields. In our work with scientists and engineers, however, we have found they almost always approach visualization pragmatically; their primary interest is in the application of available tools and techniques that can help explore, analyze, and communicate information about their data.

In accordance with our experience, *Visual Cues* shows by example the generic information that a visualization technique reveals about any data on which it is used. We have found that emphasizing what a technique reveals frees users to focus on what they want to see in their data independent of algorithm and discipline, and we believe this approach will work equally well for those in other disciplines.

We offer 150 examples that show effective techniques to use to analyze and present data. Some of the techniques may seem obvious to the computer scientist who daily works with visualization. Those in other disciplines will most likely find much that is new or not obvious. From the selection and descriptions of the images to the discussions on data visualization, output media, design, and use of color, our emphasis is on providing practical information to help you use visualization effectively and efficiently in your offices and laboratories.

We dedicate this book to our parents, who taught the value of completing the task.

PETER R. KELLER
MARY M. KELLER

Acknowledgments

Visual Cues has been accomplished with the encouragement, inspiration, and help of many. Peter credits the book's genesis to the support and encouragement he received from three of his former supervisors at Lawrence Livermore National Laboratory: John Horvath, Len Margolin, and Donald Vickers. They possessed keen insight into the direction of computer-graphics technology and its value to scientists and engineers. Each encouraged Peter's collaboration with scientists and engineers so that he might help identify unrecognized graphics needs and devise new graphics techniques to better aid their research. Because of those collaborations Peter realized that many expect to benefit from visualization without having to become visualization experts.

A source of inspiration was Minh Duong-van, a physicist at Lawrence Livermore studying the nature of chaos in a variety of application domains. Minh's contagious enthusiasm for discovering new meaning in data inspired Peter to develop visualization techniques that permit rapid data exploration and analysis and that quickly and visually "prove" a concept. This fast-paced collaboration led to the realization that graphic techniques could be considered entities, independent of the data, application, output medium, and stage of image construction.

We acknowledge the contribution of all who answered our request for examples of visualization. Without their help the writing of *Visual Cues* would have been much more laborious. Most respondents were the actual creators of the images they submitted; a few respondents recognized the significance of another's work in visualization and took time to submit an example, crediting the image creator. All individuals whose visualization examples appear in *Visual Cues* are listed alphabetically in Appendix G. Names of contributors also appear on the page with their visualization image.

During the writing of *Visual Cues* many people supported us by suggesting topics, submitting material, providing secretarial support, or reviewing the numerous drafts. We acknowledge: William Banks, Mark Blair, David Butler, Scott Carman, Kenneth Charron, Raymond Cochran, John Compton, Patrick Crowley, Michael Feit, Dorothy Freeman, Terry Girill, Kevin Gleason, Diane Governor, David Handeli, Christel Horten, John Horvath, Gene Ledbetter, Albert Miller, Amal Molik, Henry O'Brien, Patricia Parsens, Dan Patterson, Viviane Rupert, Joseph Sefcik, Thomas Thompson, Jaylene Tingley, Venkatesw (Rao) Vemuri, Donald Vickers, Claudia

Watkins, Steven Wehrend, Richard Williams, and George Zimmerman. A special thank you goes to Gary Shaw for his organization of the original book design requested by the publisher. This design was the foundation for the subsequent writing. We especially want to thank Marjan Bacé of Manning Publications for his support, guidance, and friendship throughout the development of *Visual Cues*.

Numerous people helped ensure high quality in preparation of the text, images, artwork, and design; we are especially grateful to Earl Aldrich, Rita Anderson, John Blunden, Mark Bussanich, Elizabeth Caires, Marjory Cantor, Lynn Costa, Gary Graff, Arlene Hee, Nancy J. Hill, Barbara Kahn, Paul Kahn, Christina Keller, Peter Link, David Lynch, Margaret Marynowski, and Kelly Spruiell.

Those who had a large but thankless part in reviewing all or parts of the final tome richly deserve our thanks: John Ambrosiano, Chris L. Anderson, Tom Bennett, John Blunden, David E. Breen, Stewart Brown, Robert W. Conley, Roger Crawfis, Said Elghobashi, Kirby Fong, Gary Graff, Beverly Hobson, William Hobson, Carolyn Hunt, Thomas Kelleher, Cynthia Keller, James Keller, Jackson Mayes, Umberto Ravaioli, Susan Schoenung, Nancy Storch, Roy Troutman, Richard Ward and , David Wells. We especially want to recognize Nelson Max for his technical review of the front chapters, carefully pointing out matters we had overlooked.

Any large organization has its maze of rules, regulations, and required approvals. We wish to thank those from the Lawrence Livermore National Laboratory management and staff who helped guide us through the maze, including Edward Bodily, Robert Borchers, Dennis Braddy, Scott Buginas, William Dunlop, Richard Dyer, Rex Evans, Bill Fulmer, Robert Lormand, Charles McCaleb, Coralyn McGregor, Charles Miller, Leland Minner, Ronald Natali, Dale Nielsen, David Nowak, Michael Pratt, Gerald Richards, Jack Russ, Diana Sackett, Henry Sartorio, Marty Simpson, Sandra Sydnor, and John Verity. We especially want to thank Ann Abers, William Masson, and Diana (Cookie) West whose knowledge and help were indispensable to our success.

We also want to thank other friends and coworkers who helped more than they probably realize. Their interest and occasional query, "How is it going?" or their invitations that provided refreshing breaks from the writing routine were just the tonic to help us maintain the momentum. And we cannot omit Albert "Thor" von Rott Hutte, our ever-present, always willing, but undemanding diversion and reality check.

Portions of this work were performed under the auspices of the U.S. Department of Energy by Lawrence Livermore National Laboratory under contract No. W-7405-Eng-48.

Introduction

The ever-increasing power of computers, which enable the generation and process-ing of vast amounts of data, creates an imperative for techniques that facilitate exploration, analysis, and communication of that data. More and more, that imperative is being effectively answered by using the capability of computers to present data in graphical form. Indeed, the popular media often carry colorful computer-generated images that communicate data in ways understandable to the non-expert.

The proliferation of such colorful images implies that meaningful visualization of data is routine in laboratories and offices. Although such published examples certainly provide evidence of what is possible, the reality is that how to achieve the possible is not widely known. The description of such images usually emphasizes the application, discussing what is being learned about the data; the techniques that accomplish the image are secondary and presented in terms specific to the application.

Such discussion, though certainly valid, hides the fact that the techniques could be used with a whole range of applications, disciplines, data structures, and data formats. *Visual Cues* asserts that although each discipline has its own data, the kind of information that specialists want to depict and convey about data is often universal. Physicists may want to reveal the structure of fluid flows, medical doctors may want to reveal the structure of a malignancy, geologists may want to reveal the structure of oil deposits, and meteorologists may want to reveal the structure of a tornado. Of the many techniques available that reveal structure, most can usually be applied to any data regardless of application, discipline, structure, or format. In our examples, we emphasize visual cues that communicate information indepen-dent of any specific hardware products or software techniques; most tasks could be accomplished by any of several products or techniques.

From our experience we know too that specialists usually want to focus on their field of study and have no desire to become computer graphics experts in order to use visualization. Therefore, we omit the details on how visualization algorithms are derived and instead emphasize the results that can be obtained with algorithms. Our many examples present a broad spectrum of available visual cues, most of which can be created by one of the many visualization algorithms already available. Our examples are intended to enable generation of a meaningful image by linking the knowledge of a discipline and the knowledge of visualization. Having examples that show which visual cues reveal which information can eliminate guesswork and may also suggest other meanings to look for in the data.

Purpose

Our purpose in writing *Visual Cues* is to help make the possible doable—to put visualization capability in your hands by:

- Presenting a large collection of visualization images, some of which may relate to your current work.

- Describing generically the visualization techniques used to construct images in a variety of disciplines.

- Emphasizing the kinds of information revealed by a visualization algorithm rather than details about the algorithm or the application.

- Providing a handy reference work you can peruse when actually looking for a visualization technique to illustrate data.

- Introducing a methodology for selecting a visualization technique.

- Providing basic information about output media, image design, and color, knowledge of which is vital in creating an effective image.

Scientific visualization is a broad, rapidly evolving field filled with complexity. We use our eyes to visualize the world day after day—isn't it incongruous that scientific visualization can be so complicated? In *Visual Cues*, we generally hide the complexities and instead focus on practical aspects that you can apply to data in your discipline.

Audience

Visual Cues is addressed to several audiences who can be generally classified as either the consumers of visualization or the facilitators of visualization. We include as consumers all those who benefit from the construction and viewing of an image of their data. Physicists, engineers, medical doctors, geologists, physiologists, and statisticians are examples of some of the many who might be so categorized. Facilitators of visualization are the "visualization specialists" and include, among others, computer scientists, systems analysts, artists, computer graphics programmers, and designers. Visualization specialists help consumers analyze data, perhaps by programming algorithms, suggesting image layout and design, applying knowledge of the physiology of color, or using any other combination of talent that helps bring out the meaning hidden in the data.

Visual Cues may be especially helpful for those in a research setting, who often have voluminous, novel, or poorly understood data to explore, analyze, and present. Our experience indicates that researchers need to visually validate their data, trying many representations to determine which parts of the data deserve greater study and analysis. The analysis phase tests one or more hypotheses; the results are then communicated with a visual emphasis that highlights the results. Such needs may require the use of many visualization techniques before the researcher discovers how to proceed with the data. The many examples in *Visual Cues* can be a resource for techniques to use when visually exploring data.

You do not have to be directly involved in visualizing scientific data to find *Visual Cues* helpful. Managers of organizations that need visualization will find a survey of visualization techniques that could help determine appropriate tools for their staff. Commercial artists and computer artists will find *Visual Cues* a practical source for ideas to create their artistic message. *Visual Cues* can also serve as a convenient compendium of examples of different techniques for teachers and students to use for discussion and comparisons. The book can be perused for ideas, studied for details, or used as a communication tool by anyone who sees the value of the computer as a visualization medium and communication tool.

Visual Cues has two instructive sections, seven appendices, a glossary, and a general index. In Section I, we draw on our experience and offer tips for selecting visualization techniques and designing images to clearly communicate the intended meaning. Section II consists of images using visualization techniques from contributors worldwide in disciplines as different as medicine and astrophysics and computer art. Throughout the book, the images in Section II are referenced by a boldface number, for example, **11-9**. Most of these images suggest practical ways you might use visualization to understand or communicate something about data. We have selected them not because they are flawless, but because they illustrate a technique, an approach, a solution for visualizing data that is a bit different from each of the other images. The diversity is meant to stir the imagination as well as to show what is possible. In our accompanying descriptions, we give the technique for deriving each image, including the visual cue or cues that help communicate meaning hidden in the data, the specific application using the technique, the hardware and software that created the image, hints about using the technique, and cross-references to related or contrasting examples in *Visual Cues*. **Structure**

Each appendix provides a point of entry to the book. Appendixes A and B introduce a methodical way of locating possible techniques that some consumers of visualization have found useful. The methods emphasize the advantage of determining the meaning to be derived from data before data are visualized, instead of plotting data and then looking for meaning. Other appendixes list the major goal of image; number of variables; discipline (such as solid state physics, fusion engineering, or astronomy); hardware and software used; and contributors.

We have designed *Visual Cues* so that you can obtain a quick overview or detailed information. Skimming the succinct summaries and captions next to the images in Section II can provide you with global knowledge of visualization and how to use it. More careful reading of the sections and Appendixes A and B can teach you the basic tricks of the trade and direct you to specific techniques for accomplishing your visualization goal.

In the extensive glossary we define many technical terms that appear in *Visual Cues*. But as in many new disciplines, the meaning of some common words and phrases can vary depending on the definer's emphasis or on the hardware or software product. We clarify our use of a few such words. **Vocabulary**

Scientific visualization in this book means the study, development, and use of graphic representations and supporting techniques that facilitate the visual communication of knowledge—that make computer images speak to us.

Visualization means the bringing out of meaning in data.

Data means any form of number created by or input to a computer, including scientific data, engineering data, medical data, statistical data, computed data, measured data, scanned data, simulated data, approximated data, smoothed data, sparse data, and voluminous data. Data are simply the numbers the computer knows about.

Technique is the method, rule, step, procedure, or algorithm used in the construction of an image. Among these are data-representation techniques, layout and design techniques, visualization algorithms, data-conversion algorithms, and procedures for creating or constructing contextual cues.

Background We gleaned the images in Section II from more than 1000 examples submitted by more than 100 respondents to more than 1000 requests sent to participants in major visualization conferences, schools offering degrees in computer graphics and related disciplines, and major vendors of visualization hardware and software. We chose these sources because we wanted to include mainly examples of current work. Each contributor was asked to briefly describe the image. From these initial submissions, we selected images that represented a broad cross-section of disciplines and techniques and then requested more specific information from each contributor. We rewrote that information to achieve an even standard of exposition and returned that writeup to the contributor for technical review. The complete book was then reviewed by several experts, which led to further refinements. The images themselves were collected on photo, viewgraph, printer output, and a various electronic file formats. To create a uniform graphical appearance, we converted all formats to Apple Macintosh TIFF file format. Adobe Photoshop was used to crop, size, and perform minor editing of the images for consistency and clarity. Text was composed on an Apple Macintosh IIcx, with Microsoft Word. Word and TIFF files were imported to Aldus Pagemaker for design and layout and to produce the color separations for printing.

Section I
Effective Visualization

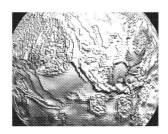

Computer hardware and software are making the visualization of numerical data increasingly easy and affordable. With these improvements also comes the capability of using more and better visual cues to reveal and depict the meaning of data. Now it is possible to impart greater meaning to visualization by using visual cues that illustrate motion, suggest relationships, or relate data to the phenomenon being studied. The challenge now is learning how to efficiently and effectively use these abundant resources and tools to reveal the meaning in the data.

We believe that successfully meeting this challenge first requires determining what meaning is to be conveyed in an image and then choosing the technique that best depicts the meaning. Another important—though often downplayed—aspect of meeting this challenge is managing such image components as size, placement, color, and labeling to ensure that an image clearly conveys the intended meaning.

Attention to such components is even more important when presenting an image to an audience. Besides providing tools for exploration and analysis, visualization offers a powerful tool for communicating meaning to others. For years, commercial advertising has used graphic presentations to sell products. Now scientists and engineers and others are beginning to recognize that visualization greatly enhances their efforts to gain support for research, to help them get needed funding. A visualization that clearly conveys the meaning of data not only helps explain the researcher's ideas but also casts a glow of credibility and capability.

In this section we draw on our experience in helping scientists and engineers meet the challenge of producing meaningful images from their data. We present our method for selecting visualization techniques. We also offer guidelines for selecting an output medium, designing an image, and handling color. We point to many examples in Section II to illustrate our advice. We are your guides as you construct effective images and avoid problems that can obscure or distort the information in your data. Many of the details we cite are easy to overlook, but ignoring them can result in a confusing or an unintelligible image.

Visualizing Data: Focusing on an Approach

The very abundance of visualization techniques can make selecting the one most appropriate for bringing out the meaning in data a perplexing search—a difficult, frustrating, and time-consuming aspect of visualization. If your thought process is like ours, you most likely rely first on experience. If nothing appropriate suggests itself, you may turn to other convenient sources: programs that colleagues are currently using or a new technique a friendly programmer offers. In each instance, you study the resulting image for any useful information it may reveal. This reflexive "try, then study" approach may eventually yield an image that reveals the meaning in the data, but it is just as likely to yield an image that is pretty but useless.

A methodology is needed for selecting visualization techniques, but the nascent discipline of scientific visualization does not yet have pat formulas for selecting appropriate techniques. A focused approach like that outlined in the following paragraphs is one we have found successful. It is meant to eliminate obstacles that may obscure valuable techniques.

In describing this approach, we have sometimes used a broad brush to depict a complex subject. Wherever we introduce a simplified view, we also refer you to texts with more detailed discussion. Our goal in simplifying is to quickly put an image of your data in your hands by shielding you from detail while building your understanding of scientific visualization.

The main points in our approach are to:

• Identify the visualization goal: We identify the meaning we seek in the data before we begin to construct an image. Knowing the goal, we may recognize new sources of techniques; meanwhile we have a focus for determining if a prospective technique is likely to reveal the meaning.

• Remove mental roadblocks: We regard data as nothing more than numbers bearing information to be visualized. When we think of data as belonging to some application or having some structure, we unnecessarily limit ourselves in imagining possible techniques.

• Decide between data or phenomena: We distinguish between data-representation and contextual-cue techniques. Data representation shows the data values independent of the phenomenon; the viewer must deduce the relationship to the phenomenon. Contextual-cue techniques relate the data values to the phenomenon being studied and add meaning to the visualization. Deciding whether data or phenomena are the focus further refines the visualization goal.

Beginning data visualization by first identifying the visualization goal may give some pause, but we believe identifying the goal is the cornerstone in constructing an effective image. The goal is the meaning you hope to derive from the image, and, if appropriate, the meaning you want to communicate to others about your data. Identifying what you want to learn helps you select techniques that will produce an image communicating that meaning if the data support it. Just as a builder must know the building plan to select the correct construction materials, so too should you identify the desired result before proceeding to select techniques for visualizing data.

Usually data visualization consists of exploration, analysis, and then presentation—if the visualization is used to communicate with others.* Identifying the ultimate visualization goal may be evolutionary, reflecting the stage in the visualization process in which we are involved. Exploration, the searching of data for new relationships, usually means many trial-and-error data representations and requires interactive adjustment of data or image. Analysis, the study of known relationships among data, may require metrics or other precise means for comparison. Analysis and exploration are generally accomplished by one person or a few, and images that result need not be pretty or refined; they may even be unlabeled and, hence, meaningless to someone not familiar with the data or problem. Presentation is the "publication" of data for the benefit of others; the image should be aesthetically appealing, properly annotated, and intelligible.

How do you identify a visualization goal? Regardless of where you are in the visualization process, you need to ask such questions as Why am I looking at these data? What is important about the data? Am I comparing, associating, locating, verifying, finding, ranking, searching? What do I hope to learn? What do I want the image to say? What do the data prove? What do I expect the data to prove? In the exploration stage, the goal may be less focused than in the analysis and presentation stages. See Appendixes A and B for possible goals.

In fact, you are already identifying visualization goals, though perhaps subconsciously, when you input data to a graphics utility you have used for similar data. The unstated goal may be, "Compare this image with the prior image." Or this idea might be at the back of your mind, "If it is wrong, I will know it," meaning, "Verify the correctness," or again, "Compare this image with the correct image." The more you can focus the goal, however, the more effectively you can construct images. **11-1** provides a good example of how the visualization goal affects technique selection. Both images are constructed from the same data, but because each image uses a different color palette, each depicts different information. In **11-1,** Figure A, the goal may have been "reveal shape," and in **11-1**, Figure B, the goal may have been "examine structure." Identifying the goal permits the selection of the appropriate color palette. The more specific the goal, the better focused and more useful the visualization.

Here again, we suggest an approach that may seem untraditional. Our experience with scientists and engineers leads us to believe that many have been conditioned to regard data as some entity with inviolate properties. This rigid thinking may

---

* Some visualization specialists distinguish types of visualizations by the terms *personal*, *peer*, or *presentation*. We prefer to distinguish types of visualization by the terms *exploration*, *analysis*, and *presentation*, which emphasize the functional aspects of visualization.

narrow the choice of techniques. We urge you instead to think of data only as numbers—numbers that a computer knows about. If data are only numbers, you can then consider any image-construction technique for the data. Treating data thus eliminates artificial constraints imposed by associating data with their origin (discipline or application), format or structure, or dimension. Instead you can consider any technique that will reveal the meaning in your data. This approach also diverts you from the common practice of using a familiar representation and then trying to figure out what you see in the representation.

Eliminating Constraints of Discipline and Application

Thinking of data as medical, mechanical-design, fluid-flow, oil-industry, satellite, or earthquake may focus you only on the image-construction techniques already used in that discipline. Techniques from a different discipline, however, might better represent data or might suggest modifications to the technique you are using. For example, if you have engineering data, you should not automatically use a CAD/CAM/CAE package for visualization. **2-4** and **2-11** visualize complex engineering data with general-purpose visualization techniques. **2-4** uses color and 3-D to visualize tensor qualities. **2-11** also chooses color and 3-D and adds glyphs. Of course, using a technique associated with the discipline from which your data come is often entirely appropriate. The important point is that you should select a technique because it produces the result you want, not because it is traditional in a discipline. Exploring the visualization techniques useful in other disciplines can enhance your ability to find those useful for your own data.

Eliminating Constraints of Format and Structure

Data-representation techniques do have specific format and structure requirements, and data in each discipline tend to be collected in specific formats and structures. For example, much of mechanical engineering data are geometry data, medicine data are image or scanned data, satellite data are signal (time-history) data. Therefore, selecting a technique with the same format and structure requirements that your data have seems logical. The data fit easily into the conventional utility requirements. But if the familiar or usual technique does not best depict your data, you should consider other techniques and not be deterred because your data are in a format or structure unacceptable for use with that technique. Data-conversion algorithms allow you to convert data to fit different requirements, and therefore to use other available techniques. It is usually easier to convert data to a technique to which you already have access than to write a new, equivalent technique.

Here's an example: you may think that an irregular (nonrectangular) array of real numbers cannot use imaging software because such software generally requires a rectangular array of integers from some image-scanning device. It is easy, however, to change the format of an irregular array from real to integer, and its structure, too, is easy to approximate with a rectangular array. The converted array can then use imaging software.

Among the images that use data conversion in *Visual Cues* is **8-4**, an example of how data with one structure can be converted for use with an algorithm that requires a different structure. An algorithm generates a 2-D slice of data through a 3-D pressure field. The 2-D slice is then pseudocolored by a conveniently available algorithm and merged with the 3-D model to relate the data to the model. **10-5** provides another example of structure conversion. The data, originally represented on a square mesh, were converted to an irregular triangular mesh to take advantage of increased rendering speed.

Other algorithms that convert or modify data take randomly positioned data and convert them to regularly positioned data, minimize noisy data with smoothing algorithms, or create planar data by passing a plane through a volume of data.

You can find algorithms for data conversion in numerical analysis and computer graphics journals. Also, each of these four books describes a few conversion algorithms: Andrew S. Glassner, ed., *Graphics Gems* (San Diego: Academic Press, 1990); James Arvo, ed., *Graphics Gems II* (San Diego: Academic Press, 1991); David Kirk, ed., *Graphics Gems III* (San Diego: Academic Press, 1992); and William H. Press et al., *Numerical Recipes* (Cambridge, Eng.: Cambridge University Press, 1986).

We urge you not to hesitate to convert data to a different format or structure because you fear that conversion may introduce errors in approximation. Such errors, though harmful if the data are to be used for continued simulation, generally cannot be discerned in the data representation of an image. Ignoring conversion errors, especially in the exploration phase of visualization, encourages rapid evaluation of techniques. Our experience shows that positional errors introduced are small and errors for data values even smaller. Whether these errors are tolerable depends, of course, on the application. An architect's plan for uniform air temperature in a small room is less critical than a surgeon's plan for risky, delicate surgery. Generally, though, errors are tolerable during exploration but must be accounted for in analysis.

Data conversion can be a complex, tedious issue that may have to be addressed for accurate analysis. But if you find a visualization algorithm you want to use, we suggest that you convert your data to the algorithm's input format and structure rather than rewrite visualization algorithms to work with the format or, worse yet, forgo constructing a meaningful image because you think your data cannot be used with the algorithm.

Eliminating Constraints of Dimension

Thinking that the representation's dimensions or number of variables must be the same as those in your data can also channel your thinking and eliminate useful techniques. For example, in selecting a representation technique you can often treat a 2-D scalar field and a (single-valued) 3-D surface as the same kind of data set. You can then use the same visual techniques for both kinds of data. **7-3** illustrates how a 2-D scalar field can be represented as a 3-D surface. Conversely, a 3-D surface can be projected on a plane and the values treated as 2-D, a technique commonly seen in U.S. Geological Survey maps, for which data on elevation are projected to a plane that is then represented as a contour map. With either data set, the 2-D representation can be a contour plot or pseudocolor plot, and the 3-D representation can be a shaded surface. The shaded surface could also include isolines and color.

Nor should the number of variables limit your representation choices. A variable is said to be a dependent if it is a function of another variable (called an independent variable). In the equation $y = f(x)$, x is the independent variable and y is the dependent variable. You can use the common x-y scatterplot to study the relationship. If you have a two-variable data set x and y (say temperature and humidity), where x and y are measured at the same point, you have two variables. There is no defined relationship. You can visually determine if there is a relationship, though, by using the same x-y scatterplot as you used to show the relationship between the independent and dependent variables. In using a visualization technique, it often does not really matter whether you have two variables or one dependent variable and one independent variable. Whether it makes sense to choose the technique is another question, determined by what you are trying to learn from the image, not by the relationship between the variables.

Multivariate data can be especially challenging because of the many dimensions or variables. We illustrate several ways of handling multivariate data in the multivariate category of Section II. Also, the dimensionality of multivariate data can sometimes be reduced by combining variables and then analyzing the data. **2-1** uses a three-variable technique effectively to analyze the relationship of four variables. On the other hand, data can be redundantly encoded to permit low-dimension data or data with a few variables to use a technique that requires higher-dimension data or more variables. **7-2** illustrates data redundantly encoded to height and color. An effective technique for handling multivariate data is to divide and conquer by representing each variable relative to another on a scatterplot. If random structures appear in some scatterplots, they may indicate a less important relationship between the variables. The variables related to the random-appearing scatterplots may be ignored for the moment, resulting in a lower-dimension data set to investigate.

Our aim is not to describe all possible ways of thinking about data, but to show that the same data set considered differently allows you to imagine different representations. The appropriateness of the representation will depend on the data.

Deciding Between Data or Phenomena

Techniques are the collection of rules, procedures, and algorithms whose systematic application produce an image that communicates the meaning implicit in data. We distinguish between the data-representation techniques that represent the numeric values of data and the contextual-cue techniques that provide additional clarifying, interpretive meaning to the representation of the data.

Data-Representation Techniques

Data-representation techniques are those well-defined algorithms that take data as input and deliver an image as output. A simple example is the 2-D contouring algorithm, which takes a 2-D array of values and returns a set of isolines. Surface plots that show shape and texture; volumetric plots, which include a number of techniques that expose relationships in 3-D; x-y plots; scatterplots, histograms, and bar charts are other techniques for representing data.

Contextual-Cue Techniques

Visualization achieved by contextual-cue techniques is somewhat equivalent to the special effects with which photographers, artists, and moviemakers deliver meaning to viewers. The cues may result from parameters in the computer program that control the output's appearance from a data-representation algorithm, or they may be the special effects introduced in the image by adding or removing other graphic elements. Contextual-cue techniques are usually applied apart from the data-representation algorithm; examples that suggest the properties of the phenomenon being studied are models, coastlines, motion blur, haze, bounding boxes, perspective, and color. The techniques can also make representations of data values and relationships more readable, such as numbered scales and grid lines that make values readable or the color, size, and position of abstract objects that suggest value and relationships.

Relating Data to Context

For an image to clearly communicate a visualization goal, you usually must incorporate both data-representation and contextual-cue techniques in an image. The need to distinguish between and to use both kinds of techniques brings to mind Hamming's statement:

The purpose of computing is insight, not numbers.

To provide insight you must do more than symbolically represent the numeric values of data; you must also relate those values to the phenomenon that the data represent. We offer the following simple example to show the additional insight communicated by using contextual cues that represent or identify the phenomenon.

Assume we have a 100×100 square array of numeric data values to examine. Pseudocoloring the values according to the visible light spectrum (blue, low; red, high) reveals a cluster of red that locates the maximum. Now we have an image that conveys the relative value of the numeric data. What does this cluster actually represent? The scientist studying the data values knows the cluster represents temperature measurements of a circuit board on which the components that are running too hot are to be identified and replaced. The meaning communicated by the image, however, is simply, "high values are located."

If on the array of colors we use contextual-cue techniques to superimpose labeled, white, rectangular outlines representing individual components on the circuit board, the cluster of red now locates and identifies the hot component and the meaning becomes "hot circuit component identified." We have changed our emphasis from relative values of the data to meaning of the data by also showing the phenomenon the data represent.

Initially in constructing an image, you may use only data-representation techniques that visualize the numeric values of data. But for effective presentation to those unfamiliar with the data, an image that represents the phenomenon is a necessity. We also believe that even for those familiar with the data, a representation of a phenomenon is more valuable than a numeric representation. A phenomenon representation more clearly reveals the meaning and more accurately presents the information. **8-4** illustrates the increased meaning available in such a representation. In the figure, color depicts numeric values of a 2-D pressure field. Those familiar with the origin of the data know that a launched space shuttle creates the pressure field. But even for them, superimposing the context, the 3-D model of the shuttle, instantly shows the relationship of the pressure field to the shuttle configuration.

Representing Phenomena

When phenomenon is your focus, you should select techniques that create cues corresponding as closely as possible to the viewer's experience with the phenomenon. Color, shape, texture, or setting may suggest the phenomenon: blue can suggest water, arrows can suggest projectiles. **2-13** and **7-8** choose color to suggest the properties of the phenomena being studied and to help the viewer draw conclusions. **10-8** applies color to suggest the planet Mars and photographer's tricks to add the depth cues. The teacup in **10-4** provides the setting that indicates the fuzzy white objects are steam. **1-1** adds lines describing the shape of the world and its continents to bring meaning to the measured ozone data. The shape the data describe can also suggest meaning, as in **10-2**, where the viewer recognizes the shape as that of a backbone.

Choosing techniques to represent the phenomenon may require some creative or artistic talent, especially if the phenomenon is abstract or has never been seen, such as the inside of a proton, or a black hole. To illustrate such phenomena, you may add abstract cues to suggest the expected environment of the phenomenon, as in **6-3**, where color represents the quark property and motion blur and position illustrate interaction in a phenomenon never seen.

Ideas for contextual cues may be found in art books, design books, television commercials, and, closer to home, in Edward R. Tufte's *Visual Display of Quantitative Information* (Cheshire, CT: Graphics Press, 1983). The data-representation techniques are usually found in graphics systems or graphics libraries, such as PV-Wave, AVS, Explorer, and NCAR Graphics. More recent data-representation techniques can be found in the *Graphic Gems* series previously cited in this section.

Constructing Ideal Images

The continuum of understandable visual techniques seems to reach from

Instantly understandable to
Takes some study time to
Requires additional schooling.

The ultimate goal of visualization is to create complete images that "speak" to the viewer without additional explanation. To demonstrate what we mean when we say "speak," we ask you to recall computer-generated images or to thumb through the images in this book. Some will simply and clearly speak to you—you will understand the images immediately. Others will require some time to view and ponder, but then you will understand. And no matter how long you study some images, they will be no more than images—they will not speak to you. We realize immediate understanding may not always be attainable, but we believe you must have such a goal for each image lest the image (and by implication, you) communicate poorly or imprecisely, or not at all. We assert that the end purpose of an image is to facilitate communication of knowledge, not merely to display or represent data.

To understand the challenge of visualization, we compare art and scientific visualization to show why visualization may be so difficult. Both have the goal of communicating visually and symbolically. The artist, in using such established tools as canvas, brushes, and oils to illustrate a point of view, benefits from the knowledge of centuries. The tools of scientific visualization—output device, data-conversion software, software to depict data—as well as the knowledge of how to use them are still evolving. The computer's power is needed to handle voluminous data, convert data, and apply visual techniques that reveal and communicate meaning hidden in data. The available computer tools, however, sometimes impair or limit ability to display data meaningfully or artistically. Scientific visualization is in its infancy. Computer artistry is a long way from representing data with the proficiency of a Michelangelo, Van Gogh, or Picasso.

Meaning and beauty are in the eye of the beholder. For any set of data, a spectrum of correct representations could accomplish the visualization goal, but even more representations would not. The correctness of a representation depends on your purpose. A complex, obscure representation might be quite adequate for personal use, but a general audience will need a simplified, obvious representation. Again, the goal for any representation is to make information about the data values or the phenomenon clear and immediately obvious to the viewer.

To facilitate constructing images that effectively communicate the meaning of the data, we advocate thinking of an image as comprising a visualization goal, one or more data sets, and a collection of techniques, each deliberately chosen to communicate the meaning that is in the data. The data are numbers that can be converted or transformed to be input to any representational technique.

Although we suggest not classifying data so that other data-representation techniques can be considered, it is certainly possible that the best visualization is the one commonly used with those data. The best solutions to problems in data visualization result from considering the possibilities and selecting the most appropriate. And if the familiar technique best communicates the meaning of the data, then it is the most appropriate. If you have a technique that works, by all means use it. Understanding is always the goal.

The relationship between the visualization goal and the choice of techniques for accomplishing that goal is just beginning to be understood. Appendix A lists generic visualization goals, suggests techniques to accomplish the goals, and points to examples from *Visual Cues* that depict the techniques. Appendix B formalizes the relationship between goal and technique by defining terminology to use in classifying the goals.

Output Media: Communicating the Visualization

Implicit in visualizing data is that the resulting image will be displayed on a medium that will make it possible to communicate about the data. Output media can range from paper to CRT* to virtual reality devices. In our discussion, output media are the final means for *rendering* images; these media are not necessarily the same as those used when *constructing* images. In fact, the two frequently are different because the medium on which an image is constructed is likely to be inconvenient for communicating to others the meaning in the data. And therein lies a problem. The image that looks great on one output medium can be unintelligible when output to another medium.

Let us next discuss problems that you may confront if you initially construct images on a CRT but then render them to different output media, and list factors for you to consider when selecting an output medium. We intend this discussion to help with routine output of data between media, not to transform you into a media maven. If your next production is to compete with a Hollywood creation, we suggest collaborating with an expert.

Types of Output Media

Output media for displaying data consist of both the traditional and the new. We discuss the media that are traditionally used and generally available: CRT, paper, transparencies, movie film, 35-mm slides, and video. For simplification, we make video synonymous with television, TV, VCR, VTR, VHS, NTSC, and others. A television set is also a CRT and monitor, but for clarity, CRT and monitor here mean high-resolution devices. Less commonly used output media such as HDTV, stereo CRT, 3-D projection, Omnimax, virtual reality, and multimedia are all possibilities to use, but are not discussed in *Visual Cues*. We assume that *the CRT is the medium used to initially construct images and that the images are then sent to other output media for the final rendering.*

Image Components Affected by Medium

Currently, images cannot be sent from one medium to another with impunity. To ensure that you will see the desired effects in the medium to which you send an image, you must adjust for the requirements of the final output medium before you send the original image to it.

---

*CRT = cathode ray tube = workstation = workstation CRT = office CRT = VDT = PC CRT = monitor.

The adjustments can be extensive and can directly affect design and composition of the original image. Also, the same image may be displayed on more than one output medium, requiring adjustments for each medium. The sooner you know the output medium or media on which your image will finally be rendered, the easier it is to accommodate differences. Even at best, several iterations are usually necessary to achieve the same communication effect in another output medium as we have on the CRT.

Constructing an image on one medium to be output to another may drastically affect the information the viewer sees: colors can change, obscuring important features or altering meanings; detail can be lost; objects can be distorted or changed, or even disappear; and timing can affect perception. Knowing how media handle color, how resolution varies among media, and how proportions and image area change with different media can prevent major problems when you switch from the CRT to other media.

Color

For practical purposes, CRTs, film,* and video create color by combining (adding) red, green, and blue (RGB model) and then directly transmit those combinations to the eye. Most printers that produce paper and transparencies create color by applying cyan, magenta, yellow, and sometimes black (CMYK model) to a medium that subtracts some color from white and reflects the remaining color to the eye. We discuss these two ways of creating color in some detail in the paragraphs on color beginning on page 26. The colors of images created additively on a CRT and output to a medium that subtractively creates color will not look the same on the second medium; in fact, they could appear radically different. For example, the red and green combination that produces yellow on the CRT produces a muddy color on a printer. Depending on the media hardware and software, this color-model difference may be minimized or avoided because technology is becoming available that will mask or avoid color incompatibilities between media.

Other problems with color may also originate with how software or hardware systems handle black, white, and clear, particularly when rendering to a transparency. If black is the background color on the CRT, it may be mapped to clear on the transparency. If the white is drawn in white it will not be seen when projected; often, therefore, white is automatically drawn in black on a transparency by the system software creating the transparency. This automatic selection of black or white may become a problem when the annotation in the image says, "Notice the white." Or suppose you have a color scheme like **5-10**, where the colors range from blue to red to white. How will rendering to a transparency treat white? If the white is converted to black, then the smoothly varying color table will abruptly change to black at the maximum. Each system is different and may or may not have optional controls over how colors are converted.

The background color of the output is sometimes determined by the medium. For example, transparencies have a clear background, and the color of paper determines its background. But the background color of the CRT may be black or white or any other color. If that background is selectable, choose one that will match the final output medium to avoid or minimize color differences between the media.

---

* For simplicity, we ignore the intermediate creation of a negative and the film chemistry.

Although CRTs and video both create color additively, the results are very different. The color encoding of the video cannot represent the very vivid colors displayable on the workstation CRT, and the video's electronics are often unable to cleanly reproduce adjacent contrasting colors. Also, abrupt changes in color can create shimmering, halolike or other ghostlike artifacts around the edges of vivid colors. Separating large areas of vivid color with neutral, black, or white lines, or limiting the color choices to pastels can minimize such artifacts. The colors produced by video are so different from those originally designed on a workstation CRT that we strongly recommend equipment that allows simultaneous display of the video image. Even with the simultaneous display, you still should preview the video on the actual equipment on which the video will be shown. Differences in hardware or in manual settings, such as tint, brightness, or contrast may require further adjusting to ensure that you see the colors you want to see.

When rendering images to film for animation, color integrity problems can arise if portions of the film are developed at different times. Temperature and chemical mixtures used to develop film are so critical that a color shift may be evident where the different batches of films are spliced. If all the film cannot be developed in one batch, we suggest that you minimize color shifts by structuring the animation as a collection of scenes (just like Hollywood) and developing a complete scene all in one batch. Using transition techniques such as fade, wipe, window, or title, from one scene to another, can diminish a color shift.

The most practical rule we can offer about color is to allow enough time to evaluate color selection in the chosen output medium and to change colors if necessary. If you are not using a turnkey system, then do not expect to get it right the first time, or the second!

Resolution

Resolution is the quantity of detail that can be clearly shown on the output device. When images are rendered to a lower-resolution medium, detail becomes less distinct and some data may even disappear. Similarly, in images rendered to a higher-resolution medium, detail supplied by dots may become too small to discern. Therefore, you must always consider how the resolution of an output device will affect an image.

Of the various output media, film and paper best match the resolution seen on the workstation CRT. Video, on the other hand, because of its much lower resolution, greatly degrades the detail seen on a CRT. Details evident on a CRT will be lost or blurry in a video. The hardware industry is eliminating some difficulties (for one, it is converting CRT to video images), but some hardware simply ignores the even or odd horizontal lines in the image. This selectivity could be a problem if important lines in an image happen to be drawn on the lines that are ignored. To preview images destined for conversion to video, we recommend constructing CRT images with a 256 × 256 pixel definition, which approximates the apparent resolution of an average video.

Another problem with resolution can occur when you create an image on a CRT and print it on a commonly available higher-resolution 300-dpi laser printer. The printer-produced details may be barely discernible because the dot sizes of the CRT may be much smaller when reproduced on the printer. Our solution is to draw the dots on the CRT as a square array of 4, 9, or 16 pixels or, if available, to invoke the specific printer command that causes wide lines or large-diameter dots to be printed.

Proportion and Image Area

Many data-representation techniques are implemented to operate on data arranged on a square grid in a 1:1 aspect ratio, but if a nonsquare output medium is used, the 1:1 ratio must be adjusted to avoid image distortion. For example, if you are constructing an image with a 1:1 height-to-width ratio, but rendering it to a slide (typically 2:3 ratio), a transparency (typically 8:10 ratio), or video (typically 3:4 ratio), you may need to rescale an axis just prior to rendering to ensure that the 1:1 aspect ratio is retained. Different proportions may also drastically alter the shape of objects and letters, requiring you to resize the components to ensure that the intended meaning remains.

The amount of information displayed can also be altered between the CRT and video or between the CRT and slides. Whereas the CRT image area shows the image edges, television hides these edges by stretching an image beyond the television screen. If the full image area of the CRT is output to video, then approximately 10 percent of each edge of the image will be plotted on the part of the television screen that is hidden from view. Crucial information may not be seen unless the image is designed with nonessential material at the four edges, or the image is plotted so as not to use the entire image area of the CRT. Our own approach is to reduce the CRT image size by 20 percent. The image is generally smaller than necessary on the video, but we have yet to lose information because the image on the television screen is stretched. Similar allowances need to be made for slide mounts, which cover the edges of an image area.

Proportions for slides and transparencies can also require adjusting if image components are plotted with vertical orientation. Although projectors allow for either horizontal or vertical displays, many conference-room and auditorium screens on which you might display the images are horizontally oriented. Consequently, you may lose part of a vertical image off the top of the screen. The safest approach is to plot all images to a horizontal orientation.

Timing

Rendering images to film or video requires other adjustments besides those that may be necessary to account for differences in color, resolution, or image size. You are probably using film or video to animate data, and so you must time images to ensure they effectively convey meaning. Image duration and the speed of the image's apparent motion are the critical timing aspects. In an animation, each frame is displayed on the screen for a fraction of a second (1/16 second for silent film, 1/24 second for sound film, and 1/30 second for video). This speed contrasts with still-frame projection (slide, print, or transparency), where information can be on the screen for several seconds or even minutes. These differences in viewing times and the physiology of the eye require that you present a limited amount of changing information in each animation frame and that you repeat the frame enough times to allow at least 1/8 second for the viewer to perceive the content. Before beginning a complex sequence we recommend advising the audience where to look in the animation for specific details.

With film or video, viewers are attempting to understand data using a sequence of images viewed at a fairly rapid rate. If apparent motion of objects is too fast, viewers can be distracted by jerky motions or the wagon-wheel effect, where motion appears to reverse. The scene's duration depends on the complexity of the changing information being shown: the more complex, the slower the animation should be.

Slow motion can be accomplished by simply replicating the images (or running at low speed), but this slowing may cause jerky movements. Smooth slow motion requires computing intermediate frames. Our solution is to prepare animations for presentation by planning to repeat a scene four times: slow, fast, slow, fast. Presenting the "slow motion" first gives us the opportunity to point out the features of interest, which then can be absorbed during the second, faster showing. Depending on the audience's reaction, we may not find it necessary to show the last one or two repeating scenes.

Scene transitions also require timing adjustments. Unless you intend to jolt the audience by abruptly switching scenes, hold the first and last images of a sequence for a second while increasing or decreasing the brightness. The movie industry calls this technique fading in or fading out. We suggest fading because it is effective and easy to implement.

Animation timing also affects text on a frame. The text, which should be minimized in animations, has to appear on screen long enough to be read. (Our rule of thumb is to leave text on the screen long enough to be read aloud.) An unchanging title need not appear on every frame; it can be an introductory title to the animation sequence. Except for a digital clock or similar conventional readouts, numbers that indicate a changing amount should be removed from frames. Setting any axis scale to some constant value and letting the data change with respect to the fixed scale eliminates a distracting, jittery image.

If you add sound or narration to an animation, the duration must be adjusted to accommodate the length of the sound or narration. We strongly recommend sound or narration because the movie and the television industries have conditioned audiences to expect such accompaniment.

Selecting an Output Medium

No output medium is ideal for all circumstances, but knowing the advantages and constraints of various media can help you select the best one for your purposes. We list and discuss some factors that could affect your choice of an output medium.

• *Purpose.* If the image is for personal use, almost any medium is acceptable because of familiarity with the data. If you are communicating with an audience, then you must consider how much detail or which features are necessary to convey your message.

• *Level of detail.* Generally, CRTs on which images are constructed provide the best quality. Film, paper, and slides can come close to the CRT, but output quality can be degraded by printer and film output devices of poor quality. Transparencies and video cannot convey as much detail because they can handle only a narrow color range. Video may also lose detail because of low resolution. And high-resolution devices may also lose detail if any dots or lines are plotted too small to be seen.

• *Quantity of text versus quantity of graphics.* With animation, text should be minimized.

• *Production time.* Once the colors are acceptable, paper or an instant print transparency is as quick as video. Film takes longer for developing and processing. Animation is time consuming because of the many parameters that need adjusting, especially the timing of the presentation.

• *Availability of projection equipment.* Most conferences and organizations can provide equipment for slides, videotape, and transparencies, all of which support color. Lead time may be needed to set up and adjust the equipment.

• *Availability of support staff and talent.* Before undertaking an involved visualization project, be sure you have or can get the necessary expertise. Animations, particularly, require specific knowledge.

• *Convenience.* Printer paper and transparency are probably most convenient. The use of other output media depends on which are integrated into your work environment.

• *Impression on viewer.* The medium that produces the highest resolution and best color reproduction will affect the viewer most. Video usually has the lowest resolution, but animation generally is more effective than a still image. Film animation can offer both high resolution and good color reproduction.

• *Color constraints.* Each medium has a different range of possible colors. Be sure that the range you want is available on the selected medium.

• *Cost.* The cost varies for each medium according to quality and features, which can range from amateur use to professional production. In general the media that cost least are the printer devices that output paper and transparencies because labor costs are minimal. Slide or film output is usually more expensive because a specialist has to handle the product. An animation, regardless of medium, is most expensive because of the cost involved with getting the correct timing of the animation.

• *Size of audience.* 35-mm film gives the brightest image for a large screen in a large hall; use of video projectors and transparencies should be limited to smaller audiences and smaller screens. (Video projectors that produce bright images, though costly, are becoming more widely available.) Paper output is best used with very small groups.

Conclusion

There are not yet any magic "turnkey" systems that cause the image to look the same when output to different media. A few innovative software developers provide procedures for calibrating color between media. This calibration may minimize the color differences between media, leaving few problems because small differences in color appearance generally will not affect the meaning conveyed in the visualization. If you want an image to convey the same information independent of output medium, then a practical rule of thumb is to design images for video using pastel colors and minimal detail.

Allowing time to create a second version, or at least periodically evaluating the image on the final output medium, is crucial. Previewing the output in actual viewing conditions is also advisable; at the minimum, know the actual viewing conditions so that you can make needed adjustments. The paragraphs on color later in this section offer more information on the effects of room lighting systems on the image's appearance.

Design: Selecting and Arranging Image Components

Jackson Mayes, Lawrence Livermore National Laboratory, Livermore, CA, was a principal contributor to this discussion.

Selecting a technique for visualizing data and a medium for conveying the resulting image is only part of the process of communicating the meaning of data. The various components that depict the data must be selected, arranged, and displayed so that the intended meaning will be easily and correctly comprehended. We next present general information about image components and their effective use as well as design principles that help produce an easily comprehended image.

Image Components

For simplicity of discussion, we group image components into four categories: color, grayscale, and black and white; lines; type; and background. Their function, use, and relative importance vary with the meaning being communicated. We discuss here how to select and use these components to best communicate the intended meaning.

Color, Grayscale, and Black and White

Color, grayscale, and black and white are appropriately used to represent properties of data, such as value or classification. Because these are often the most prominent components in design, they are frequently the first components about which you make design decisions. Color is eyecatching, but it is not always available, and even when available is not always the most effective way to visualize data. If you have access to both color and black and white, you want to choose the more effective to visualize the meaning in data.

Color does add a dimension to an image; its effectiveness is not to be ignored. We are all in marketing, whether we are promoting our ideas to gain research support or to sell a new product. Color can create excitement and a favorable bias toward ideas or products. Meaningful color can be added to a grayscale or black-and-white image to redundantly encode data and create a stronger impression. But you should avoid introducing color that does not add or support meaning; unrelated color can contribute confusion as the viewer tries to discern meaning.

Grayscale and black and white encourage simplicity. Among their advantages are the limited number of shades available for discriminating objects. Grayscale also removes such color complexities as the physiological, psychological, and media influences that are discussed in the paragraphs on color. And medical doctors prefer black-and-white x-rays to pseudocolor x-rays because of the greater range of contrast through the grayscale. Many professional journals still favor black and white to avoid the additional cost of color. In Section II are selected images that effectively use black and white and grayscale to communicate meaning. **13-9**, Figure A, shows how white quickly locates a hot spot. **4-2**, Figure B, and **13-10** use grayscale to group or cluster like meanings.

11-4 illustrates differences between effective use of color and black and white to reveal the meaning of data. In Figure A, color effectively and quickly communicates the location of extremum, but specific values are difficult to determine even though a detailed color key is part of the image. The reverse is true in the black-and-white image, Figure B, where specific values are easily identified, but the extremum are not so easily located. **2-4** and **13-3** also display the appropriateness of color and black and white. Both images use wire-frame models to depict data. In **2-4**, color clearly identifies stress points, which are the object of the study. In **13-3**, the wire-frame model depicts position; color would not greatly enhance understanding. **13-2** was submitted in both color and black-and-white versions. The color may offer more eye appeal but reveals no additional information.

Lines

In a black-and-white image, lines may be the major component, but they are also important in color images. Lines can be solid, dotted, or broken. Lines connect, show relationships, separate, delineate, indicate direction, highlight, locate, orient, suggest size, and add perspective. Line sizes range from thin to thick and are measured in points in the printing industry and in some computer software: the higher the point number, the thicker the line. Other software measures line thickness as a percentage of screen size or as fractions of an inch; still other software provides predefined widths from which to select.

Generally, a line's importance determines its thickness within the size context of the image's other components. In **13-7,** two line thicknesses provide important reference points and indicate distinctions. The bolder lines represent and locate the configuration of an experiment. The thinner, more numerous lines, without overwhelming the other components in the image, delineate changes in dot density that would otherwise be hard to distinguish. Thin lines can indicate subtle relationships, as in **5-3**, or can better define shape as the thin bounding lines do in **9-3**. The thin lines in **9-3** are necessary to define the volume and terrain, but their thinness avoids any confusion or interference with the heavier lines that indicate important locations. Dotted or dashed lines may indicate pathways, as in **5-8.**

Lines do not impact the eye as color does, but they do impact the eye's ability to discern the meaning of an image. In **1-1**, thin, solid lines outline geographic references and highlight the circumference of the circles; dotted lines indicate latitude and longitude and also suggest 3-D. Using the two kinds of lines distinguishes their functions and provides orientation cues for comparing data on the two circles. Without the lines, much more verbal explanation would be required to understand the data. **5-10** also exhibits subtle but very important lines. Without the bounding lines, the viewer would see a blob of colors; the lines tell the viewer to read the image as 3-D. **8-7** uses lines to highlight perpendicular slice planes, making it easier to distinguish their intersection. Grid lines add perspective and the bounding lines indicate the volume without detracting from the slice planes. Tick marks help identify locations. In all these examples, the lines are not the focal point of the image, but without them the images would be very difficult to understand.

Type

The adage that a picture is worth a thousand words notwithstanding, minimal annotation usually enhances understanding of even the best images. Using key words to title an image or to explain, label, or call out an image's components supports the meaning in data. Selecting the wrong type size or style, however, or using too much, or positioning type incorrectly, can detract significantly from the meaning. We emphasize that use of type in an image should not substitute for producing an image that in itself communicates the meaning of data. An image cluttered with words defeats the reason for visualizing data and is probably not effective.

The many sizes and styles of type may not all be available via the computer, but a large selection is not needed for most visualization work. Some knowledge of how to select from available options will help you create a more effective image. Type size is denoted by height, which is measured in points (72 points to the inch). This text is set in 9 point type. (In some computer systems type size is measured in fractions of an inch or characters per line, or is selected from a set of predefined sizes.) To some extent, the type size you select depends on your intended use for the image; among the factors besides legibility are personal or audience presentation, publication, or screen use. Generally, type size should be chosen for its proportion to the components to which it relates; it should also help indicate relative importance of components. All type, even the image title, should always be secondary and complementary to the image. You should carefully place type so that the primary image components occupy the principal image space. If the data representation competes with text, the image loses effectiveness.

Type styles, called *typefaces* in the printing industry, range from functional to fanciful. Typefaces are classified as *serif* or *sans serif*. Sans-serif typefaces are clean and unadorned, resembling the block letters many of us learned to print in our early school years. In contrast, serif typefaces have finishing lines or adornments at the end of line strokes, some of which may be very fanciful. Typefaces are also available in condensed or extended styles, with very narrow or very wide spacing between letters, and in different stroke weights, the most general classifications being light, medium, and bold. Weight, like size of type, may denote relative importance. A typefont collects all the characters in one size of typeface. (Some computer software, however, uses typefont to mean all the characters, regardless of size, in any one typeface.)

Using the same typeface and only two or three sizes or weights of type within an image or throughout a related series of images provides unity. Legibility, so that viewers can quickly read the annotations, is always the first guide in choosing typefaces. Typefaces characterized by heavy strokes with or without serifs tend to fill in, making them hard to read. Closely spaced words and lines of type are also hard to read. Displaying words in all capital letters obscures word shape, an aid to word recognition, and should generally be avoided. **13-11** shows good type use: the title is in the largest type, though it does not overpower the image; the cities are in the same typeface but smaller, their relative importance indicated by weight of type; and annotation is minimal.

Typefaces should also match the intended meaning of an image. For most scientific and engineering images, simple sans-serif faces are best. A serif face that does not harm legibility can also be appropriate, however. An elaborate serif typeface suggesting grace and gentility may look fine in **12-5** but would look out of place in an image displaying scientific or engineering data. If you select a good technique to represent your data and apply good design principles, then, indeed, very little type is needed.

Background

Any image has a finite area or proportions in which to arrange, size, and display the image's components. The area not filled with primary components, the background (called negative space in the art world), is not leftover space but is as important a component in the image as are any of the others. Properly used, background enhances, supports, and highlights the main elements in the image. **5-5** and **6-7** demonstrate how using the background as contrast enhances the main components of an image. **9-2** specifically colors the background to show field effects. **12-5** and **12-8** show how background provides supplementary information about the main subject of the image. **12-7**, by using background to reflect an unseen area, and **8-3**, with shadows in the background, reveal additional information but still maintain focus on the primary object in the image. The background in **5-2** adds perspective, telling the viewer to read the image as 3-D. Filling the available image area with only primary information can overwhelm and obscure meaning.

Design Principles

Design principles may mistakenly be dismissed as aesthetic rules that contribute little additional insight or meaning. In reality, even in the preliminary stages of image construction, design is vital for ensuring speedy comprehension and accurate interpretation. Significant information may be obscured if a component blends with the background instead of contrasting, or if too many data are represented in one image, or if the grayscale or colors selected do not adequately distinguish data. You may minimize application of design principles if no one else is to see your image. When an image is shown to an audience, however, you must apply design principles if you are to communicate the intended meaning. For supplementary reading we particularly recommend Edward R. Tufte, *The Visual Display of Quantitative Information* (Cheshire, CT: Graphics Press, 1983).

Complexity

In composing an image, one of the first determinations should be the quantity of information to display. The broader the audience, the less complex the image should be because usually time is too short to explain in detail a complex image to an uninformed audience. Images for your own use can be more complex because you are familiar with the subject and usually have more time to study and analyze content. **2-12** and **2-13** are complex images that are valuable to researchers who are familiar with the subject or who have time to study and understand the image. For larger, more diverse audiences, images should be simpler and more direct, and require less active participation by the viewer to understand the content, as in **1-1**, where very little additional information is needed for any viewer to understand the meaning.

A good guide for determining complexity is "The Magic Number 7 plus or minus 2."* Oriental artists typically restrict compositions to five elements. Studies indicate the human brain can best handle seven unrelated elements, more or less, simultaneously. The spread from five to nine can be a function of viewers' familiarity with the topic, viewers' fatigue, or distraction in the viewing environment. We strongly advise creating a second image whenever the number of elements exceeds seven. Simplicity and directness are always good principles of communication.

Complex images can be simplifed in other ways too. You can relate a smaller portion to the whole by zooming in on, or magnifying, a portion of the image, as in **5-3** and **8-2**; or relate a detail to the whole with cutaways, as in **9-1**. **8-11** examines the details in three orthogonal views of an object by creating the appearance of stacked cubes and then projecting the surface values of the object for subsequent visualization in the cube. **3-8** shows the detailed behavior of one point on a surface representing a snapshot in time of three-axis displacement.

Orientation

The image's orientation and the relative position of its elements can greatly affect comprehension. A horizontal, or landscape, format is preferred to a vertical, or portrait view, partially because it corresponds to the normal field of vision. Also, most output media are horizontally oriented. Some subjects, however, such as geophysical logs or tall structures, are better rendered with the long edge vertical. If you have to present a vertical subject in a horizontal format, the resulting adjustments could provide space for image elements that are not a function of height, such as text.

Positioning objects within an image is a way to focus the eye on the elements you want to be noticed. In **2-10**, the object represented in the image was rotated to position the small flipperlike glyphs in the foreground and to avoid having them obscured by the taller glyphs. This adjustment also brought the active, more interesting, more important elements to the foreground.

Viewing angles are another aspect of orientation, but rather than consider rotating and tilting the object, you can transport the viewer to another vantage point. In **11-12**, the viewer examines the data from two positions. In **4-8**, Figure A, the viewer sees the block diagram at an angle.

Conclusions

• Simple images are best for communicating; complex images risk adding confusion and should be used only with a well-informed audience.

• Background is an integral part of an image used to emphasize and support the main idea in the image.

• Type style should be simple, legible, and uniform; type size should vary according to the importance of objects it identifies and should always be secondary to objects it identifies.

• In 3-D images, symbols representing data should be oriented so that the most important information is easily seen.

• Different orientations of the same data can reveal different information.

---

* G. Miller, *Psychological Review* 63 (1956): 81–97.

• Effective, logical, pleasing design affects meaning and impact in all phases of image creation, and is a necessity in images used to communicate with audiences not familiar with the subject.

• Lines can be subtle but powerful components of the image that unify, separate, relate, and focus.

• Black and white, grayscale, and color can represent the properties of data.

• Color can classify information and is effective in distinguishing a range of values.

Color: Managing a Complex Component

Jackson Mayes, Lawrence Livermore National Laboratory, Livermore, CA, was a principal contributor to this discussion.

The availability of color greatly increases your ability to efficiently communicate the meaning in data. Correctly used, color is a kind of shorthand, allowing you to communicate in one image information that would take several black-and-white images or much explanation. But useful though color may be, it is also a very difficult element to use effectively. Artists spend a lifetime experimenting with and refining their use of color. And researchers continue to learn more about the physiological and psychological relationships between color and our perception of it. Without some knowledge of this complex element, you are as likely to contribute confusion by using color as to contribute enlightenment.

In these paragraphs we distill information from computer graphics, design, art, physiology, and psychology on three topics we believe most relevant for the consumer of visualization who wants to create effective color images: color selection, color formulation, and color differences among output media. We pass over the complexities of color-table construction and color-model transformation because available software utilities hide such detail. If you do wish to understand the detail, we refer you to James D. Foley et al., *Computer Graphics: Principles and Practice*, 2nd ed. (Reading, MA: Addison-Wesley, 1990). For a broader but still introductory survey, we recommend an easy-to-use program, Interactive Color,* available for the Apple Macintosh from San Diego Supercomputer Center. As with the other discussions in this section, we offer general information that our experience indicates will help produce an effective image.

Selecting Color Before constructing a color image, you should verify that color will most effectively communicate the content of your data. Color is best used to identify, classify, locate, and lend realism. Color may also be used to quantify a range of values, but is not so effective for fine distinctions or exact measurements. Once you have verified that color will best convey the meaning of your data, which colors do you

---

*If you are familiar with Internet and the Macintosh system, Interactive Color is available at press time by anonymous ftp from sds.sdsc.edu (or IP address 132.249.20.22) in directory sdscpub.dir/applemac.dir/graphics.dir as *interactive_color_sit.hqx*. This program must be converted with BINHEX and uncompressed with STUFFIT before execution. BINHEX and STUFFIT are publicly available from many bulletin-board systems.

select? Effective color selection is part science, part art, but some knowledge of the science of color is needed if you are to apply the art of color.

Properties of Color

Several models describe or specify the properties of color, but we discuss only the three relevant to *Visual Cues*: the HSV (hue, saturation, value) model, a simple way to describe the perceptual features of color; the RGB (red, green, blue) model, a common way of specifying colors for CRT display; and the CMYK (cyan, magenta, yellow, black) model, used to specify colors for printer output. The RGB and CMYK models relate to output devices and are discussed later in this chapter.

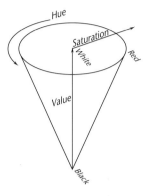

The HSV color model, represented by an inverted cone, describes the perceptual properties to consider when selecting colors to represent data. Hue is the name of a color: red, orange, yellow, green, blue, or purple. Changes in hue rotate around the axis of the cone. Saturation describes the purity or vividness of the color and is greatest at the outer edge and least at the center of the inverted base of the cone. Value (intensity) describes the lightness or darkness of color. The darkest colors are those close to the apex of the cone. On the back cover of *Visual Cues* is a color wheel, which shows actual hue changes rotating about the center of the wheel and greatest saturation at the edge of the wheel. The color wheel corresponds to the base of the inverted cone.

A main reason for color being such a complex element is that perception of color is relative both to viewing context and to the viewer's visual system. Nearby colors interact to affect hue, saturation, and value. For example, the same color appears less saturated against a dark background than against a light background. Two objects of the same size look larger or smaller depending upon their color relative to the background on which the color is placed. A light-colored object on a dark background appears larger than if the same object is dark colored and on a light background. Color also apparently changes as the ambient light level increases or decreases or when the color of light changes. The supermarket produce section takes good advantage of the latter property. Do you select nice, yellow bananas only to discover green bananas when you get them home? The bananas probably were displayed under a light that caused the eye to perceive more yellow and less green.

To further realize how relative perception of color can be, recall that red-green color blindness is prevalent enough in the population that manufacturers of traffic signals add yellow to the red and blue to the green so that people blind to red and green can still perceive a difference between the red and green signals. The differences in the physiology of each person's visual system practically guarantee that even under the same viewing conditions two viewers will perceive colors differently. A color key can minimize perceptual misinterpretations; but the relativity of color suggests that you should always evaluate the colors in your images in their final context to ensure that the intended effect is still perceivable, and that you should allow time and resources to make any necessary adjustments. The relativity also means that ultimately you must be satisfied with approximations of the colors you select.

Color Schemes

A good color scheme is one that effectively conveys the meaning of data. When possible, the color scheme should capitalize on the power of suggestion and take advantage of real-world or conventional uses of color. **7-8** is an interesting example of how real-world color associations can aid comprehension. The image relates the properties of diffusion particles to the colors of geographic features: blue in various saturations suggests oceans or lakes and represents empty areas that contain no particles; green suggests earth and represents particles connected to (or grounded to) the emitting source; yellow suggests sand or the seashore and represents a boundary between the empty areas and the grounded areas. Another familiar color association is shown in **10-8**, which depicts data about the planet Mars in red. The color scheme in **2-13** uses real-world associations by designating orange to represent oil, a color associated with motor oil, and the litmus-paper indicators red and blue to represent acids and bases. **7-2** uses the convention of blue (low) to red (high), ranging through the color spectrum, and **11-3** uses the convention of blue for cold and red for hot. Another convention is the use of dark colors for greater weight or density.

The following hints should help create useful color schemes. But regardless of how familiar you are with the rules of using color, you should not expect to produce the desired effect on the first iteration. At best, minor adjustments are usually necessary.

• *Minimize the number of colors selected.* The simultaneous use of many colors, especially colors representing unrelated objects or ideas, can overwhelm the viewer. Most often, five is the maximum number of colors that should be selected for an image, and fewer are preferred. With two broadly different saturations of one color you can depict two facets of data with just one color. With only two colors, red and blue, **9-8** depicts electron density. The two saturations of red and blue each effectively depict two electron densities.

• *Use contrast to emphasize the main objects in the image.* Contrast makes objects stand out. Color contrast may be achieved by choosing colors differing in hue, saturation, or value.

• *Minimize the number of highly saturated colors.* Saturated colors compete for the eye's attention. The large wavelength differences between red and blue and between yellow and purple make these color combinations particularly difficult for the eye to focus on simultaneously, especially if they are highly saturated. These colors do not compete as much if the saturation of one of the pair is decreased. The inability of the eye to easily focus simultaneously on red and blue or yellow and purple can be used to enhance 3-D by putting red or yellow in the foreground and blue or purple in the background. Such color choices capitalize on the eye's limited depth of field. When the eye focuses on the foreground, the background is blurry and vice versa. In the lower image of **9-8** the highly saturated red and blue enhance the 3-D effect, and the less saturated blue provides good contrast.

• *For backgrounds, choose neutral colors that provide adequate contrast to the main components of the image.* Good choices are the cool colors (green, blue, purple), which appear to recede, seem small, and suggest a passive or less active status. The neutral grayish-blue tone in **9-8** provides an unobtrusive, contrasting background. **12-10** illustrates how warm reds and oranges emphasize major components and how cool blues depict less important components and provide contrast for the more important ones.

• *Use like colors to suggest like meanings.* Color should have a consistent meaning within an image. **11-9** illustrates this point by coloring like objects the same in both figures. Use of the same color can be extended to background color to group related components within an image or even among images in a series. See **4-2**, Figure B, which uses gray to group related components, and **4-5**, which uses the same background color to relate a series of images.

• *When distinguishing classes of objects, select complementary colors evenly distributed on the color wheel (see back cover)*. This matching ensures that the color combination will be visually pleasing yet will differ sufficiently to provide good contrast, as **7-3** demonstrates.

• *Use additional cues to delineate shape.* The color system of the eye is not sensitive to shape, but contrast differences can help the eye discern edges. Outlining an edge is another way to help the eye discern the division between two colors. **11-9**, Figure A, uses all three cues: saturated red, yellow, and green are good contrasting colors; brightness varies among and within the colors; and the green shapes are outlined in yellow. Blues are difficult for the eye to focus on, and thus are a poor choice where shape recognition is important, particularly for letters.

• *Use adjacent colors, especially with the same saturation, on the color wheel (see back cover) to suggest subtle difference.* **3-7** uses similarly saturated adjacent colors to show varying densities.

• *Gradually increase or decrease color saturation to effectively show a continuum of change.* **2-10** varies the saturation of purple to show gradual hardening of plastic. The ease with which the eye detects slight changes in saturation varies across the spectrum. To see this effect, compare the number of distinct colors you can distinguish as you move closer to the center of the color wheel (see back cover).

• *Use pastels (less saturated hues) to convey continuity.* They tend to blend and wash into one another.

• *Use a sudden color change to mark a critical level.* **7-6** uses a sudden color change to show change of sign, and in **3-7** a sudden color change reveals the location of a shock wave.

• *Be aware of potentially misleading color illusions or effects.* Gray regions may appear to have a hue opposite that of the surrounding color; for example, a gray region surrounded by green will appear reddish. The eye also mixes the colors of adjacent small areas of color; for example, on a CRT the eye may perceive small areas of red interleaved with small areas of green as yellow. When small areas are an integral part of the image, it is better to use black, white, or gray to denote the area. For example, in **13-10**, the small black-and-white blocks are very distinct, but if color were used, the distinctions probably would not be so sharp. Another misleading effect, *mach bands*, occurs where two colors of different intensities meet and give the illusion of intensity changes where none exist. Suspected new features observed in an image should be verified by selecting different color schemes and observing areas of potential illusions.

Formulating Color

Once you choose a color scheme, you need to select the colors of the objects that are to be depicted. There are two general ways of selecting color: direct color and indexed color. With direct color, which allows the use of millions of colors, you individually specify the intensities of red, blue, and green each time you select a color. With indexed color, the color intensities are already specified and are arranged (indexed) in arrays called color tables.

The color table is similar to an artist's palette on which a painter places pigments preselected to create a painting. Colors are indexed (often 0 to 255) and are frequently arranged according to a logical plan for their use in an image. The order of colors, often used to show relative values as in **3-7** and **7-6,** is generally more important than the exact intensity values. A computer program may be able to access several color tables, each a different list of ordered intensities of red, green, and blue to create specific effects. Generally though, only one color table is used to create an image.

Colors are selected by choosing an index number in the selected color table; data to be plotted in color are mapped to the color index. Lacking a predefined color table, you can design your own in software by creating an indexed list of ordered colors. The previously cited *Computer Graphics and Principles* can provide help in creating color tables. In *Visual Cues*, we focus on indexed colors and suggest here uses for some easily created color tables. In many instances, we point to examples of these color tables in Section II. You can use these same arrangements of color with direct color, but you must specify the individual intensities of red, blue, and green each time you select a color.

• *Light spectrum (rainbow):* Follows the order of hues in the rainbow and has the convention of "cool" (blue, cyan) to "warm" (yellow, red) colors. **3-3** indicates sea-surface temperature with this color table.

• *Modified light spectrum (rainbow):* Defines hues from dark to light and also orders hues according to the rainbow. Such a color table is useful if an image is to be published in a black-and-white journal because it lets us use color on the CRT and also plots well as a black-and-white image.

• *Contrasting colors at extremes passing through gray:* Ignores midrange values, a useful strategy when studying deviations from a mean. Figure iv, page 41 illustrates the use of this color table.

• *Color bands:* Creates a contouring effect and helps quantify a range of values. **3-4** and **6-4** indicate contour shape with this color table.

• *Discontinuous color:* Shows values above and below a threshold; the contrast provided by the discontinuity is an attention-getting device. **7-6** uses a discontinuous color table to show change in direction, and **5-12** uses discontinuity to distinguish sea from land.

• *Random colors or sequences of contrasting colors:* Helps identify structure or order in what at first appears to be noise. These color tables are particularly useful in displaying data that exhibit chaos. **11-1**, Figure B, shows structure with such a color table.

• *Matrixed colors*: Consists of 8 rows of 32 colors, each illustrating the interaction of two variables. (The 8 × 32 matrix was selected because the eye can better discriminate hue than saturation.) Choosing a color in this table is somewhat more complicated. The value of one variable (such as density) is defined as a row in the matrix, and the value of the second variable (such as temperature) is defined as a column in the matrix. **1-4** illustrates density versus vorticity with this color table.

• *Dark to light (blue, red, yellow, and white):* Indicates densest to least dense and appeals to the notion that lighter colors are "higher" or "more active." **5-10** effectively applies such a color table to indicate "inactive," "active," and "threshold exceeded."

• *Black to white or white to black:* Provides maximum contrast. This color table is good for showing density (black, dense; white, light). **1-8** illustrates an application of this color table.

Throughout, we treat the CRT as the primary medium for creating and viewing images. But selecting and arranging colors to produce an effective image on a CRT is just the beginning of the need to adjust color if you also intend to reproduce the image on another medium. We discuss some general guidelines for adjusting color for the more commonly used output media of print, film, and video. More details about output media are given earlier in this section under the Output Media heading; see pages 14 to 19.

Creating Color

Output devices create color either by adding light energy to black (additive method) or by subtracting light energy from white (subtractive method). On a CRT, colors are created by adding red, green, and blue (RGB color model) light energy in various ratios to produce the colors that are perceived by the eye. In contrast, printer-produced output creates colors by mixing cyan, magenta, yellow, and, sometimes, black (CMYK color model) and applying these pigments to a medium. The pigments on the medium absorb (subtract) some light energy and reflect other light energy. The eye perceives the reflected light energy as color.

Problems of color integrity occur when color is created by one method but reproduced by another method. Volumes are written on methods that transform one color model to the other. If you are interested in the details, we particularly recommend James D. Foley et al., *Computer Graphics: Principles and Practice*, 2nd ed. (Reading, MA: Addison-Wesley, 1990). Software is even becoming available for calibrating output devices to a standard. The important point is that color CRT output will seldom look the same as color printer output because the colors are created differently. Therefore, it is always wise to verify color integrity between media. An exact color match may seem desirable and may sometimes be an imperative, but usually all you need is enough color definition to reliably discern the information.

You should also be aware that color integrity problems can arise even when color is created on one CRT and displayed on a different one. The perceived color from a CRT depends upon the emission wavelength intensities of the primary RGB screen phosphors that produce the image. These intensities can vary greatly among manufacturers and even with the same manufacturer. Therefore, if color accuracy is critical, we suggest you verify colors whenever you are showing your image on a CRT different form the one on which you created the image.

Besides knowing that differences in color creation methods among output media affect color reproduction, you should also be aware of other complications when combining colors. Depending on the software or hardware used, a color may print on top of an existing color or completely replace the existing color with the new color, or the overlapping colors can combine to produce yet a different color—all the more reason to preview work.

Projecting Color

Different color models are not the only complication. The projector on which an image is displayed may affect how color is perceived. The colors are not immediately reflected to the eye, but are first projected onto a screen by way of a lamp. Red, orange, and yellow appear much brighter than blue and violet, a crucial consideration when choosing colors to highlight key points in a presentation. Placing a piece of white paper behind a transparency gives a fairly accurate idea of how the colors will appear when projected, but the only way to know how a color slide or film animation will project is to preview it.

Slide projectors can cause a special problem because many portable projectors have inadequate lamps that further lower the overall image contrast, thus diminishing color discrimination. Whether a meaningful image can be projected with a slide projector depends on the colors selected, the detail in the image, the brightness of the projected image, the size of the projected image, and the ambient light in the viewing room. We strongly urge you to preview with the actual projection equipment and to allow time to revise presentations.

Some printer-produced transparencies are made by wax transfer, yielding brilliant colors. If these transparencies are shown with older overhead projectors that heat the projector table, the wax melts and runs after two or three minutes. Imagine your embarrassment if your image conspicuously melted during a presentation. Newer technology is always being developed. Anyone applying relatively new technology may encounter traps, and should put the room, the medium, and the equipment through a dry run.

Lighting Adjustments

Besides allowing for complexities introduced by how different media create color, you must also adjust images for the ambient lighting conditions in which they are to be viewed.

For a dark room, you should select sharply contrasting colors. Dark blue is a good choice for backgrounds because it recedes more than other colors, provides good contrast, and does not detract from other elements in the image. Other effective background colors are black, dark gray, forest green, and scarlet. Yellow, white or clear, and pink provide good contrast for text; pastels and bright colors give good contrast for data.

In rooms with more ambient light, particularly when audiences need light for taking notes, lighter colors for background and darker colors for text provide good readability. Some satisfactory background and text combinations are light yellow and dark blue, magenta and black, light green and saturated green, and white or clear and dark green. Dark and fully saturated colors provide good contrast for data.

As in any composition, use the brightest colors in the color table to draw attention to specific elements or objects and less saturated or subdued colors for the less important objects or text. Subtle changes in saturation and highlighting are not effective in brightly lit places because the eye can distinguish only a narrow range of colors.

The physiological, psychological, environmental, and mechanical complexities of color use are controllable, especially if you are organized in your approach. Remember to:

Conclusions

- Use color for the functions it performs best.

- Use realistic, logical color schemes.

- Limit the number of colors, especially the saturated colors.

- Make the most important information the most prominent color.

- Be sure that important detail is clearly evident.

- Be consistent in the meanings you assign to color.

- Be aware that context influences color perception.

- Be aware that color schemes must be adapted to output media.

- Allow time and resources to review color in actual viewing conditions and to make necessary adjustments.

Finally, if you lack background in using color and time to learn about it and are undertaking an involved project, we suggest consulting an artist, a designer, or someone else trained in using color. You will save time, dollars, and sanity.

Additional References

1. Gerald Murch, et al., Tektronix Laboratories Inc., "Human Factors Research," *Tekniques* 10, 2.

2. Gerald E. Jones, "Color Use, Abuse in Presentations," *Computer Graphics World* (May 1986).

3. Morris L. Samit, "The Color Interface," *Computer Graphics World* (July 1983).

4. SuperGen® Owner's Manual, © 1988 Digital Creations.

5. George A. Agoston, *Color Theory and Its Application in Art and Design, 2nd* ed. (New York: Springer-Verlag, 1987).

6. R. W. G. Hunt, *The Reproduction of Colour in Photography, Printing, and Television,* 4th ed. (London, Eng.: Fountain Press, 1987).

Section II
Illustrated Techniques

In this section we present examples consisting of images and accompanying descriptive text that cumulatively represent a broad range of techniques for visualizing data. Our purpose is to provide a logically organized, convenient reference source and a cross-section of examples that can help you choose a technique that will reveal the meaning hidden in your data. We have purposely chosen images from many disciplines to demonstrate by example that the techniques for displaying data are usually not specific to a discipline. The selected images illustrate visual techniques already in use that may facilitate visual communication of information in any discipline. We describe the techniques generically to encourage broad application. Most of the images are from current, general-interest research applications and show pretty much what the researcher sees during the exploration and analysis stages of visualization. The images thus may not gleam with the polish of a finished product. We present them first and foremost for ideas to show the kinds of information that scientific visualization can depict.

Organization of Examples

Examples are grouped in thirteen categories expressing common ways of thinking about data or visualization. Within each category, images are arranged from simple to complex. Although each category is distinct, relationships among some categories should be explored, as explained in these descriptions of categories.

These two categories can be explored for techniques that compare or relate data:

• *Comparisons and Relationships:* Techniques for comparing or relating two data sets.

• *Multivariate:* Techniques for handling many variables in one data set or for handling many data sets. Other names for data of this kind are multidimensional data or *n*-dimensional data.

The next four categories show techniques for depicting change over time:

• *Time:* Techniques for showing the passage of time in one image.

• *Process:* Techniques for showing behavior, performance, or operation of a system.

• *Animation:* Techniques to use when dynamic data values are to be animated.

• *Motion:* Techniques for conveying movement in one image.

The next four categories show techniques for representing dimensions of data:

• *2-D:* Techniques for illustrating 2-D data. Such data do not have to be displayed in 2-D. Treating a scalar field as a height field may lead to a 3-D surface or model.

• *Surface and Slice:* Techniques using surface and slice algorithms to illustrate 3-D data. Surface and slice techniques can also be used to study multivariate data.

• *Volume:* Techniques for representing data throughout a volume and for gaining an understanding of the complete volume.

• *Models:* Techniques for representing models derived from data or for using models to represent data. Generally, we use models to show qualitative information, to provide a frame of reference, or to provide a context within which to understand data. Models are especially helpful for presentation or publication because they can supply a context that will help explain the phenomenon that the data represent.

The final three sections, though not related to one another, include special techniques that may be applied to any visualization.

• *Multiform Visualization:* Images that use different techniques or different applications of one technique to represent the same data. These images show how important it is to know the visualization goal of an image before selecting the technique for representing the data. Although each technique accurately represents the data, the meaning communicated is vastly different. Representing data in multiple ways may result in deeper understanding of the data.

• *Artistic Cues:* Techniques from the art world that can be applied to scientific visualization. Often an artist can represent the data or information about the data, and also make the data tell a story, emphasize a point, create a bias, or set a mood.

• *Black and White:* Techniques to use specifically if black and white or grayscale is a constraint. But many of the techniques could also be adapted to color. Representing data in black and white (and shades of gray) is not obsolete even though color is less costly than it used to be. Our purpose in this section is not to teach the merits of black and white, but to use these examples to further illustrate application-independent techniques; these examples just happen to be black and white.

Presentation of Examples

Each image and its accompanying text are on the same page. Images are identified at the outr top margin by a bold, two-number visual cue that facilitates locating example references in the text. The two numbers identify image placement within a category. Images are uniformly described by:

• A summary at the top outside margin that lists the number of variables* in the image, gives a short generic description of the meaning conveyed by the image (which we call the visualization goal), and names the discipline from which the example is taken.

---

* The variable count in the summary is intended to help if you are looking for techniques that can be applied to data having a specific number of variables. Notice that the count reflects the number of variables illustrated in the image. We choose not to count variables that may be part of the example's data set but that are not part of the image, such as time if the image is a frame of a movie. The variable count is not intended as a precise description of the data set. Consequently, we claim artistic license for some of the counts. Complicating the count are images of models, images with more than one data set, the concept of rank (Is one 2-D vector counted as one or two variables?), as well as variable counts that can also be a function of one's point of view. A variable representing speed and direction (a vector) is usually represented as a unit and therefore is counted as one. If the specific components of a vector are examined independent of the others, the count is indicated by the variable's rank.

• A short caption in discipline-independent language that states the technique used to achieve the goal. The summary and caption condense the content.

Accompanying explanation describes:

• The application or specific research area, such as global climate modeling, medical imaging, pollution, or oil exploration; the names of the variables being represented; what the researcher means to communicate with the image; and hardware and software used for the application and the image.

• Level of compute power we suggest to use the technique efficiently. An icon appearing on the same line as the Technique heading denotes which of five general classes of compute power could comfortably accomplish the job. We may indicate less power than that actually used by the creator of the image. You can always use a more powerful computer. Lesser compute power might also have produced the image, but at a high cost in time. The classes are:

IBM PC/Macintosh class, generally costing less than $10,000.

IBM PC/Macintosh class with specialty hardware, such as accelerators, extra memory, or 24-bit color.

Workstations from Silicon Graphics, Hewlett-Packard, IBM, Sun, and others; widely varying in price and usually supporting some flavor of UNIX.

Workstations with specialty hardware.

Mainframe and supercomputer class, costing $1,000,000 and up and used along with a workstation.

Our ratings are relative judgments meant to create classes of machines that are three to four times faster, better, and thus costlier than those in the preceding group. Compute requirements for an image depend on the choice of visualization algorithm, quantity of data, resolution, and time in which to do the visualization. If time is not critical, then a low-power computer can do the job. But, just as in the $$ restaurants with medium-priced entrées, we often want other items and wind up spending much more.

• The techniques for deriving the image and the contextual cue(s) used to emphasize relationships or meanings in the data.

• Hints about ways of using the technique or similar techniques. Also included are cross-references to other images in the book that use other techniques to accomplish the goal or that use similar techniques to accomplish a different goal. When appropriate, contrasting techniques are also referred to so as to further clarify the description.

• References supplied by the contributor for additional information about the application and techniques.

Using the Examples

The examples provide many ways to help you visualize data. Identifying the example that accomplishes a visualization goal has the twofold benefit of suggesting possible visualization goals as well as describing techniques for accomplishing these goals. These images may enable you to create your own images for visualizing data. Or these images may serve as a tool for communicating to a visualization specialist the type of image you want. For visualization specialists, the images provide ready examples showing what is possible. For all readers, the examples and accompanying images provide a quick survey of how to visualize the meaning in data.

To create effective visualizations of data, you generally need not learn how to create visualization algorithms. Most visualization needs can be met with visualization algorithms that are widely available in books and journals, or are implemented as commercial software products. Visualization utilities are available for the IBM PC and the Apple Macintosh as well as for workstations and mainframes. Also, weekly and monthly computer magazines, besides offering articles and product reviews, carry advertisements describing visualization utilities. Some examples in *Visual Cues*, however, are from current research in visualization and may require you to seek out the research paper or the contributor in order to produce the algorithm.

If you prefer to understand the algorithm behind the image or to do your own programming, we list some useful and informative texts:

• *Projective Geometry and Its Applications to Computer Graphics*, Michael A. Penna and Richard R. Patterson (Englewood Cliffs, NJ: Prentice-Hall, 1986).

• *Fundamentals of Interactive Computer Graphics*, James D. Foley and Andries Van Dam (Reading, MA: Addison-Wesley, 1982).

• *Principles of Interactive Graphics*, 2nd ed., William M. Newman and Robert F. Sproull (New York: McGraw-Hill, 1979).

• *Procedural Elements for Computer Graphics,* David F. Rogers (New York: McGraw-Hill, 1985).

• *Mathematical Methods in Computer Graphics and Design,* K. W. Brodlie (London, Eng.: Academic Press, 1980); United States edition by Academic Press, Orlando, FL.

• *Graphics Gems*, ed. by Andrew S. Glassner (San Diego: Academic Press, 1990); *Graphics Gems II*, ed. by James Arvo (San Diego: Academic Press, 1991); *Graphics Gems III,* ed. by David Kirk (San Diego: Academic Press, 1992).

• *Volume Visualization*, IEEE Computer Society Press Tutorial, Arie Kaufman, ed. (Washington, DC: IEEE Computer Society Press, 1991).

• *Computer Graphics: Principles and Practice*, 2nd ed., James D. Foley et al. (Reading, MA: Addison-Wesley, 1990).

• Conference Proceedings of ACM SIGGRAPH and the IEEE VISUALIZATION.

Computer Science Resources

For scientists and engineers who are not programmers themselves and who want help in visualizing data, we recommend enlisting the assistance of a computer scientist, preferably one with graphics knowledge. If such a person is not readily available, some of these alternatives may help.

• Internet-available bulletin board called "Netnews" and accessed by the UNIX utility "RN," called "read news." The read news directories of COMP.GRAPHICS, COMP.GRAPHICS.RESEARCH, and COMP.GRAPHICS.VISUALIZATION provide electronic question/answer and sources for possible collaboration.

• Annual conferences, such as Visualization, sponsored by IEEE, or ACM SIGGRAPH. Both are potential sources of professionals in the visualization field who may accept small research grants.

• National Laboratories under the direction of the Department of Energy. Some of the Labs are leaders in graphics research and are opening their doors to collaborative research in many areas.

• Colleges and universities with computer-science departments frequently look for small grants and projects for student theses.

IEEE and ACM SIGGRAPH, two professional societies, have extensive visualization libraries of books, videos, and slides that may interest you. To request a catalog, write to:

- IEEE Computer Society Press, 10662 Los Vaqueros Circle, P.O. Box 3014, Los Alamitos, CA 90720-1264, USA.
- ACM Order Department, P.O. Box 64145, Baltimore, MD 21264, USA (Conference Proceedings, Visual Proceedings, and slide sets).
- SIGGRAPH Video Review, c/o 1st Priority, P. O. Box 576, Itasca, IL 60143-0576, USA (video reviews).

The Process of Visualization

Looking at the images in this chapter, you might think that effectively visualizing data is fairly simple. In reality, discovering the technique that best fulfills a visualization purpose is often an evolutionary process involving time, trial-and-error, and the blending of several types of expertise.

The images on pages 41 and 42 submitted by Wes Bethel of Lawrence Berkeley Laboratory, Berkeley, CA, illustrate the incremental progress you may expect as you seek the best way of visualizing data. The sequence also demonstrates how goals may change as new or unexpected information appears.

The data Bethel uses in the accompanying images are deviations of average compressional velocity derived from measurements of earth movement taken at different depths at each of more than 8000 seismic (earthquake) sensing stations worldwide and from the location of the earthquake epicenters. The data are from more than 46,000 earthquakes that occurred between 1962 and 1987.

The simple two-tone, 2-D plots of Figure i, page 41, typify the kinds of images with which researchers often begin to explore data. In Figure i, the researcher[*] has created a plot for each of three depths to show seismic velocity. Velocity is represented by a color range correlated to an annotated color bar below the plot. The continents and tectonic plates are outlined in black to provide contextual information. These plots are packed with data but are hard to interpret. Exploration is further complicated because the velocity at various depths is really 3-D data, but the plots depict the velocity in 2-D; the researcher can approximate 3-D only by physically arranging in the air the papers on which the plots are printed—somewhat inconvenient. Although these plots show information, the researcher needs other visualization techniques to progress further in exploring the data.

In Figure ii, Bethel begins to experiment with other techniques to make the data more legible. He creates a scatterplot depicting the velocity data as discrete squares according to the latitude and longitude of the sensing stations. The plot lessens color in the image and also verifies that the data accurately describe actual station locations. Bethel also changes the color range to lessen the amount of saturated blue or red in the image, thus reducing the areas competing for attention, and outlines the continents in white to make them more visible than in Figure i. The tectonic plates are not shown. In seeking the best visualization, Bethel plots the data in several ways to help the researcher determine what really needs to be displayed.

In Figure iii, Bethel adds more data to the image. A yellow dot marks each summary station. (A summary station is the average of several regional sensing stations;

---

[*] R. Jay Pulliam, Earth Sciences Division, Lawrence Berkeley Laboratory, Berkeley, CA, USA.

hence it does not physically exist.) Green dots locate epicenters and cluster to form lines because of the large number of earthquakes. The tectonic plates are again drawn in as white lines. After studying this image, the researcher verified that the information was approximately what he expected to see. Because the image is still crowded with extraneous information, Bethel seeks yet another form of representation to facilitate analysis of the data.

To take advantage of available graphics tools, Bethel converts the 3-D scattered data from the seismic measurements into regular 3-D gridded data. The data are estimated for a regular latitude–longitude grid and for regularly spaced depths down to the core–mantle boundary, using an algorithm developed at the Center for Computational Seismology at Lawrence Berkeley Laboratory. The pseudocolor plot in Figure iv, a 2-D slice of data taken from the 3-D gridded data, is the first experimental image of a slice taken of the gridded data. A different color encoding for the velocity causes the values close to zero to appear in gray, diminishing their importance and effectively hiding them while accentuating the more significant velocity extremes.

Seeking to further simplify the image and to show the data more meaningfully, Bethel introduces the researcher to the possibility of using spherical (Figure v) and Mollweide (Figure vi) map projections. Adding pseudocolored slice planes to Figure v reduces the quantity of data presented to the viewer from any desired viewing position and depicts the data in 3-D. Bethel also adjusts the color table to enhance structure. The researcher likes the spherical projection, Figure v, and so Bethel adds the contextual cues of epicenter and summary stations. Using different slice planes and depth-of-velocity measurements permits further examination and analysis of the data. Now the researcher decides to focus the investigation on a previously undiscovered, ancient geologic subduction zone, where continental plates abut and one plate is pushed down into the mantle. By cropping away some of the foreground data, Bethel can compute isovelocity surfaces (blue and red) corresponding to that subduction zone to produce Figure vii, which the researcher can use to present the discovery (indicated by arrows).

This sequence is typical in its use of imaging techniques and data-conversion techniques that allow the use of current graphics tools. Some images in the sequence provide significant scientific insight into the underlying data and others require considerable study for the viewer to gain understanding. At each step, though, the insight gained leads to additional visualizations.

In the examples that follow beginning on page 41, we present images from various stages in visualization. Some images provide instant understanding, some may take some study, and others may require reading the text, the references, or other sources of knowledge. All images illustrate techniques used to accomplish a visualization goal.

Figure i

P-Velocity (0-200 km)

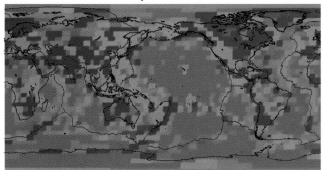

P-Velocity (200-400 km)

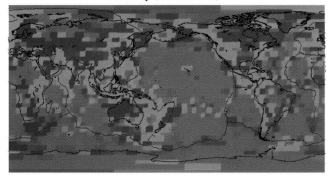

P-Velocity (400-600 km)

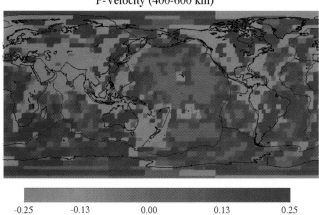

-0.25   -0.13   0.00   0.13   0.25

Figure ii

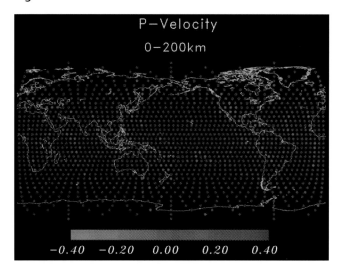

Figure iii

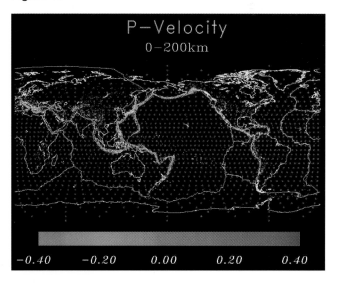

Figure iv

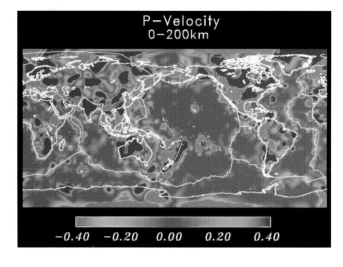

Figure v

P−Velocity

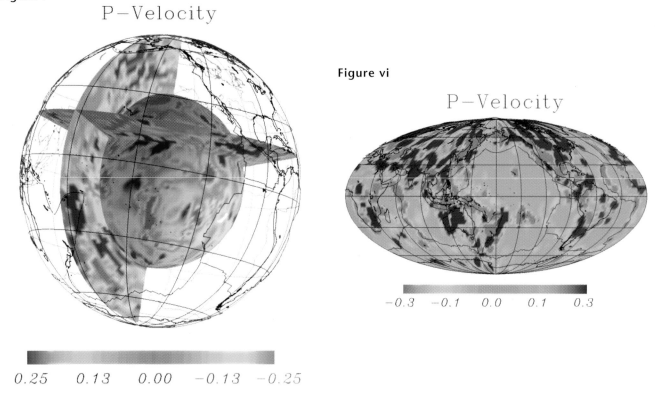

0.25   0.13   0.00   −0.13   −0.25

Figure vi

P−Velocity

−0.3   −0.1   0.0   0.1   0.3

Figure vii

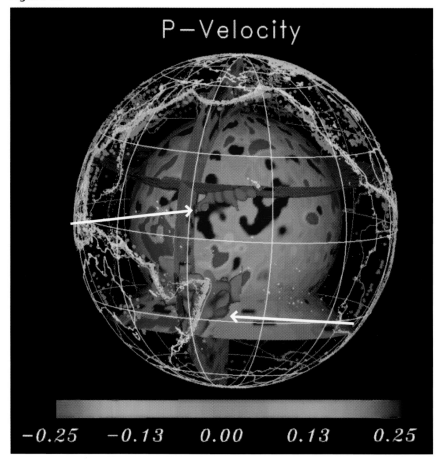

P−Velocity

−0.25   −0.13   0.00   0.13   0.25

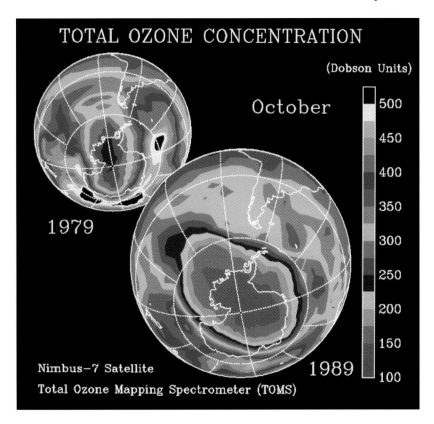

1 dependent variable
2 independent variables
Compares scalars
Atmospheric Science

Annotation makes comparison of scalars self-explanatory.

Mark Abrams, Cheryl Craig, and Bill Mankin; submitted by Lee Carter and Bob Lackman, National Center for Atmospheric Research, Boulder, CO, USA.

Application (Global Climate Modeling)

This image compares global ozone concentrations of October 1979 with those of October 1989. The dominance of blue, green, and yellow areas on the 1989 globe shows the overall decrease in ozone levels. The data were collected by the NASA Total Ozone Mapping Spectrometer (TOMS) on the Nimbus-7 satellite. The image was created with the National Center for Atmospheric Research (NCAR) graphics package, executing on a Cray Y-MP supercomputer.

Technique

Color-filled isolines compare two data sets. The variable is named in the title and keyed to a color scale of values; the data source and instrumentation are noted. Relative size suggests relative importance. White grids and reference lines allow positional comparison of the two data sets.

Hints

Self-explanatory images are effective and desirable for publications or formal presentations. ◊ In this image the relative sizes of the globes emphasize importance; relative size could also help emphasize the before-after aspect of data.

1 dependent variable
2 independent variables
Compares images
Computational Physics

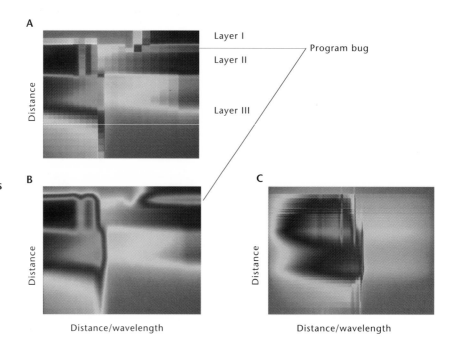

A

Layer I

Layer II

Program bug

Distance

Layer III

B

C

Distance

Distance

Distance/wavelength

Distance/wavelength

Visualization techniques compare simulations to experiments and help validate program development.

Viviane C. Rupert, Edward Garelis, and Peter R. Keller, Lawrence Livermore National Laboratory, Livermore, CA, USA.

[1] Gregory A. Baxes, *Digital Image Processing: A Practical Primer* (Denver, CO: Cascade Press, 1984), pp. 50–51, 140.

Application (Material Mix Dynamics)

The accuracy of a material-mix simulation program is verified as the program is being developed. The program images are compared to the researcher's mental image of the program's expected behavior and to pseudocolored radiographs from experiments (not shown). The image from the simulation was created on a Cray 1 supercomputer and displayed on a Tektronix 4125 high-resolution color terminal.

Technique

Three in a series of pseudocolor raster images used to verify accurate development of a computer program are shown. Figure A, a coarse-grained image, identifies gross features to allow comparison of the image pixel values to expected results before continuing with the program's development. (The unexpected horizontal bluish lines to the top and right of center identified a program bug, which was corrected before creating Figure C.) Figure B, which facilitates visual comparison between the simulated image and the radiograph from the experiment, results from using a low-pass filter[1] that smooths the image, removing the coarse, block-shaped format. Errors discovered by the processes used in Figures A and B are corrected, and Figure C, a fine-grain simulation, is created to reveal greater detail for even more accurate comparison with the radiograph in the experiment.

Hints

Using intermediate steps to verify accuracy of the computer program eliminates errors and dramatically shortens time for completion; such a technique is particularly valuable when extensive computer time is needed to create the ultimate image. ◊ The smoothing technique used in Figure B has the disadvantage of also removing the sharp spectral lines. ◊ Because the researcher is familiar with this color table, it is not drawn as part of the image. ◊ Pseudocolored radiographs are easier for some people to compare than black-and-white radiographs.

21 variables
Relates position and scalars
Physiometry

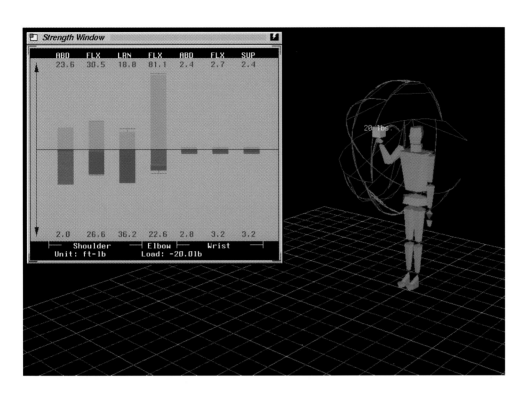

The positions of a 3-D model are related to measured data.

Susanna Wei, Saint Joseph's University, Philadelphia, PA, USA; Norman I. Badler, University of Pennsylvania, Philadelphia, PA, USA.

Application (Muscle Group Strength)

Actions safe and unsafe for the body are studied[1] relative to the amount of weight lifted and posture. The image was rendered on a Silicon Graphics workstation using the University of Pennsylvania's *Jack*™.

Technique

A colored trace shows a weight's (blue) path and indicates unsafe actions (red) and safe actions (green) relative to the position of a stylized, polygonal 3-D model of the human body. The model is flat shaded for rendering speed. A base grid, highlights, and perspective enhance 3-D effect. A color-coded bar graph at the upper left allows correlation of various measured values based on the body's posture, the position of the weight, and the amount of weight.

Hints

Multiple levels of presentation facilitate the study of large data sets by providing, first, a quick look and then, if desired, a more detailed look. This image, as well as **4-3**, has two levels of presentation. Here, posture and colored traces provide the primary information, and a bar chart provides secondary information. In **4-3**, a flow chart provides primary information, and the secondary information is called up on demand. ◊ We strongly support the use of familiar conventions, as in this image: red for unsafe and green for safe.

[1] Susanna Wei and Norman I. Badler, "Graphical Displays of Human Strength Data," to be published in the *Journal of Visualization and Computer Animation.*

2 dependent variables
2 independent variables
Compares scalar fields
Computational Physics

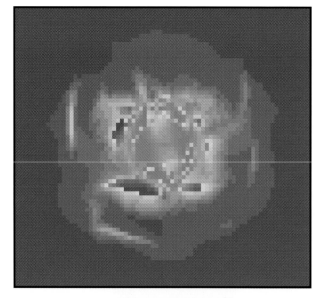

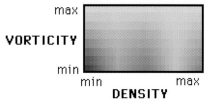

Hue and saturation
show relationships
between two variables.

James A. Viecelli and Peter R.
Keller, Lawrence Livermore
National Laboratory,
Livermore, CA, USA.

Application (Computational Fluid Dynamics)

The image shows the distortion of a shock front propagating outward from the center and the shock front's relationship to vorticity (a measure of turbulence). The data were generated and the picture was created with a Cray 1 supercomputer. The image was displayed on a Tektronix 4125 high-resolution color terminal.

Technique

In a pseudocolored cell array, hue and saturation individually correspond to two variables. Each cell is colored according to the visible light spectrum to represent density: blue, low; red, high. The color saturation changes from low (saturated color) to high (pale or gray) to show the magnitude of vorticity of each cell. A color key shows the relative density and vorticity values. Although a snapshot in time is shown here, a dramatic animation was created to study the relationship between the two variables over time.

Hints

In this example we matched the colors of the density variable to a range familiar to the researcher, thus making it easier to absorb the large amount of information in the image. On the other hand, in applications comparing temperature and density, we suggest using the visible-light spectrum for temperature (blue, cold to red, hot) and using intensity for density (dark, dense material to light, light material.) ◊ When three variables are being compared, a ternary color key of red, green and blue as in **2-6**, Figure A, could be used.

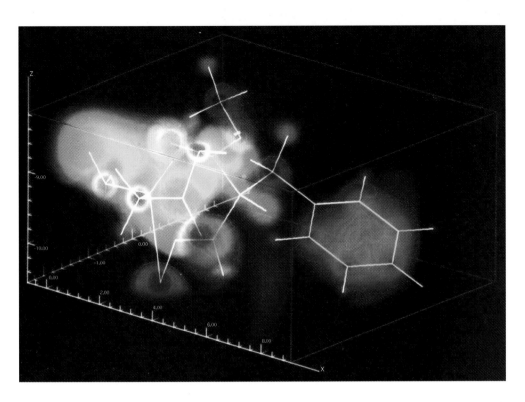

1 dependent variable
3 independent variables
Associates 3-D geometry
    and volume data
Computational Chemistry

**3-D geometry rendered
with volume data
permits correlation.**

Vincent Argio, Vital Images,
Inc., Fairfield, IA, USA;
submitted by Maggie Vancik,
Vital Images, Inc.

Application (Molecular Modeling)

The electric-charge distribution of a NutraSweet molecule in a $133 \times 122 \times 68$ volume of data and the 3-D chemical-bonds geometry are simulated by molecular modeling software[1] on a supercomputer. The image was rendered on a Silicon Graphics IRIS workstation using VoxelView®/ULTRA.

[1] Data courtesy of Gary Griffin, using molecular modeling software from BIOSYM Technologies, Inc.

Technique

Embedding traditional geometric graphics (lines in this case) in a 3-D volume provides the accuracy of the geometric positioning with the information content of the volume rendering. The pseudocolored cloudlike features represent the charge distribution. Numbered axes provide a mechanism for approximating the size of the features. The perspective bounding box provides the cue to read the molecule as a 3-D representation.

Hints

Interactive control of volume translucency permits shifting of the focus between the volume data and the geometry data.

1 dependent variable
2 independent variables
Correlates scalars and
    position
Meteorology

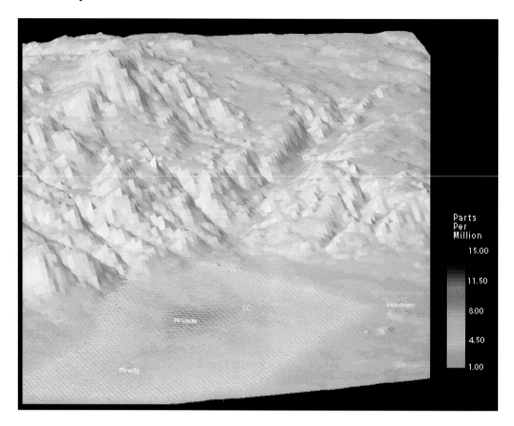

**Color and texture
correlate data.**

Sudhanshu K. Semwal, L. Ted
Ryder, Keith Seyler, University
of Colorado, Colorado Springs,
CO, USA.

[1] Ambient Monitoring Data,
Colorado Springs Utilities,
Environmental Services
Department, Colorado Springs,
CO.

[2] "Data Standards, Digital
Elevation Models," National
Mapping Program, United
States Department of the
Interior, Geological Survey of
the Interior, Circular 895-B
Geological Survey, Reston, VA.

[3] James D. Foley, et al.,
*Computer Graphics: Principles
and Practice* (Reading, Mass.:
Addison-Wesley, 1990), ch. 16.

Application (Air-Quality Assessment)

Carbon monoxide concentrations in the Colorado Springs vicinity including Pikes Peak[1] are visualized in 3-D space to show how terrain might influence pollution concentrations. The image was modeled and rendered on a Hewlett-Packard HP 9000 series 300 workstation using Hewlett-Packard's Starbase graphics package.

Technique

A translucent, colored grid showing carbon monoxide distribution is combined with a 3-D terrain map.[2] Grid color, correlated to a color key at the right, indicates densities of carbon monoxide. The translucent grid permits viewing of the terrain, which is generated from United States Geological Survey Digital Elevation Model data. The angle of the sun shades the terrain[3] and shows time of day. Pollution-monitoring sites, though difficult to see on an image of this size, are identified by a label and a single dot.

Hints

The terrain map is a 3-D data set being compared to a 2-D data set. Instead of using a 3-D terrain map as a reference, we could have used a 2-D map and depicted the pollution in 3-D, as in **5-7**. ◊ See **1-7** and **5-12** for other techniques of showing 3-D terrain with a translucent representation of 3-D data.

2 dependent variables
2 independent variables
Compares surfaces
Geology

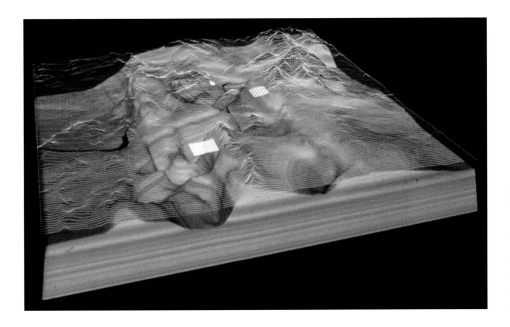

Superimposing a transparent surface on a solid surface permits comparison.

Melvin L. Prueitt and Scott Baldridge, Los Alamos National Laboratory, Los Alamos, NM, USA.

Application (Geophysics)

This image of the Rio Grande Rift area, which includes the cities of Albuquerque, Santa Fe, and Los Alamos, is used to compare the current surface topography with the ancient bedrock. The earth's crust is tearing apart as crustal plates shift, and sediment fills the gap as it widens. We learn that approximately 15,000 feet of sediment fills the ancient canyon beneath Albuquerque (largest white grid). The in-house GRAFIC code runs on a Cray supercomputer to create the image, which is rendered on a Dicomed film recorder.

Technique

The surface topography is modeled as a collection of white lines derived by intersecting the surface with a regularly spaced vertical plane. The bedrock surface is modeled as a solid. The white grids representing city locations are reference marks. Colors on the solid surfaces represent altitude. Black is sea level.

Hints

Using rows of lines to represent a translucent surface allows the surface below to be easily seen. ◊ The contextual cues of lines and pseudocolor help distinguish the two surfaces.

1 dependent variable
3 independent variables
Reveals differences
Visualization

Subtraction reveals differences between images.

Gregory M. Nielson and Thomas A. Foley, Arizona State University, Tempe, AZ, USA; David Lane, NASA Ames Research Center, Moffett Field, CA, USA.

[1] Thomas A. Foley, David Lane, and Gregory M. Nielson, "Towards Animating Ray-Traced Volume Visualization," *Journal of Visualization and Computer Animation* 1, 1 (1990): 2–8.

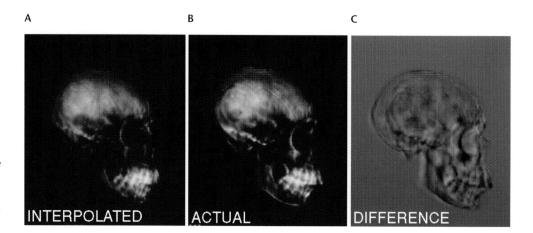

A   B   C

INTERPOLATED   ACTUAL   DIFFERENCE

Application (Image Interpolation)

Spherical interpolation (Figure A) techniques[1] that approximate ray-cast volume renderings (Figure B) are studied. The approximation technique revealed no noticeable degradation in quality. In-house software using the DORÉ graphics package and the X Window environment was executed on the Ardent Titan, the Cray X-MP supercomputer, and the IBM 3090 Processor Complex Model 500E.

Technique

Differences between Figures A and B, although not readily apparent to the untrained eye, are revealed by rendering a new pixel array (Figure C). Figure C is obtained by taking the absolute value of the difference between corresponding pixel values from Figures A and B. Brightness is adjusted on the new rendered array to emphasize the differences.

Hints

This fast interpolation technique is useful for animation or interactive viewing to spot a potentially interesting feature. If accuracy in the rendering is important, then the true volume-rendered image should be computed. ◊ Small differences in images are nearly impossible to perceive in side-by-side comparisons. Consider using this technique to reveal differences, or try a glyph technique, as illustrated in **13-9**.

2 dependent variables
2 independent variables
Locates clusters
Agriculture

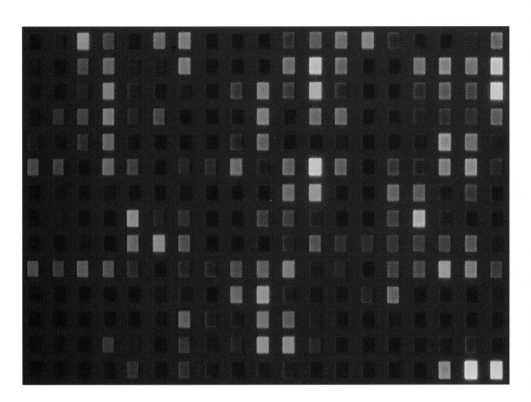

Colored rectangles locate clusters of similar value.

Donna J. Cox, University of Illinois, Urbana, IL, USA; Ray Idaszak, NCSA, Urbana, IL, USA; and David Onstad, University of Illinois, Urbana, IL, USA.

Application (Entomology)

A simulation models the population dynamics of corn borers. The image represents a cornfield. Some locations contain normal corn-borer larvae; some contain larvae infected with a microsporidium for pest control; other locations contain both types of larvae; and some contain no corn-borer larvae. The simulation was computed on a Cray supercomputer and the image rendered on a Silicon Graphics workstation.

Technique

Each colored rectangle represents a location in a cornfield. To understand how a rectangle is colored, we can think of adding an amount of red or green corresponding to the two populations of corn borers. The greater the sum, the brighter the color; the smaller the sum, the darker the color. A rectangle whose sum is near zero is black. Reddish or greenish rectangles have more of one type or another of corn borer. Brown to orange to yellow rectangles indicate approximately equal populations.[1–3]

Hints

The success of this technique depends on the viewer's understanding how colors are added; e.g., adding a medium green to a medium red results in orange; adding a bright green to a bright red results in bright yellow. ◊ We should also be aware that the physiology of the eye may respond better to certain colors; different colors may facilitate locating the cluster boundaries. ◊ The technique of adding colors is also useful for discovering relationships between two physically different scalar fields, such as temperature and density.

[1] D. Cox, "Using the Supercomputer to Visualize Higher Dimensions: An Artist's Contribution to Scientific Visualization," *Leonardo: Journal of Art, Science and Technology* 21 (1988): 233–242.

[2] D. Cox, "The Art of Scientific Visualization," *Academic Computing* (March 1990): 20–40; references at end of journal.

[3] G. Meyer and D. Greenberg, "Perceptual Color Spaces for Computer Graphics," Proceedings of SIGGRAPH '80, in *Computer Graphics* (July 14–18, 1980).

4 variables
Locates regions
Mathematics

A
B

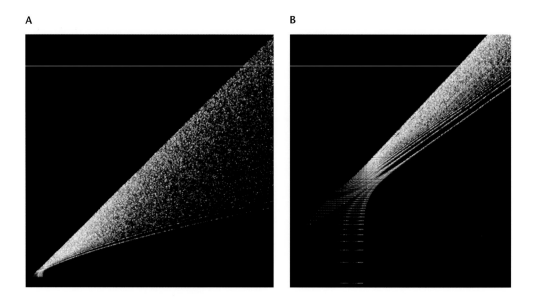

A scatterplot locates regions of interest.

John Compton and Peter R. Keller, Lawrence Livermore National Laboratory, Livermore, CA, USA.

[1] V. L. Gardiner, R. B. Lazarus, and P. R. Stein, "Solutions of the Diophantine Equation $x^3 + y^3 = z^3 - d$," *Math. Comp.* 18 (1964): 408–413.

Application (Number Theory)

Visualization of the Diophantine equation $x^3 + y^3 = z^3 - d$; [1] (x, y, z, d are integers) discloses information that leads to significant progress in finding solutions to the equation. The data were calculated by a highly vectorized Cray supercomputer code and the image was computed using in-house graphics libraries. The image was output to 35-mm slides.

Technique

The equation is studied by mapping the solutions to a scatterplot where color represents the magnitude of d, the abscissas represent $\log(z)$, and the ordinates represent $\log(x\text{-}y)$. Parallel, spatially separate jets leading from the base of the image to the upper right in Figure B were revealed by zooming in to the lower left-hand corner of Figure A. Discovery of these jets led to increased speed in searching the solution space because the regions between the jets where no solution could fall were not searched. This optimization, realized through visualization plus some program optimization, allowed study of a solution space that was larger than that in Gardiner et al.[1] by a factor of 50,000.

Hints

When searching for patterns in data, apply functions that capitalize on the eye's physiological ability to find patterns. In this example we applied the log of a difference that causes straight-line patterns to appear. ◊ Although the discovery of the parallel jets seems straightforward, we created hundreds of scatterplots by transforming the data in various ways. These scatterplot graphics, though elementary, were crucial in teasing out hitherto unseen patterns in the data set. Because patterns may exist on numerous scales, we must examine plots at various magnifications. ◊ Axes were not labeled because only qualitative results were sought.

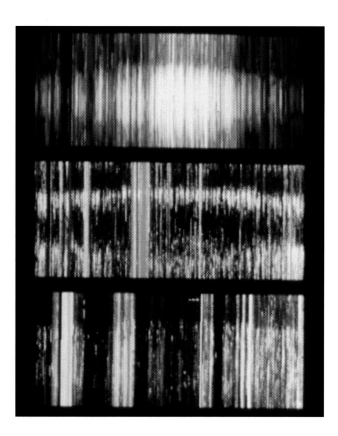

3 dependent variables
1 independent variable
Compares scalars
Meteorology

Three 1-D data sets plotted as 2-D facilitate comparison and analysis of periodic behavior.

Submitted by Lew Harstead, Precision Visuals, Inc., Boulder, CO, USA.

Application (Air Pollution)

Air-quality data for Colorado Springs, Colorado, are studied. Data consist of temperature, carbon monoxide, and sulfur dioxide measurements collected daily at 10-minute intervals for 365 days. The data were rendered on a Sun Microsystems workstation using Precision Visual's PV-WAVE.

Technique

Three pseudocolored plots, each representing a different dependent variable, are created by reformatting the variables from a 1-D array into a 2-D array. The *y*-axis is the 24-hour day, representing one complete cycle of a periodic event. The *x*-axis is the date. The resulting 2-D arrays are displayed as histogram-equalized images[1] to equally distribute the colors over the data to bring out detail. The colors range from blue (low) to red to yellow to white (high.) The three images are stacked to facilitate comparison among the variables.*

Hints

This technique allows one to visualize large data sets quickly and to interpret relationships among variables. ◊ See also **3-1**, which uses a similar technique for studying discrete events. ◊ The axis selection facilitates observance of periodic events.

[1] Azriel Rosenfeld and Avinash C. Kak, *Digital Picture Processing* (San Diego, CA: Academic Press, 1982), pp. 231–237.

* The top image reveals that high temperatures occur at midday and at midyear. In the center image, the bright horizontal bands show higher carbon monoxide levels during the morning and evening rush hour throughout the year. The bottom image shows sulfur dioxide peaking randomly, indicating no apparent relationship to time or the other variables.

3 dependent variables
3 independent variables
Shows multiple relationships
Electrical Engineering

**Multiple visualization
techniques facilitate the
study of relationships.**

Ed Buturela, IBM Simulation
Technology Group,
Burlington, VT, USA; submit-
ted by Catriona Gaeta and
Mike Wilson, Wavefront
Technologies, Santa Barbara,
CA, USA.

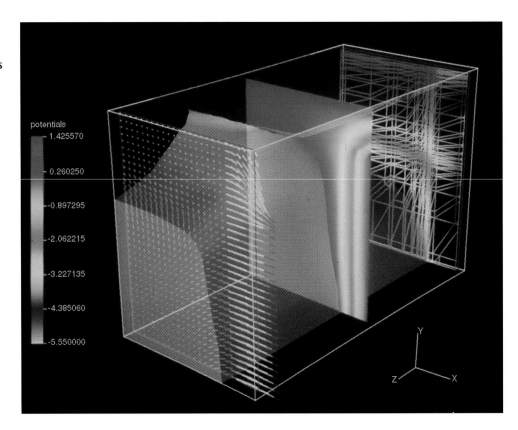

Application (Performance Simulation)

Performance simulation of a semiconductor is modeled using the IBM Field Day
package with an 8000-element unstructured grid. Visualization techniques are
helping to reduce costs and time to market. The simulation data were rendered on
an IBM RS6000 workstation using Wavefront Technologies' Data Visualizer.

Technique

Combining three 2-D slices locates values in 3-D and reveals a more complete
picture of the variables. The foreground slice is a vector plot showing orientation
and magnitude of the electric field. The second slice, a pseudocolor plot, shows the
magnitude of the electric field. The third slice, a mesh plot, relates the information
seen in the image to the computational mesh of the program. On each slice, the
magnitude of the electric field is indicated by the color key at the left. The grayish,
translucent isosurface of the electropotential field shows the shape of the field
without hiding the three slices. The x-, y-, z-axes help orient the viewer to the data.

Hints

This format could have illustrated as many as six variables. The vector plot could
have used arrows of different lengths to represent orientation and magnitude. Each
slice could have used color to represent three variables, and the isosurface could
have represented the sixth. ◊ Multiple-technique images such as this one, that show
numerous relationships give a more comprehensive description of the data and save
analysis time for those who are experienced in reading the complex image. However, the complexity can confuse an uninitiated viewer. Multiple techniques are
used for a more thorough description of the data. See **2-9**, **11-1**, **11-7**, and **11-11**
for other multiple-technique images.

6 dependent variables
3 independent variables
Compares variables
Mechanical Engineering

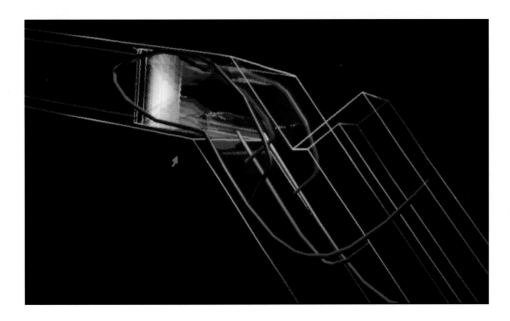

Two distinct rendering techniques allow comparison of variables.

Robert R. Dickinson, Pacific Visualization Systems, Montreal, Canada.

Application (Stress Analysis)

The stress induced in a 3-D guide bracket is studied. The stress tensor data from ANSYS software by Swanson Analysis, Inc., was input to the machine-independent *Via* field data exploration software system.[1]

Technique

A wire-frame model of straight blue, green, and purple lines describes a 3-D guide bracket and is colored according to the visible light spectrum to show stress intensity (blue, low; red, high), where stress intensity is a scalar function of the stress tensor. The curved red and blue tubes,[2] highlighted to help locate them in 3-D, represent the direction in which stress is transmitted. The blue tubes are parallel to the maximum compressive stress. The red tubes are parallel to the maximum tensile stress. The area of maximum stress intensity, located by the red arrow, is made visible by rendering stress intensity as a collection of colored translucent isosurfaces.

Hints

This image shows how simple techniques can effectively depict complex data. ◊ The wire-frame model locates variables of interest without obscuring data, and the arrow directs attention to the area of interest.

[1] *Via* was developed by Visual Edge Software Ltd., Montreal, Canada.

[2] Robert R. Dickinson, "Interactive Analysis of Stress Field Data," submitted to *ASME Journal of Pressure Vessels and Piping* (1991). Also presented at ASME, PVP '91 and published in ASME, PVP special publication Vol. 209, "Computer Graphics and DataBase Management" (June 1991).

4 variables
Locates clusters
Visualization

A 19039

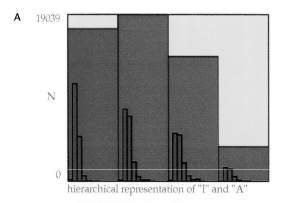
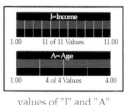

N

0

hierarchical representation of "I" and "A"

values of "I" and "A"
(both ordinal)

**Nested histograms
locate clusters in
multidimensional space.**

T. Mihalisin and J. Schwegler,
Temple University, Philadel-
phia, PA, and Mihalisin
Associates, Inc., Ambler, PA,
USA.; J. Timlin, Mihalisin
Associates, Inc.

B 8248

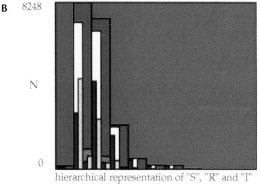

N

0

hierarchical representation of "S", "R" and "I"
for "A" fixed at second bracket

values of "S", "R", "I" and "A"
("S" and "R" are categorical)

[1] T. Mihalisin, J. Timlin, and J.
Schwegler, "Visualization and
Analysis of Multi-Variate Data:
A Technique for All Fields," in
Visualization '91, (Los
Alamitos, CA: IEEE Computer
Society Press, 1991).

Application (Multivariate Analysis)

Visual techniques[1] for analyzing multivariate data are studied. Data are taken from
a survey of approximately 54,000 people. Figure A shows distribution of income
within each of four age ranges. Figure B shows the distribution of income, race, and
gender in the second age range only. The data were displayed on a Sun Microsystems
SPARCstation 1GX using the Temple Multi-Variate Visualization System.

Technique

Bar charts (histogram within histogram within histogram) and slider bars (horizontal scales) locate clusters in multidimensional space, allowing display of multiple
views of the data set. In the bar charts each variable is identified by bar width and
color. The total in a cluster, shown by bar height, is indicated by the scale on the
y-axis. The bar is correlated to the slider by color. Each slider bar, representing a
variable, is labeled to show that variable's minimum and maximum. The length and
placement of the slider indicate the subset of the variable being plotted. (U.S. Patent
Pending.)

Hints

This technique can be extended up to 20 dimensions. ◊ Analysis of continuous
variables can be made by first mapping to a discrete variable. ◊ Market analysis and
sociological investigations are two uses for this technique.

4 dependent variables
3 independent variables
Locates regions
Reservoir Engineering

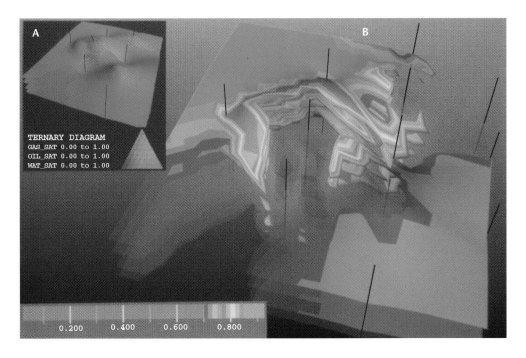

Color bands and translucency locate regions of interest.

Olin Lathrop, Cognivision, Inc., Westford, MA, USA.

Application (Steam Injection)

A simulation of steam injection into an oil reservoir to locate areas with oil or gas concentrations is analyzed. The simulation was executed on a Cray supercomputer and the image rendered on an Apollo DN10000 using Cognivision, Inc., FOTO.

Technique

In Figure B, four stacked, colored surfaces representing oil saturation at different depths are correlated to a color key skewed to emphasize the highly saturated regions. Surface height cues provided by lighting and shading represent relative amounts of pressure. Making areas with oil saturation of less than 0.5 transparent, 0.5 to 0.7 semitransparent, and greater than 0.7 opaque further emphasizes areas of interest and cuts away unimportant areas in the image. Figure A, with ternary color mapping, shows three scalar fields mapped to the primary colors: gas, red; oil, green; and water, blue. Each color in the ternary color key depicts the concentration of the three scalars. Both images represent existing wells with dark gray vertical lines.

Hints

Although the ternary color key could be used to compare three independent scalar fields, the key works best when used to visualize a mixture, as in this image, where the percentages of gas, oil, and water add up to 100 percent. ◊ See also **1-4**, which shows color used to depict two scalar fields that are not a mixture.

2-7 Multivariate

3 dependent variables
2 independent variables
Locates clusters
Agriculture

Multicolored rectangular shapes locate clusters of similar values.

Donna J. Cox, University of Illinois, Urbana, IL, USA; Ray Idaszak, NCSA, Urbana, IL, USA; David Onstad, University of Illinois, Urbana, IL, USA.

[1] Donna J. Cox, "Interactive Computer-Assisted RGB Editor (ICARE)," *Proceedings for the 7th Symposium on Small Computers in the Arts* (October 8–11, 1987): pp. 40–45.

[2] D. Cox, "Using the Supercomputer to Visualize Higher Dimensions: An Artist's Contribution to Scientific Visualization," *Leonardo: Journal of Art, Science and Technology* 21 (1988): 233–242.

[3] D. Cox, "The Art of Scientific Visualization," *Academic Computing* (March 1990): 20–40; references at end of journal.

[4] See additional references at the end of Section II, p. 182.

Application (Entomology)

A simulation models the population dynamics of corn borers. The image represents a cornfield. The corn rows are infested with normal corn-borer larvae and with larvae that have been infected with a microsporidium for pest control. The simulation was computed on a Cray supercomputer and the image rendered on a Silicon Graphics workstation.

Technique

Each colored, rectangular shape represents each of the two kinds of corn borers in combination and the density of frass (a measure of the infestation). Each of the dependent variables is assigned a color: red, green, or blue. The intensity of color is determined by the magnitude of the variable. The rectangular shape is colored according to the sum of the colors. The sum of the three variables also determines the height of the box, which corresponds to the magnitude of the infestation. A shape whose sum is near zero is black. Reddish, greenish, or bluish shapes stand for greater numbers of one type or the other of corn borer or of frass. Black to gray to white indicates approximately equal but increasing distributions.[1–4]

Hints

Changing the colors of the variables may help locate the boundaries of the clusters because the physiology of the eye may respond better to some colors. ◊ The success of this technique depends on the viewer's understanding how colors are added; adding a medium green to a medium red to a dark blue results in orange; adding a bright green to a bright red to a bright blue results in white. ◊ This technique, similar to that of **1-9**, is useful in discovering relationships among three physically distinct variables. Four variables could also be represented, using height as the fourth.

5 dependent variables
2 independent variables
Correlates variables
Computer Graphics

Multiple visualization techniques allow correlation of three scalar fields, one vector field, and mesh topology.

Roger A. Crawfis and Michael J. Allison, Lawrence Livermore National Laboratory, Livermore, CA, USA.

Application (Visualization)

Visual techniques are explored to see how five fields can reasonably be correlated by using textures for some of the fields. The image was created and rendered on a Silicon Graphics workstation.

Technique

On a regular grid, pseudocolor, surface height, and a bump map isoline[1] each represent a scalar field; a vector bump[2] represents a vector field. A bump map is a collection of bumps (a texture) used to enhance a graphical element (isolines and vectors in this image) to help the eye perceive that element. The bump map depends on lighting because it is a 3-D distortion of geometry seen only as highlights and shadows. A vector bump is a rectangular cell having texture and color and made to look like an arrow. In this image, vector bumps are placed to show the gradient, but they could have shown other vector quantities. Lighting, perspective, and a square grid that distorts as the surface distorts enhance 3-D understanding.

Hints

Bump-map appearance can range from an almost smooth surface, like an orange rind, to a rugged, surreal landscape, to bumps occurring along lines or within regions. However, using bumps on an already rough surface could be distracting. ◊ Bump-map appearance is highly dependent on the texture created by the size, position, and density of the bumps and the light source; therefore, we recommend interactive adjustment of these parameters for effective use of this technique. ◊ See **5-4** and **10-7** for other examples of effective bump-map usage.

[1] Roger A. Crawfis and Michael J. Allison, "A Scientific Visualization Synthesizer," in *Visualization '91* (Los Alamitos, CA: IEEE Computer Society Press, October 22–25, 1991).

[2] James F. Blinn and Martin E. Newell, "Texture and Reflection in Computer Generated Images," *Communications of the ACM* 19, 10 (October 1976): pp. 542–547.

4 dependent variables
3 independent variables
Correlates scalars
Computational Fluid
   Dynamics

**Multiple images
correlate scalars.**

Verlan K. Gabrielson, Sandia
National Laboratories,
Livermore, CA, USA.

[1] Greg Evans and Ralph Greif,
"Unsteady Three-Dimensional
Mixed Convection in a Heated
Horizontal Channel with
Applications to Chemical
Vapor Deposition," *International Journal of Heat and Mass
Transfer* 34 (1991): 2039–2051.

[2] V. K. Gabrielson, "GGP: A
Graphics Program for
Specialized Displays and
Animation of Finite Element
and Finite Difference Analysis," SAND 91-8223, Sandia
National Laboratories,
Livermore, CA, USA.

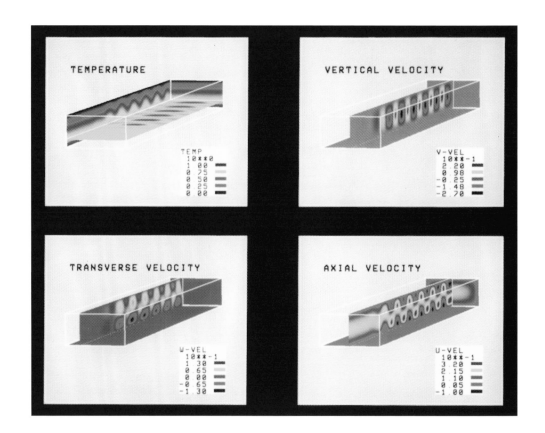

Application (Chemical Vapor Deposition)

The fluid flow and heat transfer that occur during channel flow in chemical vapor deposition are simulated for conditions typical of microelectronics processing. The image shows a snapshot in time of data computed for a 3-D Navier-Stokes flow in a channel.[1] The analysis and visualization using GGP[2] were executed on a Cray supercomputer.

Technique

Each of four variables in the channel is represented in a rectangular box delineated in white to allow correlation among any of the variables: temperature and the three velocity components of the flow. For each box, two bounding faces and one slice plane of the 3-D volume are colored according to the value of the variable labeled in the image. Color keys help estimate the values for each variable. This 3-D image is rendered using 2-D techniques: the (x,y,z) locations were plotted as $(x\text{-}z, y\text{-}z)$.

Hints

Using only two bounding faces and one slice plane greatly simplifies the graphics programming and avoids the problem of occluding boundaries.

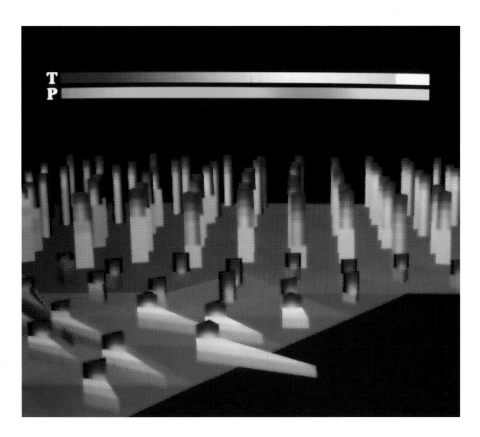

Glyph plot correlates variables.

Donna J. Cox, University of Illinois, Urbana, IL, USA; Richard Ellson, Eastman Kodak Company, Rochester, NY, USA; Ray Idaszak, National Center for Supercomputing Applications, Urbana, IL, USA.

Application (Plastic Injection Molding)

Plastic injection molding[1, 2] is simulated to predict and optimize the flow phase in the molding process. The simulation ran on a Cray supercomputer, and the final image was rendered on a Silicon Graphics workstation using Wavefront Technologies software.

Technique

3-D glyphs represent depth of mold and behavior of plastic during the molding process. Glyph height indicates depth of the mold; color indicates temperature, which is keyed to the upper color scale labeled "T"; orientation indicates direction of flow; and length indicates velocity of flowing plastic. When the plastic begins to harden, velocity becomes zero, shortening the length. Shading the glyphs redundantly encodes velocity: smooth shading is zero velocity; flat shading (or faceted shading) is positive velocity. Smooth shading of the stagnant plastic makes the glyphs appear rounded and visually distinguishes them from the angular glyphs of the flowing plastic. The angular, flat-shaded glyphs in the foreground that look like pinball flippers represent areas of the mold that are still filling. The color of the plane below the glyphs represents pressure and is keyed to the lower color scale labeled "P."

Hints

As many as six variables could be represented. The velocity variable, counted as one, is actually two variables: speed and direction. And the type of color shading, not counted as one of the four dependent variables, is used redundantly. ◊ Glyph techniques are useful when representing many variables. ◊ Orienting the image so that the glyphs indicating flow are in the foreground puts the important information where it is easy to read.

[1] R. Ellson and D. Cox, "Visualization of Injection Molding," *Simulation* 51, 5 (1988): 184–188.

[2] R. Ellson and M. Olano, "Injection Molding: Supercomputing and Supergraphics," *Cray Channels* 11, 3 (1989): 2–5.

2-11 Multivariate

7 dependent variables
2 independent variables
Relates scalars and tensors
Computational Solid
   Mechanics

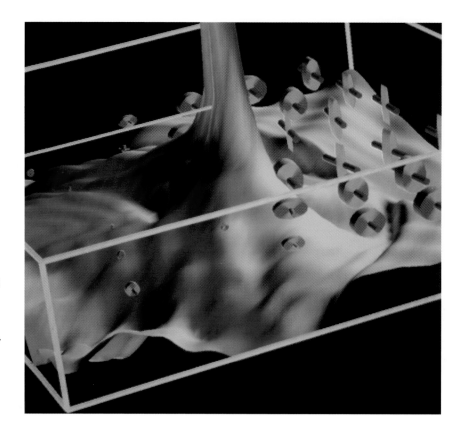

Pseudocolor surface and glyphs relate scalars and tensors.

Robert B. Haber, Hyun M. Koh,
Hae Sung Lee, Department of
Theoretical and Applied
Mechanics, University of
Illinois at Urbana-Champaign,
Urbana, IL, USA.

[1] Hyun M. Koh and Robert B.
Haber, "Dynamic Crack
Propagation Analysis Using
Eulerian-Lagrangian Kinematic
Descriptions," *Computational
Mechanics* 3 (1988): 141–155.

[2] Robert B. Haber, "Visualization Techniques for Engineering Mechanics," *Computing
Systems in Engineering* 1 (1990):
37–55.

Application (Fracture Mechanics)

Rapid crack propagation in a brittle material is simulated[1] to create and then study two scalars (strain energy density and kinetic energy density) and one 3-D second order symmetric tensor (stress). The image is rendered on an Alliant VFX-80.

Technique

Color and height show the fields for singular strain energy density and kinetic energy. The stress content of the elastic wave pattern emitted at the growing crack tip (pointed to by a line at the approximate center of the volume) is revealed by the shape, orientation, and color of the glyphs. The lighting model is adjusted to reveal the subtle elastic wave pattern. The glyphs are drawn at selected locations.[2] The principal stress directions and magnitudes are computed for each of these locations and encoded into the geometry and color of the glyphs. A perspective-bounding box and lighting provide the 3-D depth cues. A zoom operation magnifies the image to bring out the detail.

Hints

Lighting adjustments, glyph location selection, and orientation are best made in an interactive environment. ◊ The wide antialiased lines avoid the distracting jagged-ness often seen in diagonal lines. ◊ The glyphs provide a means for viewing the stress tensor as a unified object. See also **2-10**, **6-11,** and **13-9** for other glyph-encoding schemes.

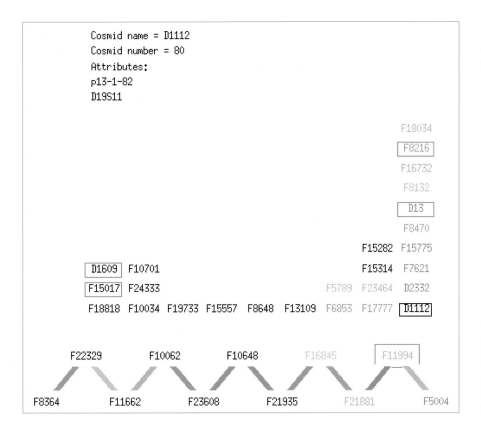

Cosmid name = D1112
Cosmid number = 80
Attributes:
p13-1-82
D19S11

Miscellaneous
Shows relationships
Genetics

Color, location, and legend show relationships.

Mark C. Wagner, Lawrence Livermore Laboratory, Livermore, CA, USA.

Application (Human Genome)

An interactive analysis tool[1] assists comprehension and manipulation of DNA data for the Human Genome Project. (This tool helped confirm the recently discovered structure of a common type of genetically caused muscular dystrophy.) This image was created by the Human Genome Browser and rendered on a Sun Microsystems SPARCstation 1.

[1] Mark C. Wagner, "Human Genome Browser: A Graphical Tool for Viewing DNA," DOE Contractors Meeting, Santa Fe, NM, February 1991.

Technique

A zigzag line represents overlap in an approximate ordered segment of DNA. The alphanumeric notations at the top and bottom of the zigzag lines encode clone locations in the DNA segment. The colors of the bars represent the relative amount of DNA common to both clone locations. Other alphanumeric notations above the zigzag notations locate other clones in relation to the ordered DNA segment. The column of text in the upper part of the diagram indicates the clone being studied and gives some biologically significant information about it. The colors of the other clones indicate the relative amount of DNA common to the selected clone. Red rectangles highlight the clones that have properties of special interest to the clone under study.

Hints

Using the very simple image elements of lines, identifying text, position, and color facilitates discovery of relationships among the elements in this very complex image.

20 dependent variables
1 independent variable
Depicts patterns
Biology

A modified bar chart, called a *sequence logo*, depicts patterns.

Thomas D. Schneider, National Cancer Institute, Laboratory of Mathematical Biology, Frederick Cancer Research and Development Center, Frederick, MD, USA.

[1] T. D. Schneider and R. M. Stephens "Sequence Logos: A New Way to Display Consensus Sequences," *Nucleic Acids Research* 18 (1990): 6097–6100.

[2] R. E. Dickerson and I. Geis, *Hemoglobin: Structure, Function, Evolution, and Pathology* (Menlo Park, CA: Benjamin/Cummings, 1983).

[3] T. D. Schneider, G. D. Stormo, L. Gold, and A. Ehrenfeucht, "Information Content of Binding Sites on Nucleotide Sequences," *Journal of Molecular Biology* 188 (1986): 415–431.

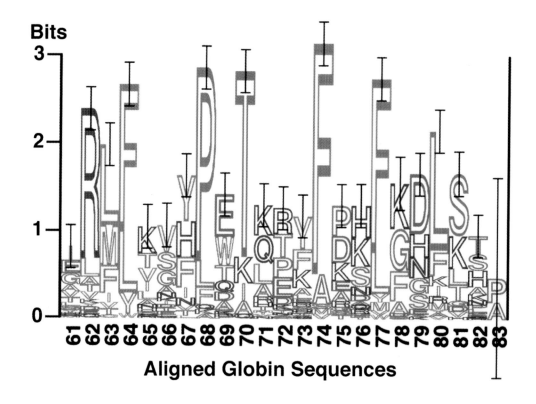

Aligned Globin Sequences

Application (Protein Patterns)

A "sequence logo"[1] showing positions 61 to 83 of the amino acid sequences of globins that capture and store oxygen[2] is the subject. A machine-independent program written in either C or Pascal constructs the logos in Postscript.*

Technique

The sequence logo, a way of representing the amino acid combinations at various positions, is constructed from 20 colored letters, each representing an amino acid. At each position a stack of letters is created. The height of the stack represents the Shannon information[3] indicated by the vertical scale. A black error bar positioned at the top of each stack indicates the expected variation in height. The height of a letter is proportional to the frequency with which the amino acid occurs at that position. The letters are sorted by frequency and color coded to indicate the properties of the amino acids: blue is basic, red is acidic, green is neutral, purple is ambivalent, and orange is oily.

Hints

The sequence logo is application-independent and can be used to study frequency distributions of various multivariate datasets. ◊ The logo can easily be extended to two independent variables by creating a 3-D modified bar chart. ◊ The amino acid color classification is also a memory aid: blue and red are the litmus-test colors for base and acid; green is at the middle of the color spectrum; purple is sometimes represented at either end of the color spectrum as magenta (a little brighter than red) or as a darker blue; and orange is the hue of some oils. ◊ Complex logos take time to decipher and may not be appropriate for general audiences.

---

* For those familiar with Internet, UNIX, and either C or Pascal, the sequence logo program is available (at press time) on Internet by anonymous ftp from ncifcrf.gov in directory pub/delila. Files makelogo.c.Z. and makelogo.p.Z are the sources.

11 variables
Identifies periodic events
Business

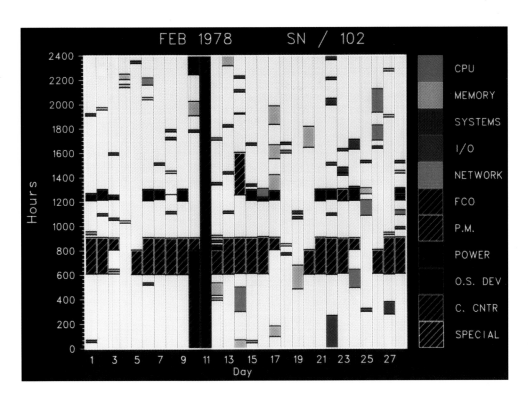

A bar-charting technique is used to identify periodic events.

Author unknown. Contributed by Donald Vickers, Lawrence Livermore National Laboratory, Livermore, CA, USA.

Application (Time Accounting)

Computer availability and downtime were analyzed over a one-month period. The bar-charting application ran on a Control Data Corporation CDC7600 and constructed an image file using Computer Associates' DISSPLA graphics library. The image file was then output to a slide on a Dicomed film recorder.

Technique

A bar-charting program is adapted to show correlation of events over a fixed cycle. All bars are equal in length and each represents one day in a time-history. The cycles are laid out side by side. Events, encoded on the bars by color and patterns to indicate frequency and duration, are identified on an accompanying key. White signifies "up and available." Cyclical events are seen as recurring patterns.

Hints

Dramatically different colors distinguish the events. ◊ This technique fails if events are simultaneous.

3 dependent variables
1 independent variable
Correlates variables
Computational Astrophysics

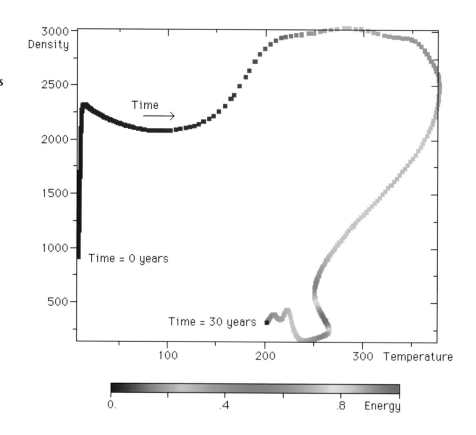

Time-ordered colored squares show the relationship of three variables over time.

Richard A. Ward and Peter R. Keller, Lawrence Livermore National Laboratory, Livermore, CA, USA.

[1] I. Iben, Jr., "Thermal Pulses: p-Capture, α-Capture, s-Process Nucleosynthesis, and Convective Mixing in a Star of Intermediate Mass," *Astrophysical Journal*, 196, 2, Part 1 (1 March 1975): 525.

[2] I. Iben, Jr., "Thermal Pulse and Interpulse Properties of Intermediate-Mass Stellar Models with Carbon-Oxygen Cores of Mass 0.96, 1.16, and 1.36 M," *Astrophysical Journal*, 217, 3, Part 1 (1 November 1977): 788.

Application (Plasma Physics)

An ionized stellar plasma undergoing a helium shell flash[1,2] is simulated. The data were calculated and the picture was computed on a Cray Y-MP supercomputer using in-house graphics libraries. The computed picture was sent to an Apple Macintosh II for display by a modified version of the University of Illinois, National Center for Supercomputing Applications utility, IMAGE.

Technique

A labeled Cartesian plot shows relations among three variables over time. Density and temperature are calculated separately as a function of time. The color of each square on the curve is proportional to the rate of nuclear energy generated by helium burning (red being the greatest). Each square shows the value of two variables (read on the x- and y-axes), locates the approximate value of a third variable (read from the color scale), and indicates the relation among those three variables. An arrow indicates the direction of time. The colored squares are plotted at equal time steps; the gaps indicate the relative rate at which the variables are changing.

Hints

The "curve" could also be annotated with several numbered tick marks to show time. ◊ The size of squares can be larger or smaller to accommodate different amounts of data. ◊ If the curve appeared discontinuous, the squares could be connected with a thin line.

1 dependent variable
2 independent variables
Reveals pattern
Atmospheric Science

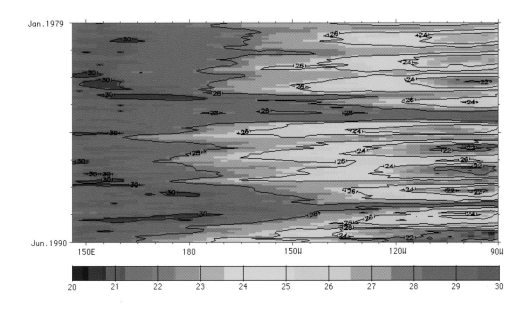

A time-history of a 1-D slice reveals periodic patterns.

Dean N. Williams and Robert L. Mobley, Lawrence Livermore National Laboratory, Livermore, CA, USA.

Application (Global Climate Modeling)

The measured temperature of the sea surface is pseudocolored to study the El Niño effect in the Pacific Ocean. The in-house Program for Climate Model Diagnosis and Intercomparison rendered the image on a Sun Microsystems workstation.

Technique

This image illustrates several straightforward, simple, but good methods for presenting data. The surface temperature of the Pacific Ocean is measured daily on a regular grid over a number of years. A subset of the 2-D time history along a 1-D slice reveals recurring cycles. The data are pseudocolored to emphasize the cyclic behavior. Black isolines highlight the cycles and are annotated to show temperature values.

Hints

Attention to small, easily accomplished detail such as the breaks in the isolines that improve readability of the number makes an image more comprehensible. ◊ See also **3-1** and **3-7** for other examples for discovering time-dependent behavior.

1 dependent variable
2 independent variables
Locates scalars
Atmospheric Science

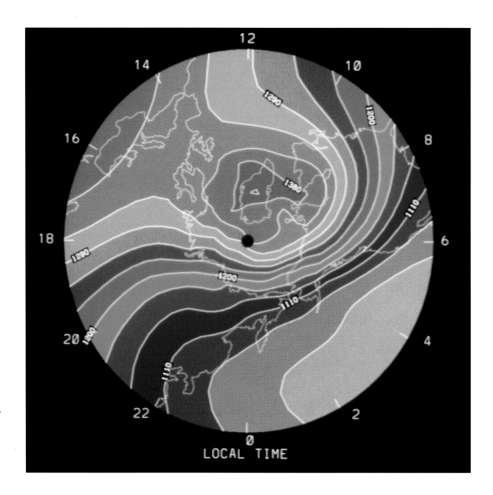

Labeled colored bands locate regions with same values.

Bob Dickinson, Ben Foster, Cicely Ridley, and Ray Roble, National Center for Atmospheric Research, Boulder, CO, USA; submitted by Lee Carter and Bob Lackman; National Center for Atmospheric Research.

[1] NCAR Graphics Package: *NCAR Graphics Version 3.1 Update Packet,* June 1991; *NCAR Graphics Guide to New Utilities,* Version 3.00, October 1989; *NCAR Graphic User's Guide,* Version 2.00, August 1987; *AUTOGRAPH: A Graphing Utility,* Version 2.00, August 1987; National Center for Atmospheric Research, Scientific Computing Division, Boulder, CO, USA.

Application (Global Climate Modeling)

A variety of upper-atmosphere processes during a geomagnetic storm are simulated on a Cray X-MP supercomputer. The graphics were created with the National Center for Atmospheric Research (NCAR) graphics package.[1]

Technique

Several simple, good methods clearly visualize data. A labeled, color-contour band plot quickly identifies regions of equal temperature. A black dot at the center clearly locates the North Pole, a position of interest to meteorologists. Outlining the continents, shown in white, provides a reference for the variable. The white isolines, slightly thicker to distinguish them from the continent reference lines, help show the shape of the temperature field. A rectangular black background on top of the temperature colors makes the labels on the isolines more legible. Numbers around the circumference provide time-of-day reference.

Hints

This image illustrates the importance of correctly matching purpose and technique. Using a few discrete, saturated colors bounded by white lines clearly shows shapes of regions and distinguishes different values. Choosing pastels or more hues would make it difficult to see bands of equal temperature. ◊ In contrast, **1-2**, **7-6**, **11-3**, and **11-4,** Figure A, effectively use more than 250 discrete colors, but their purpose is to convey continuity and locate highs and lows.

1 dependent variable
3 independent variables
Reveals structure
Astronomy

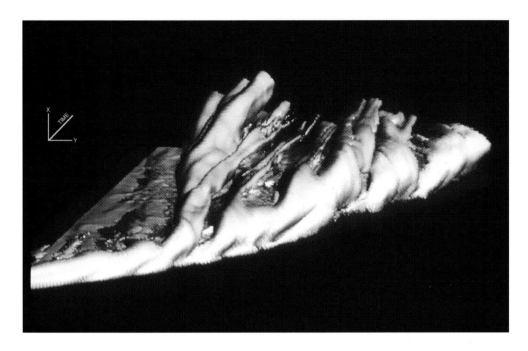

Volume visualization shows time-history structure.

T. Todd Elvins, San Diego Supercomputer Center, San Diego, CA, USA.; David Payne, Jet Propulsion Laboratory, Pasadena, CA, USA.

Application (Computational Astrophysics)

Computer models of a cosmic jet's magnetic fields reconstruct the jet's evolution using fluid-dynamics techniques to discover why the jet continues in a thin stream as it penetrates a relatively low-density medium. The image was generated with Sun Microsystems's voxvu software on a Sun Microsystems 4/370 with a TAAC accelerator.

Technique

Successive 2-D slices in time are combined to form a volume for studying the entire simulation in one static image. Ray casting enhances the 3-D shape. This image shows the progression through time of a 2-D scalar field moving from the front lower left face of a transparent cube to the back upper right face of the cube.

Hints

This technique can be used to study the shape of fluid flow over time on a single image. Watching the evolution as an animation would be more effective, however.

3-6 Time

1 dependent variable
3 independent variables
Reveals structure
Computational Physics

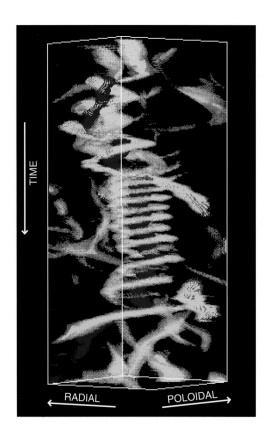

Opacity and color reveal structure.

Chris L. Anderson, James A. Crotinger, and Alice E. Koniges, Lawrence Livermore National Laboratory, Livermore, CA, USA.

[1] A. E. Koniges, J. A. Crotinger, and P. H. Diamond, "Structure Formation and Transport in Dissipative Drift-Wave Turbulence," Submitted to *Physics of Fluids*, Part B.

[2] Ch. Filippas, P. Ritz, A. E. Koniges, J. A. Crotinger, and P. H. Diamond, "Detection of Coherent Structures in the Edge of the Text Tokamak Plasma," *Proceedings of the 18th European Physical Society Conference on Controlled Fusion and Plasma Physics*, Berlin, June 3–7, 1991.

[3] *SunVision Reference Manual*, Sun Microsystems, Inc., 1990.

[4] Marc Levoy, "Volume Rendering: Display of Surfaces from Volume Data," *IEEE Computer Graphics and Applications* 8, 3 (May 1988).

Application (Plasma Turbulence)

Coherent structures in tokamak plasmas[1, 2] are studied using a magnetohydrodynamics code running on a Cray 2 supercomputer. The image was rendered on a Sun Microsystems workstation with SunVision.[3]

Technique

Four hundred time slices of 2-D vortex data are concatenated to form a 3-D volume representing the time-history of a 2-D slice. The voxels in the volume are rendered by assigning a color and opacity to each using ray casting[4] with light-source shading. The low vortex values are colored bluish-purple and opaque, the high vortex values are colored yellow and opaque, and the remaining voxels are made transparent. White lines outline the volume bounds and help to suggest 3-D.

Hints

Conceptually, coloring high values yellow and low values blue is a very simple technique, but the researcher must interactively adjust colors, opacity, and volume orientation to derive meaningful information. ◊ If more than one value is to be studied, as in this example, contrasting colors should be used to more readily distinguish one colored feature from another. ◊ See **3-5**, **6-10**, and **11-8** for other ways of revealing structure in volumes.

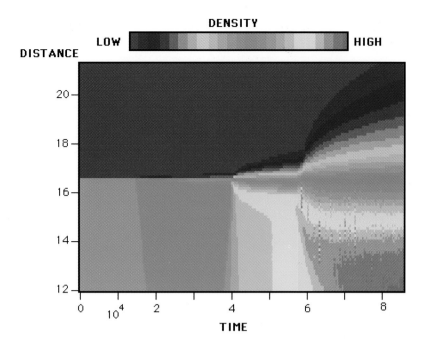

1 dependent variable
2 independent variables
Illustrates time history
Computational Physics

Pseudocolor length-versus-time plot illustrates 2-D time-history.

W. Patrick Crowley, Thomas S. Carman, and Peter R. Keller, Lawrence Livermore National Laboratory, Livermore, CA, USA.

Application (Compressible Mix Dynamics)

A shock-tube experiment to study how materials of different densities mix is simulated. A shock wave enters at the upper left and passes through, first, a layer of nitrogen and, second, an adjacent layer of helium. In this image we examine the effects of the shock but show only its effect on the helium. For graphics purposes, the nitrogen density is zero. The data were generated and the picture was computed with a Cray 1 supercomputer. The image was displayed on a Tektronix 4125 high-resolution color terminal.

Technique

At each raster point in the image, the density of helium is colored according to the visible light spectrum (purple, low; red, high). Labeled axes locate density features, and a color key indicates relative density. Although only density is plotted, the image reveals relations among shock waves, material density, and time, as well as the extent of mixing. The shock wave causes the straight lines that seem to demarcate color changes. The progressive blurring along the time axis indicates that helium is mixing with the nitrogen layer. Sloping lines indicate physical move-ment; horizontal color change indicates change in density at a specific location. Although the length-versus-time plot may seem unusual, this visualization is modeled upon diagnostic equipment called a streak camera. The streak camera sequentially records on film the changes observed in an experiment seen through a narrow slit.

Hints

Unexpected features in an image should be investigated. The bubble-like structures in the red-through-green spectrum in this example were traced to a numerical instability in the simulation and were corrected. ◊ Although we use a pseudocolor plot with a length-versus-time axis, as in **3-3**, our knowledge of the shock-induced variations in density allows us to read more out of the image. ◊ Using the streak-camera technique to examine data sets that change with time can avoid the need for animation.

3 dependent variables
1 independent variable
Depicts motion
Geophysics

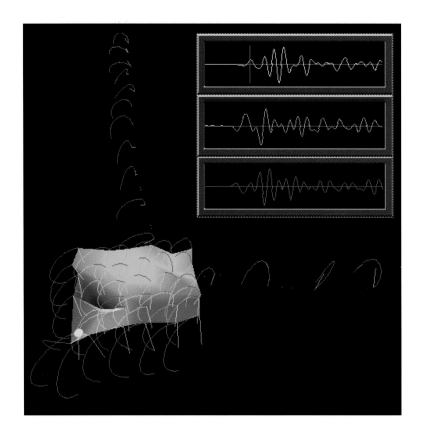

Multiple visualization techniques depict 3-axis displacement over time.

Brian C. Kaplan, Paul N. Anderson, and Gary L. Pavlis, Center for Innovative Computer Applications, Indiana University, Bloomington, IN, USA.

Application (Seismology)

Earthquake-generated seismic data, recorded by a closely spaced array of 60 three-component seismometers, were animated to study the seismic-wave character. The data were manipulated and rendered with in-house software combined with Stardent's Application Visualization System (AVS) on a Stardent Titan computer.

Technique

The image combines a pseudocolored surface representing a snapshot in time of amplified earth displacement, particle traces representing motion of seismometers, and three *x-y* plots representing amplitude of motion over a window in time. The vertical red line in the yellow *x-y* plot indicates the time of the snapshot. The colors of the surface plot and the *x-y* plots represent motion in the three orthogonal directions: yellow and blue correspond to horizontal ground motion, and red corresponds to vertical motion. A yellow dot on the surface identifies the seismometer location of the motion depicted in the three *x-y* plots. One end of a green "stick" represents the original location of a seismometer and the other end follows the seismometer's displacement, indicated by the green particle trace. (Green appears yellow when drawn on the surface.)

Hints

The path described by the green particle traces could be better understood by using interactive rotation or animation. ◊ The surface could be made translucent to reveal the particle traces without changing their color. ◊ The technique of using a time-history window as well as a snapshot in time allows us to analyze surface distortion over time.

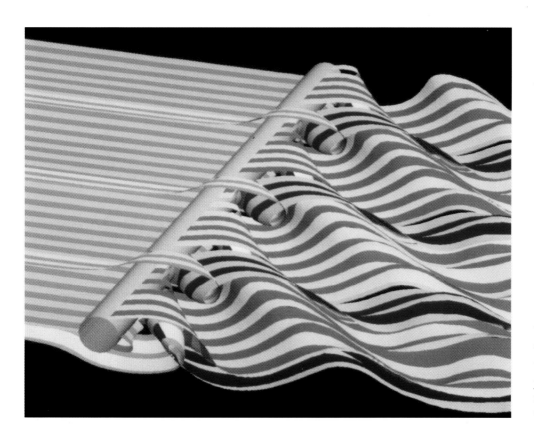

1 dependent variable
3 independent variables
Depicts flow
Visualization

**Topological surfaces
depict time history of
2-D flow.**

James L. Helman and
Lambertus Hesselink, Stanford
University, Stanford, CA, USA.

Application (Fluid-Flow Visualization)

Visual techniques for representing the time-dependent behavior of a computed 2-D flow around a cylinder are studied. The image was rendered on a Silicon Graphics 4D/220-GTX using in-house software.

Technique

Topological visualization uses dynamical systems theory[1] to help understand 2-D fluid flow past a cylinder.[2] Time increases from top to bottom (back to front). Colored bands, lighting, and shading enhance the 3-D effect to help visualize fluid flow. The critical points in the flow (points at which the magnitude of the velocity is zero) are classified by type,[3] and those points are joined with tangent curves. Each surface is colored to depict its relation to a critical point. The light and dark candystriping provides cues to shape.

Hints

Understanding this technique requires some knowledge of dynamical systems theory; therefore, it should be used only with selected audiences. ◊ Displaying vector fields as a set of tangent surfaces is much simpler and cleaner than presenting the fields as a set of arrows or curves. ◊ **6-11** also demonstrates flow fields with dynamical systems theory.

[1] R. H. Abraham and C. D. Shaw, *Dynamics: The Geometry of Behavior*, Parts 1–4 (Santa Cruz, CA: Ariel Press, 1984).

[2] S. Rogers and D. Kwak, "An Upwind Differencing Scheme for Time Accurate Incompressible Navier-Stokes Equations," in *Proceedings of the AIAA 6th Applied Aerodynamics Conference*, American Institute of Aeronautics and Astronautics, Paper 88-2583 (June 1988), pp. 492–502.

[3] James L. Helman and Lambertus Hesselink, "Surface Representations of Two- and Three-Dimensional Fluid Flow Topology," in *Visualization '90* (Los Alamitos, CA: IEEE Computer Society Press, October 1990), pp. 6–13.

4-1 Process

1 dependent variable
2–3 independent variables
Determines shape
Visualization

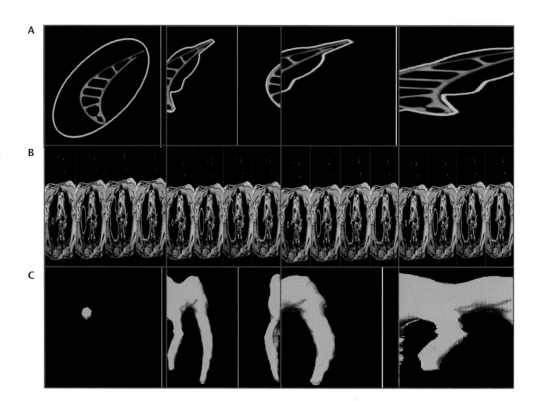

An algorithm deforms a polygon or polyhedron to determine the shape of an object.

James V. Miller and David E. Breen, Rensselaer Design Research Center, Rensselaer Polytechnic Institute (RPI), Troy, NY, USA; William E. Lorensen, General Electric Company Corporate Research and Development, Schenectady, NY, USA; Robert M. O'Bara and Michael J. Wozny, Rensselaer Design Research Center, RPI.

[1] J. V. Miller, D. E. Breen, W. E. Lorensen, R. M. O'Bara, and M. J. Wozny, "Geometrically Deformed Models: A Method for Extracting Closed Geometric Models from Volume Data," *Computer Graphics*, 25, 4, (July 1991): 217–226.

[2] J. V. Miller, D. E. Breen, and M. J. Wozny, "Extracting Geometric Models Through Constraint Minimization," in *Visualization '90* (Los Alamitos, CA: IEEE Computer Society Press, 1990), pp. 74–82.

[3] J. V. Miller, "On GDMs: Geometrically Deformed Models for the Extraction of Closed Shapes from Volume Data," M.S. Thesis, Rensselaer Polytechnic Institute, Troy, NY (December 1990).

Application (Feature Extraction)

A time series of deformation steps is studied to evaluate an algorithm that determines shape. This algorithm extracts a geometric model from arbitrary 2- and 3-D scalar data sets that may then be visualized or analyzed to produce quantitative information. The original data are from computed tomography (CT) and magnetic resonance imaging (MRI) machines. The images were rendered with Silicon Graphics GL library and Raster Technologies PHIGS+ software.

Technique

The geometrically deformed model (GDM) algorithm[1-3] converts data-set features into geometric models through steps that deform a polygon (for 2-D data sets) or a polyhedron (for 3-D data sets) until it reveals the shape portrayed in the data. In Figure A, the GDM algorithm generates a polygon of an approximately closed 2-D feature. The yellow line represents the polygon. The light green regions represent a feature within a scalar field—that is, a feature defined by values ranging from 50 to 125. The yellow polygon, when subjected to the GDM algorithm, defines the feature by deforming inward, giving it a geometric shape that can be measured or subjected to geometric operations. Figure B shows a similar example with the polygon deformed outward to reveal the shape of a cavity. Figure C depicts the GDM algorithm used to define a 3-D geometry.

Hints

An unexpected geometry requires further investigation. For example, in engineering, the unexpected geometry may be caused by a physical defect or a break in the object; in medicine, a malformed organ may indicate a tumor pressing against an organ. ◊ Notice that here we illustrate the behavior of an algorithm using shapes that represent shape, but **4-6** uses shapes that represent values.

A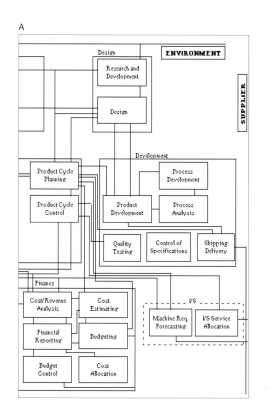

B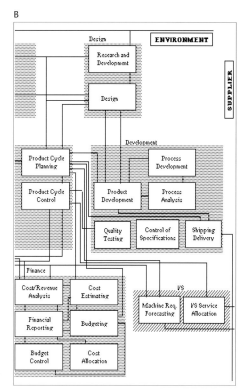

Miscellaneous
Distinguishes classes
Business

**A gray backdrop
distinguishes classes to
make an image more
comprehensible.**

Gerald L. Lohse, The Wharton
School, University of Pennsylvania, Philadelphia, PA, USA.

Application (Business-System Analysis)

The network diagram depicting relationships and information flow was developed on an Apple Macintosh II using MacDraw II.

Technique

A complex diagram of rectangles and lines (Figure A) is simplified by surrounding related blocks with shading (Figure B). The diagrams, both containing the same information, illustrate how effectively a simple technique such as background shading can differentiate groups and make an image more understandable.

Hints

The human brain quickly comprehends 7 ±2 pieces of information. To aid comprehension of a complex image, we should use techniques that visibly group similar kinds of information. Colors or dotted or dashed lines could also clarify connections among boxes.

Miscellaneous
Depicts behavior
Process Simulation

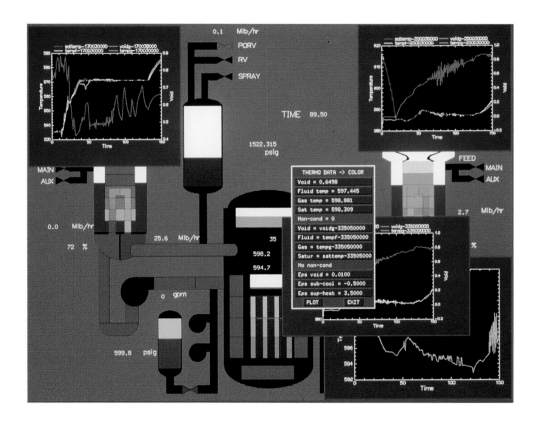

Stylized interconnected components depict complex-system behavior.

Dale M. Snider, William H. Grush, and Kurt L. Wagner, Idaho National Engineering Laboratory, Idaho Falls, ID, USA.

[1] V. H. Ransom, et al., *RELAP5/ MOD2 Code Manual*, Volumes 1 and 2, NUREG/CR-4312, EGG-2396 (August 1985 and December 1985).

Application (Process Control and Analysis)

This Nuclear Plant Analyzer (NPA) program simplifies a display of complex data depicting a nuclear-reactor system in a potentially dangerous, transient condition so that an analyst can quickly interpret the data. The image was rendered on a DECstation as the simulation progressed, using the NPA software linked to the RELAP5 nuclear-reactor transient code.[1]

Technique

Data from a simulation of a complex system are used to drive an easy-to-read display of color-filled polygons that represent the state of the system's components. Detailed data can be called up and displayed in various formats (strip charts, dials, color bars, time-history plots, tables). Call-ups indicate in more detail what is happening at selected locations.

Hints

This image is a good example of how data can communicate visually at two levels of understanding: the large icons provide an overview of the system and the callouts display data in application-specific detail. This example demonstrates the power of simple graphic representations. ◊ See **4-6** and **4-8,** Figure A, for different examples that use simple graphic elements in analyzing software systems.

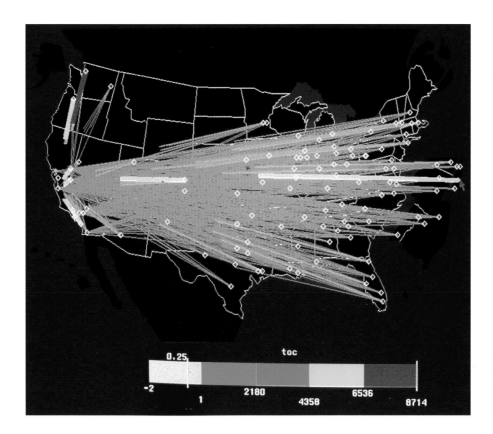

1 dependent variable
4 independent variables
Reveals behavior
Visualization

Network visualization reveals system behavior.

Stephen G. Eick, Richard A. Becker, Eileen O. Miller, and Allan R. Wilks, AT&T Bell Laboratories, Murray Hill, NJ, USA.

Application (Network Analysis)

Increased volume of telephone traffic shortly after the 1989 Loma Prieta, California, earthquake is used to help develop visual techniques for analyzing a network.[1-4] The image was rendered on a Silicon Graphics IRIS workstation using in-house software.

Technique

Color and line width indicate telephone traffic between cities, which are drawn as white diamonds. To show direction of the traffic, a line emanates from the source halfway to the target, helping to reduce visual clutter. An accompanying color key helps quantify colors (blue, lowest volume; red, highest volume). Heavier traffic stands out because the lines are made wider and are plotted "on top of" the other lines. A reference map, drawn in white, helps locate nodes and provides a bird's-eye view for zooming. For greater clarity, a portion of the East Coast is magnified at the right.

Hints

The amounts of data and graphic detail need interactive adjustment to analyze peak periods. ◊ The half-line technique, used to show activity between points, could be applied to other networks, such as water-distribution systems, highways, and computer networks.

[1] Richard A. Becker, Stephen G. Eick, and Allan R. Wilks, "Basics of Network Visualization," *IEEE Computer Graphics and Applications* 11, 3 (May 1991): 12.

[2] Richard A. Becker, Stephen G. Eick, Eileen O. Miller, and Allan R. Wilks, "Dynamic Graphics for Network Visualization," in *Visualization '90* (Los Alamitos, CA: IEEE Computer Society Press, October 1990).

[3] Richard A. Becker, Stephen G. Eick, Eileen O. Miller, and Allan R. Wilks, "Network Visualization: User Interface Issues," *Proceedings SPIE Conference on Extracting Meaning from Complex Data,* San Jose, CA (February 1991).

[4] See additional references at the end of Section II, p. 182.

Miscellaneous
Identifies direction
Computational Chemistry

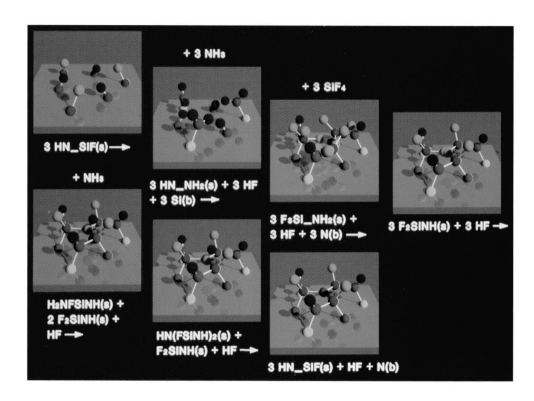

Annotated sequence of images identifies the direction of a process.

Verlan K. Gabrielson, Linda Armijo, and R. J. Kee, Sandia National Laboratories, Livermore, CA, USA; John Mareda, Sandia National Laboratories, Albuquerque, NM, USA.

[1] J. R. Strife, et al., "Application of Intelligent Processing to Chemical Vapor Deposition," First Thermal Structures Conference, Charlottesville, VA (November 15, 1990).

[2] B. E. Barker, "TEXT, A Guide to Automated Preparation of Visual Aids," SAND-8009, Sandia National Laboratories, Livermore, CA, USA (1982).

[3] Peter A. Watterberg, "MESA: A Ray Tracing and Rendering Package, Programmers Manual," unpublished report, Sandia National Laboratories, Albuquerque, NM (1988).

Application (Reaction Modeling)

The chemical reactions of depositing silicon nitride by chemical vapor deposition[1] are illustrated. This image was created on the VAX 780 and rendered to film on a film recorder.

Technique

This composite image is constructed from seven individual images to describe a process. Text for the composite image was generated with a Computer Associates' DISSPLA graphics library tool called TEXT,[2] which was rasterized into a large raster buffer. The individual images were rendered into small raster buffers using the MESA package[3] and then inset into the proper place in the composite image. The step-down arrangement of the individual images and the arrows in the chemical equation indicate the sequence of the process. In each individual image, color classifies materials (atoms), white connectors identify relationships (bonds), and a perspective translucent plane showing reflections and shadows enhances the 3-D model.

Hints

The cut-and-paste operation of a workstation word processor could also be used to move pictures into a text document to create a pictorial narrative.

Miscellaneous
Illustrates algorithm
   dynamics
Computer Science

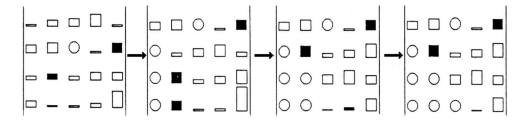

**A tree graph illustrates
algorithm dynamics.**

Konstantinos Konstantinides,
Hewlett-Packard Laboratories,
Palo Alto, CA, USA.

Application (Algorithm Visualization)

A tree graph[1] that shows the final four stages of a Gaussian elimination for a matrix of real data[2] is used to study the behavior of the algorithm. The data were calculated and displayed on a Hewlett-Packard HP9000 series 370 workstation, under the X Window environment.

Technique

In this image, data are represented as rectangles; height denotes value and color denotes sign (black, negative). Elements of zero value are drawn as circles. The positions of the circles and rectangles represent the data at various stages of the algorithm. The vertical, parallel lines at the right and left of each graph visually suggest matrices. The arrow signals the beginning of the next iteration.

Hints

Treating submatrices as blocks and providing a zoom feature into submatrices of interest would allow viewing of larger matrices. ◊ Visualizing matrix algorithms[3] can significantly help in identifying problems with numerical stability or convergence rate.

[1] K. Konstantinides, "Algorithm Visualization Using Tree Graphs," *The Visual Computer* 7, 4 (July 1991): 220–228, Springer International.

[2] R. Sedgewick, *Algorithms* (Reading, Mass.: Addison-Wesley, 1983), ch. 5.

[3] A. Tuchman and M. Berry, "Matrix Visualization in the Design of Numerical Algorithms," CSRD Tech. Report no. 826 (1989).

2 dependent variables
4 independent variables
Reveals behavior
Visualization

A

B

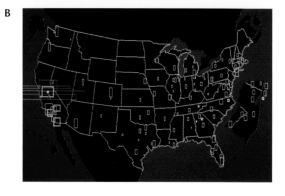

Network visualization reveals system behavior.

Stephen G. Eick, Richard A. Becker, Eileen O. Miller, and Allan R. Wilks, AT&T Bell Laboratories, Murray Hill, NJ, USA.

[1] Richard A. Becker, Stephen G. Eick, Eileen O. Miller, and Allan R. Wilks, "Dynamic Graphical Analysis of Network Data," *Interface '90 Proceedings*, East Lansing, MI (May 1990).

[2] Richard A. Becker, Stephen G. Eick, Eileen O. Miller, and Allan R. Wilks, "Network Visualization," *Fourth International Symposium on Spatial Data Handling Proceedings*, Zurich, Switzerland (July 1990), pp. 285–294.

[3] Richard A. Becker, Stephen G. Eick, Eileen O. Miller, and Allan R. Wilks, "Network Visualization," *American Statistical Association '90 Conference Proceedings*, Anaheim, CA (August 1990).

[4] See additional references at the end of Section II, p. 182.

Application (Network Analysis)

The volume of telephone traffic before and shortly after the 1989 Loma Prieta, California, earthquake is used to help develop techniques for visual network analysis.[1-4] The image was rendered on a Silicon Graphics IRIS workstation using in-house software.

Technique

In these charts from two frames of an animation showing network traffic, rectangles locate cities in the network. Rectangle widths represent the number of calls received by a city, and height represents the number of calls originating within a city. Color emphasizes the meaning of the width and height. Red cities are primarily recipients of calls; green cities are primarily originators of calls. White cities have roughly the same number of inbound and outbound calls. A reference map, drawn in white, helps locate the cities during zooming. For greater clarity, a portion of the East Coast is magnified and drawn to the right. Connections between cities are not drawn because each city is connected to every other. Figure A depicts normal traffic volume (Omaha, in red, is a major 800 answering center). Figure B depicts traffic volume (calls into the disaster area) shortly after the earthquake.

Hints

The rectangle color and aspect ratio used to show activity between cities could be used in other networks where input and output numbers are important. Amount of data and graphic detail may need to be interactively adjusted to analyze peak periods.

A

B

Miscellaneous
Depicts concurrent
   processes
Computer Science

**A 3-D block diagram
seen through virtual
reality depicts
concurrent processes.**

Michitaka Hirose, University
of Tokyo, Tokyo 113, Japan;
Haruo Amari, Tokyo Electric
Power Company, Tokyo 104,
Japan.

Application (Concurrent Software)

Virtual reality is developed to program concurrent software.[1, 2] Figure A shows just one of many viewpoints presented to the user. The user experiences 3-D through the StereoGraphics CrystalEye shown in Figure B, or an Ikegami 80-inch stereo projector, controlled by in-house software running on a Silicon Graphics IRIS 4D 210-VGX workstation.

Technique

A 3-D block diagram combines two representations: a 2-D block diagram showing how concurrent software processes are interconnected, and a time chart showing the synchronization of those processes. Rectangle color differentiates processes (or computers). Rectangle length denotes execution time. Adjacent text, which is barely visible in this image, identifies the process. Lines in the y-z plane connect rectangles to indicate communication paths. Lines parallel to the x-axis recede to a point in the past and represent the time history. Much fuller understanding and control of the 3-D block diagram is achieved with virtual reality by wearing the StereoGraphics CrystalEye headset and the VPL DataGlove. The red glove in the image moves as the user's hand moves the VPL DataGlove to allow direct manipulation of the software processes and interconnections. Virtual reality gives the user interactive control and a sense of being part of the 3-D scene.

Hints

A virtual-reality environment can be used for such tasks as designing distributed computing software, programming massively parallel computers, or designing automated factories. ◊ Virtual reality allows the user to experience the environment of a 3-D object or scene from any point of view within the environment; imagine watching a computational fluid-dynamics simulation from the eye of a vortex.

[1] Michitaka Hirose, "Visualization Tool Applications of Artificial Reality," Proceedings of International Symposium on Artificial Reality and Tele-existence, Tokyo (July 9–10, 1991).

[2] Michitaka Hirose, "Development of Virtual 3D Visual Environment for Control Software," *Human Machine Interfaces for Teleoperators and Virtual Environments*, NASA Conference Publication 10071 (1990), p. 571.

5-1 Animation

1 dependent variable
3 independent variables
Locates scalars
Meteorology

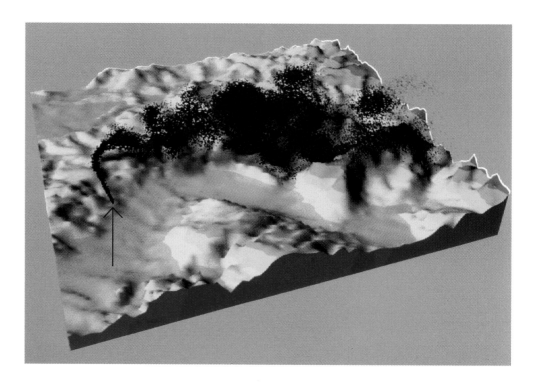

Shadows help locate a 3-D scalar field.

Melvin L Prueitt, Susan Bunker, and Tetsuji Yamada, Los Alamos National Laboratory, Los Alamos, NM, USA.

Application (Air Pollution)

A computer simulation of air-pollution particulates from an oil shale plant in Colorado is studied. The in-house GRAFIC code running on a Cray supercomputer created the image, which was rendered on a Dicomed film recorder.

Technique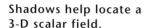

On a particle plot, the particulate density is represented by the number of blue dots per unit volume. The topography of the area surrounding the oil shale plant (indicated by an arrow on the image) becomes the reference plane below the dots. Surface height is keyed to color to redundantly encode height. Shadows from the dots are cast directly below to locate their x-y position on the reference plane. Perspective, shading, and the dark slice on the front edge, colored red to emphasize height, help create the 3-D effect.

Hints

Animating the particulates and rotating the viewpoint greatly improves understanding and the 3-D effect. ◊ The technique of drawing shadows onto a reference plane can be used to locate other kinds of data; the topography could just as easily be a pipe, an experimental container, or an abstract surface. ◊ This image also illustrates how shape can be used to show direction: the narrow base of the plume indicates the origin and the growing plume indicates the direction.

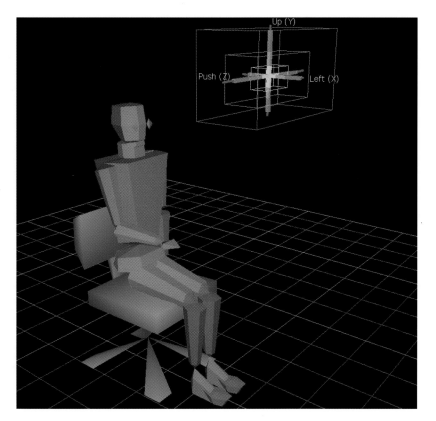

6 variables
Relates position and scalars
Physiometry

The position of a 3-D model is related to measured data.

Susanna Wei, Saint Joseph's University, Philadelphia, PA, USA; Norman I. Badler, University of Pennsylvania, Philadelphia, PA, USA.

Application (Hand Strength)

The effect of body posture on hand strength is studied.[1] Data are rendered on a Silicon Graphics workstation using the University of Pennsylvania's *Jack*™.

Technique

Labeled bars represent measured data in each of six directions of hand movement relative to the posture indicated by a stylized, polygonal 3-D model. The length of the red line at the end of each bar shows the difference between the maximum force of the entire range of hand movements and the force of the current body position. Color-correlating the bars to nested bounding boxes, which represent a population's percentile range, helps convey qualitative values. The 3-D model is flat-shaded for speedy rendering. A base grid, highlights, and perspective enhance 3-D understanding. The model's posture is interactively adjustable to permit quick analysis of measured data relative to posture.

Hints

The image is interesting because it portrays the six measurements directionally. A labeled bar chart having six bars could also be used but would communicate the directional information less directly. ◊ **13-6** also relates data to a model, but uses the model to classify, rather than to understand, data.

[1] Susanna Wei and Norman I. Badler, "Graphical Displays of Human Strength Data," to be published in *Journal of Visualization and Computer Animation*.

2 dependent variables
3 independent variables
Relates objects
Computational Fluid
   Dynamics

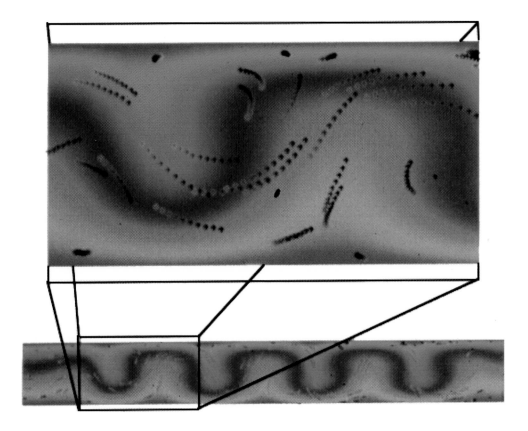

**Thin lines relate
magnified portions of
the image to the whole
image.**

Verlan K. Gabrielson and Greg
Evans, Sandia National
Laboratory, Livermore, CA,
USA.

[1] Greg Evans and Ralph Greif,
"A Study of Traveling Wave
Instabilities in a Horizontal
Channel Flow with Applica-
tions to Chemical Vapor
Deposition," *International
Journal of Heat and Mass
Transfer* 32, 5 (1989): 895–911.

[2] V. K. Gabrielson, "GGP: A
Graphics Program for
Specialized Displays and
Animation of Finite Element
and Finite Difference Analy-
sis," SAND 91-8223, Sandia
National Laboratories,
Livermore, CA, USA.

Application (Chemical Vapor Deposition)

Fluid flow and heat transfer as they occur in channel flow during chemical vapor deposition[1] are simulated for conditions typical of microelectronics processing. The flow and traveling wave move left to right. The analysis and visualization using GGP[2] were executed on a Cray supercomputer.

Technique

In this plot combining pseudocolor and particle traces, thin lines guide the eye from the magnified portion of the image to its location in the whole image. The color (blue, low; red, high) indicates relative values of the 2-D scalar field (temperature). Marker particles show speed, time, and direction of the flow. For this example a hypothetical particle is tracked for the ten previous time increments; the spacing of the markers indicates relative speed. Markers placed at each time step are succes- sively darkened to indicate direction of flow.

Hints

Connecting lines are an effective way to relate objects visually. ◊ This example also illustrates a pleasing way to fill a nearly square space with graphics that are long and narrow. ◊ See **6-7** for another effective use of marker particles. In that image the color of the particle can represent a scalar other than direction because context reveals direction.

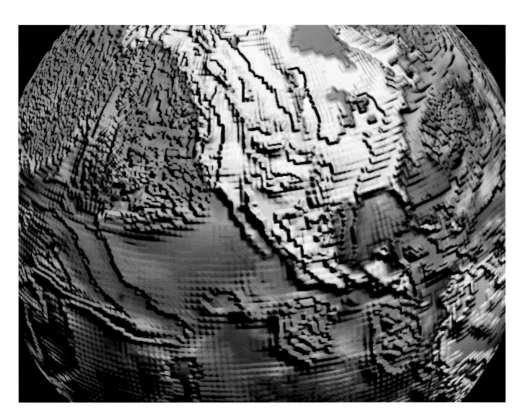

2 dependent variables
2 independent variables
Correlates variables
Atmospheric Science

**Color and textures
correlate variables.**

Roger A. Crawfis and Mike J.
Allison, Lawrence Livermore
National Laboratory.
Livermore, CA, USA.

Application (Global Climate Modeling)

A computer model[1] is used to study the correlation between wind velocity and heat leaving the earth (outgoing long-wave radiation) to better understand global climate models. In-house software rendered the image on a Silicon Graphics 4D 35 workstation.

Technique

Textures[2] are used to construct a combined reference map, velocity field, and heat scalar field. A chaotic roughness appears where wind velocities are high. A color-coded representation of the outgoing long-wave radiation (blue, low; red, high) is masked by the white continents, and the resulting color image and chaotic bump map are rendered on the globe. Notice the two hurricanes (circular, rough texture, blue to green) west of Central America.

Hints

Animating this technique shows dramatically the wind velocity.

[1] Modeling data provided by Gerald Potter, Lawrence Livermore National Laboratory, Livermore, CA, USA.

[2] Roger A. Crawfis and Michael J. Allison, "A Scientific Visualization Synthesizer," in *Visualization '91* (Los Alamitos, CA: IEEE Computer Society Press, 1991).

2 dependent variables
3 independent variables
Depicts interaction
Astronomy

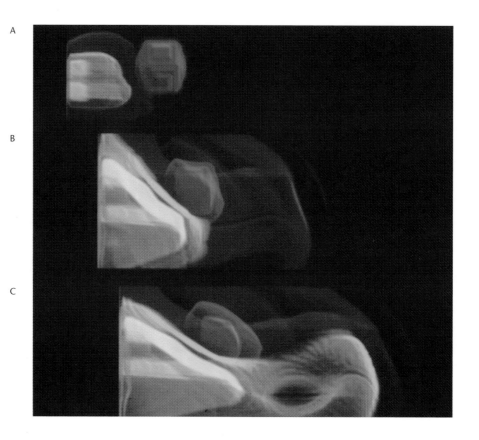

A

B

C

Color and opacity illustrate interaction of material.

T. Todd Elvins, San Diego Supercomputer Center, San Diego, CA, USA; David de Young, Kitt Peak National Observatory, Tuscon, AZ, USA; Anke Kamrath, San Diego Supercomputer Center.

[1] R. Derbin, L. Carpenter, and P. Hanrahan, "Volume Rendering," *Computer Graphics* 22, 4 (August 1988): 65–74.

Application (Computational Astrophysics)

A cosmic jet's evolution is modeled with computational fluid dynamic techniques to show a jet encountering a region of space having a different density. This computation is an attempt to determine why these jets bend as they move through space at nearly the speed of light. This simulation disproved a long-accepted theory that density inhomogeneities in the intergalactic medium cause the jets to bend. The computation was run on a Cray Y-MP supercomputer, and the image was rendered with Pixar's ChapVolumes software[1] on a Pixar Image Computer.

Technique

In this volume visualization, yellow represents the cosmic jet. Green represents the region of space having a different density. Figures A, B, and C represent the time evolution of the jet moving from left to right. Color and opacity differentiate the two densities (the more opaque, the more dense) and reveal the effect of the collision.

Hints

This visualization technique is more effective when viewed as an animation. Further information may be gained by rotating the image and viewing the animation from different vantage points. ◊ Opacity and color can also be used to model the mixing behavior of different materials.

1 dependent variable
3 independent variables
Reveals patterns
Computational Fluid
Dynamics

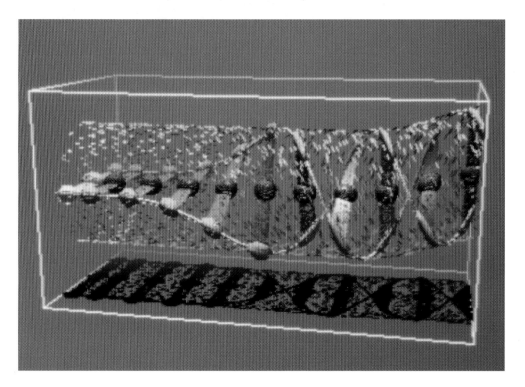

Temporal behavior of objects reveals flow dynamics.

Jarke J. van Wijk, Netherlands
Energy Research Foundation
ECN, Petten, The Netherlands;
Johan Stolk, Delft University
of Technology, The Netherlands.

Application (Fluid-Flow Visualization)

A flow field is visualized and studied by introducing objects that are carried along with the flow.[1] The images were calculated and rendered on a Sun Microsystems SPARCstation IPC using in-house software.

Technique   1 10 100

A 3-D flow field is visualized by having it move several objects with different origins and shapes. All objects are built up from surface particles, each of which is a small facet, modeled as a point with a surface normal. The normal is used for shading calculations. The surface particles with defined spatial and temporal behaviors are created at different origins. The red and yellow spheres, whose shapes are distorted by the flow, result from spherical sources with a discrete release time. The stream tube that resembles a white string connecting the yellow spheres results from continuously released small spheres. A large, almost transparent stream tube bounds the objects to reveal the shape of the flow. Ribbonlike rectangular objects connecting the large red spheres to the yellow spheres help show relative motion. A 2-D projection of the 3-D flow field is cast like a shadow to make the 3-D simulation more understandable. A white rectangular bounding box, perspective, and depth cueing enhance the 3-D effect.

Hints

Both placement of objects in the flow and specification of their spatial and temporal behavior are subjective. ◊ This image shows spheres being distorted according to speed, but in other applications sphere size and color could suggest, for example, spatial and temporal changes in pressure and temperature. ◊ See **5-3**, **6-7**, and **6-9** for other ways of using objects to study fluid flow.

[1] Johan Stolk and Jarke J. van Wijk, "Surface-Particles for 3D Flow Visualization," *Proceedings Second Eurographics Workshop on Visualization in Scientific Computing*, Delft, The Netherlands, April 22–24, 1991. To be published in F. H. Post and A. J. S. Hin, eds., *Advances in Scientific Visualization* (New York: Springer-Verlag, 1992).

1 dependent variable
3 independent variables
Depicts change
Meteorology

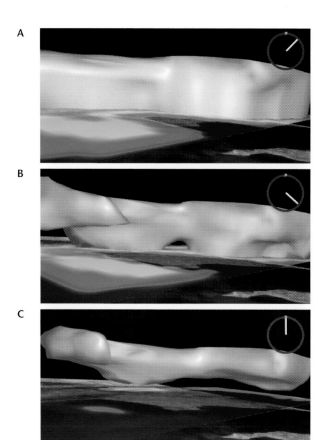

A

B

C

Isosurfaces depict time-dependent behavior of a 3-D scalar field.

Christopher Nuuja and Gray Lorig, Pittsburgh Supercomputing Center, Pittsburgh, PA, USA; Gregory McRae and Armistead Russel, Carnegie Mellon University, Pittsburgh, PA, USA.

Application (Ozone Pollution)

An animation simulating the time-dependent behavior of ozone measured over Los Angeles reveals that as night approaches, ozone merely floats higher in the atmosphere rather than disappears, as previously thought. These images were ray traced on the Cray Y-MP supercomputer with the Cray rendering system.

Technique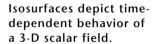

Three images from the animation show a gray isosurface of ozone computed at the EPA limit of 0.12 ppm and a pseudocolor slice depicting ozone measurements at ground level. The slice is colored according to the visible light spectrum (blue indicates no pollution; red exceeds the EPA limit) and is made translucent to reveal the terrain reference map below. A clocklike icon annotates the images for time comparison. Perspective and highlights enhance 3-D.

Hints

Although these three images point to differences in location of ozone, the animation was much more dramatic. ◊ Side-by-side comparisons are most effective when the images are dramatically different. ◊ See **1-8** for a technique comparing two very similar images.

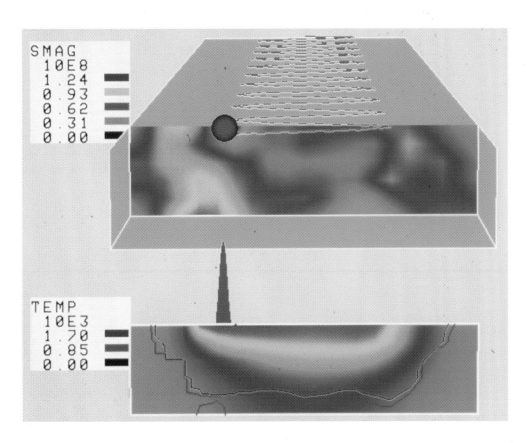

3 dependent variables
3 independent variables
Correlates variables
Mechanical Engineering

Multiple visualization techniques facilitate correlation of variables.

Verlan K. Gabrielson and Lee Bertram, Sandia National Laboratories, Livermore, CA, USA.

Application (Weld Simulation)

A weave weld[1] simulation studies the correlation among stress, temperature, and yield surface. The analysis was done on a Cray supercomputer with the in-house PASTA2D code[2] and rendered with the GGP code.[3]

Technique

Varied contextual cues, including an isoplot and two pseudocolor plots, relate three variables—stress, temperature, and yield surface—to one another and to a welding tip, which is a time-dependent input parameter. Stress (upper plot) and temperature (lower plot) are pseudocolored; their values are keyed to adjacent color keys. On the upper plot, a red sphere depicts the location of the welding tip, whose time-history is shown by a red zigzag line. On the lower plot, the thin red triangle locates the heat source and the isolines represent the yield surface. White lines and perspective indicate that this is a 3-D simulation.

Hints

The technique for showing a path is useful in relating the location of an input parameter to scalar field output parameters. ◊ See **2-3**, **2-9**, **2-12**, and **11-7** for other correlations of multiple variables.

[1] L. A. Bertram, "Thermal Simulation of 3-D GMA Weave Welds," SAND90-8210, Sandia National Laboratories, Livermore, CA, USA.

[2] W. S. Winters and W. E. Mason, "PASTA2D: Applications," SAND 89-8217, Sandia National Laboratories, Livermore, CA, USA.

[3] V. K. Gabrielson, "GGP: A Graphics Program for Specialized Displays and Animation of Finite Element and Finite Difference Analysis," SAND 91-8223, Sandia National Laboratories, Livermore, CA, USA.

2 dependent variables
3 independent variables
Correlates isosurface and flow
    path
Meteorology

**Color distinguishes
flows correlated to an
isosurface.**

William L. Hibbard and David
A. Santek, Space Science and
Engineering Center, University
of Wisconsin, Madison, WI,
USA.

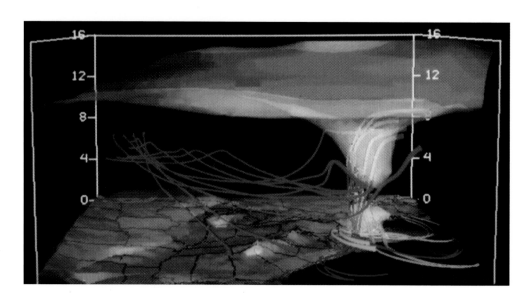

[1] W. Hibbard, L. Uccellini, D.
Santek, and K. Brill, "Applica-
tion of the 4-D McIDAS to a
Model Diagnostic Study of the
Presidents' Day Cyclone,"
*Bulletin American Meteorological
Society* 70, 11 (1989): 1394–
1403.

[2] W. Hibbard and D. Santek,
"The Vis-5D System for Easy
Interactive Visualization," in
Visualization '90 (Los
Alamitos, CA: IEEE Computer
Society Press, October 1990),
pp. 28–35. Also in 1991
Preprints, Conf. Interactive
Information and Processing
Systems for Meteorology,
Oceanography, and Hydrol-
ogy, New Orleans, American
Meteorology Society, pp. 129–
134.

Application (Weather Simulation)
This simulation of a cyclone as flows converge to create a crisis event[1] was executed on a Control Data Corporation CDC205, and the image was rendered on an IBM 4381 using the in-house 4-D McIDAS software.

Technique
Color-coded particle traces, selected by trial and error to find a representative sample demonstrating convergence,[2] illustrate the origin of converging high- and low-vorticity flows causing the cyclone. An isosurface of potential vorticity is made translucent to reveal the flows. Shading, highlights, and a white perspective cube enhance 3-D understanding. Locating the terrain map beneath the isosurface provides a reference. A height scale helps indicate the height of the isosurface.

Hints
This technique can be used to correlate scalar fields and flow fields. ◊ Fog and cloudlike features are created and used in many ways; see **5-7**, **5-10**, **6-6**, **9-2**, **9-7**, **10-4**, **12-1**, **12-2**, **12-7**, and **12-8**.

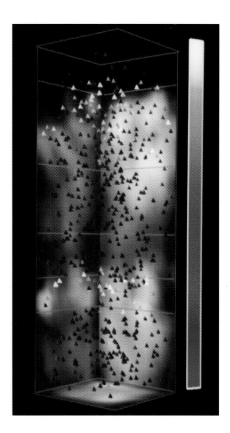

1 dependent variable
3 independent variables
Locates regions
Biology

Treating objects as light sources locates regions of interest.

Jesse W. Driver, III, Center for High Performance Computing, Austin, TX, USA.

Application (Neurobiology)

A computational model of the cat cortex,[1] created on a Cray supercomputer, uses tetrahedrons to represent the locations of 584 neurons. A Stardent computer rendered the image, which is one frame from an animation, with the DORÉ graphics package and I-nets.

Technique

A radiosity technique called I-nets[2, 3] creates a glow in regions of interest. Numerous colored tetrahedral light sources represent neurons. White tetrahedrons represent the firing of a neuron. The I-nets technique permits the use of many more tetrahedrons than can be seen because the glow from hidden tetrahedrons illuminates the surrounding region. The color scale (blue to red to white) corresponds to increasing neuronal activity. Dramatically increasing the intensity of white accentuates the occurrence of the important event, the firing of the neuron.

Hints

This technique is especially useful when modeling objects smaller than a pixel or objects hidden from view because the light cast by the objects indicates their location by illuminating the neighboring environment. ◊ Lowering the intensity of the lighted objects reveals regional effects. One lighted object will not be seen, but if several dim objects are in the area, the region will be noticed. ◊ Animating the time-dependent firing of the neurons reveals patterns of neural activity.

[1] P. Patton, E. Thomas, and R. Wyatt, "Computational Dynamics of Signal Propagation in the Visual Cortex," in *Proceedings of the Twenty-sixth Semi-annual Cray Users Group*, K. Winget, ed. (Bethpage, New York: Cray Users' Group, Inc., 1990), pp. 22–38.

[2] C. Buckalew and D. Fussell, "Illumination Networks: Fast Realistic Rendering with General Reflectance Functions," Proceedings of SIGGRAPH '89, in *Computer Graphics* 23, 3 (1989): 89–98.

[3] J. Driver and C. Buckalew, "Radiative Tetrahedral Lattices," *Proceedings SPIE Conference on Extracting Meaning from Complex Data: Processing, Display, Interaction* Vol. 1459 (1991).

5-11 Animation

5 dependent variables
3 independent variables
Depicts flow
Computer Graphics

Cloudlike streaks
facilitate understanding
of fluid flow.

David S. Ebert, Department of
Computer and Information
Science, Ohio State University,
Columbus, OH, USA.

[1] David S. Ebert, "Solid Spaces:
A Unified Approach to
Describing Object Attributes,"
Ph.D. Dissertation, Ohio State
University, Columbus, OH
(1991).

[2] David S. Ebert and Richard E.
Parent, "Rendering and
Animation of Gaseous
Phenomena by Combining
Fast Volume and Scanline A-
Buffer Techniques," Proceed-
ings of SIGGRAPH '90 in
Computer Graphics 24, 4
(August 1990): 357–366.

A

B

Application (Fluid-Flow Visualization)

Visual techniques for animation[1, 2] are developed to study a simulation of a gas volume entering a vortex. The EDGE graphics library developed at Ohio State University is used to support an animation tool. The images were rendered on a Hewlett-Packard HP 9000 series 370 TSRX workstation.

Technique

Wisplike clouds represent a gas. Wisp shape represents velocity: the narrower the wisp, the greater the velocity. These two frames from an animation illustrating convergence of gas flow show a low-velocity gas flow in Figure A and a high-velocity flow in Figure B. The opacity of the wisps represents the density of the gas. The convergence of the wisps locates the vortex. The tightness of the spiral represents amount of turbulence, strength of vortex, and vortex fall-off power. The cloudlike appearance helps suggest gas flow.

Hints

Computation expense and image quality are optimized by increasing the model resolution just enough that aliasing artifacts are no longer apparent. ◊ These still-frame images are difficult to interpret, but animation greatly improves understanding. ◊ Using all five variables to determine the shape of a wisp may seem like overkill, but it creates a more realistic model; see **13-13** for similar attention to detail.

2 dependent variables
3 independent variables
Correlates 3-D and 2-D
Atmospheric Science

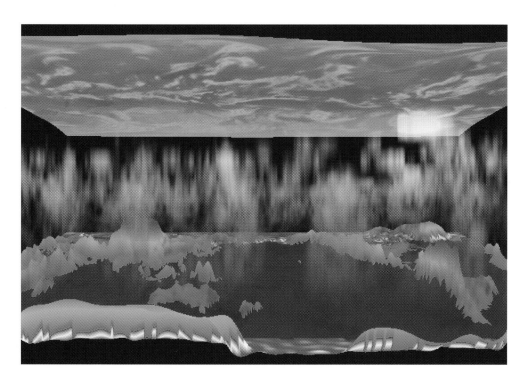

Depth cues and position correlate 3-D to 2-D.

Roger A Crawfis, Nelson Max, and Dean Williams, Lawrence Livermore National Laboratory, Livermore, CA, USA.

Application (Global Climate Modeling)

A computer model[1] is used to study the correlation between cloud cover and quantity of heat leaving the earth (outgoing long-wave radiation) to improve understanding of global climate models.[2] The image was rendered on a Silicon Graphics 4D 35 workstation using in-house software.

Technique

A linear transformation converts a rectangular volume of cloud cover to a prism, allowing the pseudocolored (yellow, low; red, high) scalar field of heat leaving the earth to be drawn on the top face, facilitating correlation. In this frame from an animation, clouds are modeled with volume rendering on a curvilinear 3-D grid. Cloud position and graytone provide altitude cues. Opacity is proportional to percentage of cloudiness. A 3-D terrain reference map indicates height according to the visible light spectrum. Cyan is removed to create a discontinuity, clearly distinguishing land mass from water. White in the reference map represents sea ice.

Hints

This image is best understood in a movie because the translucent clouds without their relative motion lose their depth cue. ◊ See **5-6**, **5-7**, **8-4**, and **8-7** for other techniques relating 3-D to 2-D.

[1] Modeling data provided by Gerald Potter, Lawrence Livermore National Laboratory, Livermore, CA, USA.

[2] Nelson Max, Pat Hanrahan, and Roger Crawfis, "Area and Volume Coherence for Efficient Visualization of 3D Scalar Functions," *Computer Graphics*, ACM Press, 24, 5 (November 1990).

2 dependent variables
3 independent variables
Correlates scalars
Computational Fluid
    Dynamics

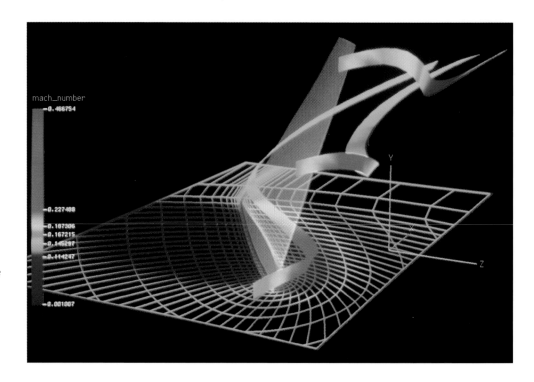

**Pseudocolored flow
ribbons correlate flow
to speed.**

L. N. Sankar, Georgia Institute
of Technology, Atlanta, GA,
\USA, A. Sugavanum, IBM,
Dallas TX, USA. Submitted by
Catriona Gaeta and Mike
Wilson, Wavefront Technolo-
gies, Santa Barbara, CA, USA.

[1] NAV3D developed by L. N.
Sankar, Georgia Institute of
Technology.

Application (Aircraft Wing Design)

A simulation of an airfoil at a 36° angle of attack (a critical angle, at which the wing
is in danger of losing lift) was run on an IBM ES/3090 using the in-house Navier-
Stokes code, NAV3D.[1] The image was rendered by Wavefront Technologies' Data
Visualizer on a Silicon Graphics 4D 25-GT workstation.

Technique

Three flow ribbons, each consisting of several particle streamlines, show the
twisting flow of air past an airfoil. The airfoil is made translucent so that the
ribbons, pseudocolored according to the color key to indicate airspeed, can be seen
and correlated to the airfoil. Instead of smoothly varying the color hue of the
ribbons from blue to yellow to red, detail is brought out by skewing the color table
so that most of the color changes occur approximately in the middle of the range.
A slice of the computational grid is shown to help relate the airspeed to the
simulation algorithm. An x-, y-, z-axis helps orient the data.

Hints

Drawing the flow ribbons at only three locations allows visual interpolation of the
flow between the ribbons and thus provides an uncluttered way of correlating parts
of a 3-D vector field to a scalar. ◊ See **6-11** for another uncluttered way of
representing 3-D vector fields.

3 dependent variables
3 independent variables
Correlates vectors and
    scalars
Visualization

A
B

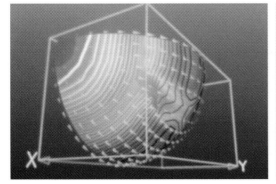

**Multiple visualization
techniques relate
several variables.**

Olin Lathrop, Cognivision
Inc., Westford, MA, USA.

Application (Airflow)

Airflow over a sphere is shown on an Apollo DN10000 using the Cognivision, Inc.,
FOTO software package, and is output to 35-mm slides using a Polaroid CI-3000 film
recorder.

Technique

Color bands, isolines, and directional glyphs are combined to show relationships in
Figure A. Shear magnitude is shown as color. Pressure appears as an isoplot overlaid
on the color; a critical value is drawn with a bold line (lower center) to call attention
to that value. White arrowheads shaped like "paper planes" suggest velocity; their
size indicates relative speed. The enclosing wire-frame rectangle is drawn in
perspective to enhance 3-D, and orientation is supplied by coloring the x-axis red,
the y-axis green, and the z-axis blue. Lighting on the arrowheads helps indicate 3-D.
Figure B, a magnified portion of the sphere, is a detailed view of the change in
velocity.

Hints

The eye does not easily relate the magnified area (Figure B) to the larger image
(Figure A). See **5-3** for a technique that relates the magnified portion to the original
image. ◊ The number and size of paper planes need interactive adjustment to create
enough of them to depict the field without occluding each other or the pseudocolor
and isoplot.

3 variables
Depicts interaction
Theoretical High-Energy
  Physics

Motion blur depicts 3-D interaction.

Jean-François Colonna, Lactamme (CNET, École Polytechnique), France.

[1] Paul Haeberli and Kurt Akeley, "The Accumulation Buffer: Hardware Support for High Quality Rendering," Proceedings of SIGGRAPH '90, in *Computer Graphics* 24, 4 (August 1990).

Application (Strong Interaction Theory)

The computed interaction of gluons, quarks, and antiquarks is studied. The computation and the visualization were executed on a Silicon Graphics 4D 20 workstation with K, a machine-independent language.

Technique

In this 3-D model a simple shape (sphere) represents several types of particles. Sphere color identifies and differentiates each particle's properties. Sphere fuzziness, achieved by randomly displacing the surface points and then applying a low-pass filter, suggests the notion of probability. Cometlike tails created by a motion-blur technique[1] indicate velocity and suggest motion. Perspective and shading help create the illusion of depth.

Hints

Motion blur can be used to depict motion of any object. Here color and motion blur represent velocity of individual particles. ◊ See **5-3**, **5-6**, **6-1**, **6-6**, **6-7**, **6-9**, **12-6**, and **12-10** for other ways to illustrate motion.

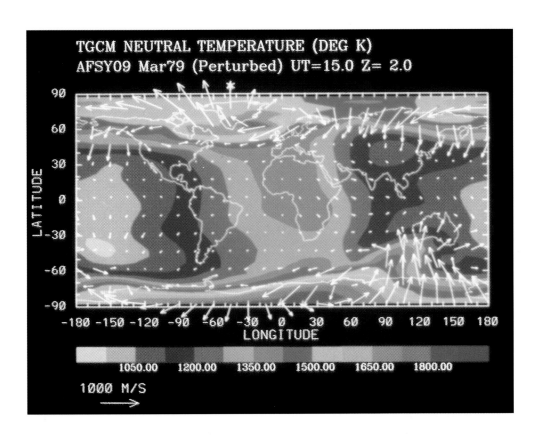

2 dependent variables
2 independent variables
Correlates variables
Atmospheric Science

Arrows and colors correlate two variables.

Bob Dickinson, Ben Foster, Cicely Ridley, and Ray Roble, National Center for Atmospheric Research, Boulder, CO, USA; submitted by Lee Carter and Bob Lackman, National Center for Atmospheric Research.

Application (Global Climate Modeling)

This simulation of various upper-atmosphere processes during a geomagnetic storm depicts data at an altitude of approximately 300 kilometers and correlates temperature with wind velocity. The simulation was run on a Cray X-MP supercomputer, and the graphics were created with the National Center for Atmospheric Research (NCAR) graphics package.[1]

Technique

Combined pseudocolor and velocity plots show the relationship between temperature and wind velocity. The arrow at lower left calibrates the vector field. Discrete colors create a contour-banding effect to demonstrate shape. Outlining the continents in white helps locate the values of the variables. Precise locations may be determined by reading the axis scales.

Hints

Interactively minimizing the number and length of arrows can reduce clutter but still provide information on velocity. ◊ Fourteen colors are created in the color key; some adjacent colors are difficult to distinguish though not critical in this example. ◊ If many distinctions have to be made, color alone is not a good tool for identifying objects .

[1] NCAR Graphics Package: *NCAR Graphics Version 3.1 Update Packet*, June 1991; *NCAR Graphics Guide to New Utilities*, Version 3.00, October 1989; *NCAR Graphics User's Guide*, Version 2.00, August 1987; *AUTOGRAPH: A Graphing Utility*, Version 2.00, August 1987; National Center for Atmospheric Research, Scientific Computing Division, Boulder, CO, USA.

2 dependent variables
3 independent variables
Depicts vector field
Computational Physics

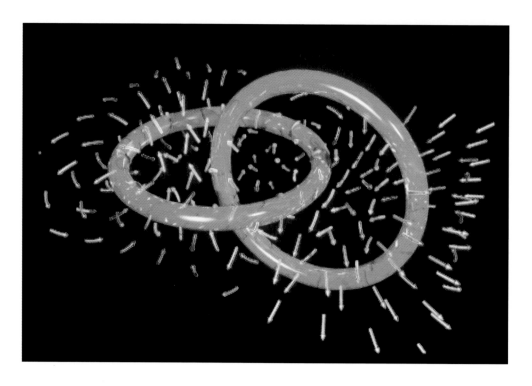

Color and regularly spaced, equal-length arrows depict a 3-D vector field.

Melvin L. Prueitt, Los Alamos National Laboratory, Los Alamos, NM, USA.

Application (Magnetic Fields)

3-D magnetic fields around conductors are visualized. In-house software running on a Cray Y-MP supercomputer created the image, which was rendered on a Dicomed film recorder.

Technique

A 3-D vector plot shows the magnitude and direction of vectors at locations in a volume. Equal-length arrows, curved to follow the magnetic lines, represent the vector field. The arrows are colored magenta, blue, green-yellow, and red to indicate the magnitude of the variable (low to high). Arrows are computed on a lattice of equal width and length to enhance the 3-D effect when lighting and perspective are applied. The conducting rings that affect the magnetic field are texture-mapped and colored differently to differentiate them from the arrows.

Hints

The number of arrows may need to be adjusted; too many will clutter the image, too few will not show the field. ◊ This technique can be used to model 3-D fields having orientation and magnitude. ◊ Excellent depth perception is possible with stereo pairs of slides and a stereo viewer.

2 dependent variables
3 independent variables
Correlates isosurface and
    vector field
Meteorology

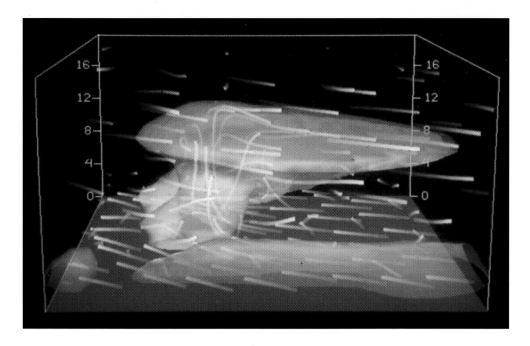

**Motion-blurred
trajectories are
correlated to an
isosurface.**

William L. Hibbard and David
A Santek, Space Science and
Engineering Center, University
of Wisconsin, Madison, WI,
USA.

Application (Weather Simulation)

This atmospheric simulation of a thunderstorm[1] was executed on a Cray X-MP
supercomputer, and the image was rendered on an IBM 4381 using the in-house 4-D
McIDAS software.

Technique

An isosurface of water vapor density and a vector plot are combined to permit their
correlation.[2] Making the isosurface translucent permits viewing of part of the vector
field that would otherwise be hidden. Cometlike objects representing the vector
field show direction and speed. The length of the tail is proportional to speed.
Motion blur adds to the sense of motion of the comets. The perspective edges of the
bounding box convey a sense of 3-D, and a vertical scale helps estimate height.

Hints

Scaling for comet tail fade-out is a trial-and-error adjustment. ◊ Motion blur can be
used to study 3-D vector fields or to correlate scalar fields with vector fields. ◊ Fog
or cloudlike features are created and used in many ways; see **5-7**, **5-9**, **5-10**, **9-2**,
9-7, **10-4**, **12-1**, **12-2**, **12-7**, and **12-8**.

[1] Atmospheric model written
by Robert Schlesinger,
University of Wisconsin
Meteorology Department,
Madison, WI, USA.

[2] W. Hibbard, "4-D Display of
Meteorological Data,"
(SIGGRAPH Proceedings, 1986
Workshop on Interactive 3D
Graphics), Chapel Hill (1986):
23–36.

2 dependent variables
3 independent variables
Correlates vector and
    scalar values
Computational Fluid
    Dynamics

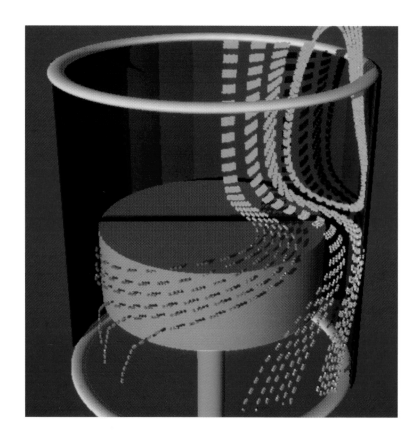

**Colored marker
particles correlate
vector and scalar
values.**

Verlan Gabrielson and Greg
Evans, Sandia National
Laboratory, Livermore, CA,
USA.

[1] Greg Evans and Ralph Greif,
"A Numerical Model of the
Flow and Heat Transfer in a
Rotating Disk Chemical Vapor
Deposition Reactor," *Journal of
Heat and Mass Transfer* 109
(1987): 928–935.

[2] Peter A. Watterberg, "MESA:
A Ray Tracing Rendering
Package, Programmers
Manual," Sandia National
Laboratories, Albuquerque,
NM, 1988.

Application (Chemical Vapor Deposition)

Data represent the flow-field solution of a Navier-Stokes equation in a cylindrical geometry. A simulation of flow and heat transfer in a rotating-disk chemical vapor deposition reactor[1] effectively reproduced laboratory experiments. The analysis was computed on a Cray supercomputer, and the visualization was computed on VAX 780 using the MESA package.[2]

Technique

Marker particles representing fluid particles are colored to show relative temperature (blue, cool; red, warm) and positioned to show relative speed. Relative speed is indicated by spacing the marker particles (close, slow; farther apart, fast). Two narrow tori describe the simulation boundary.

Hints

This image shows how effectively a collection of simple geometric shapes can communicate complex concepts. ◊ Because the researcher knows the flow direction from experience, no directional cues are needed. ◊ See **6-3** where color and motion blur show type of particle and relative velocity.

2 dependent variables
2 independent variables
Reveals orientation and
    coherence
Flow Visualization

**Line segments reveal
orientation and
coherence of flow.**

A. Ravishankar Rao, IBM T. J.
Watson Research Center,
Yorktown Heights, NY, USA.

Application (Feature Extraction)

Automatic extraction of information from fluid flow images is studied. The image was rendered on an IBM RS6000 workstation using in-house software.

Technique

A computer program interprets a coarse grayscale image of a fluid flow to extract an orientation field,[1] shown as red line segments. Orientation is calculated at each point in the image, but to avoid clutter the image shows only a sampling of points. The line segments do not have directional markings because of an inherent directional ambiguity. Line segment length, determined by the degree of visual contrast around the point, is proportional to coherence (strength of orientation). The orientation field is overlaid on the original image to visually validate the computer program.

Hints

The orientation field is a more abstract description of the grayscale image and provides useful, uncluttered topological information about the flow field. ◊ This feature-extraction study suggests that other computer images could be automatically interpreted to provide additional information for the viewer. The reader may want to consider assembling experts in the discipline of computer vision to read the image, experts in pattern recognition to discover patterns in the image, and experts in scientific visualization to illustrate the automatically extracted information.

[1] A. R. Rao and B. G. Schunck, "Computing Oriented Texture Fields," *Computer Vision, Graphics and Image Processing— Graphical Models and Image Processing* 53, 2 (March 1991).

3 dependent variables
4 independent variables
Locates path
Medicine

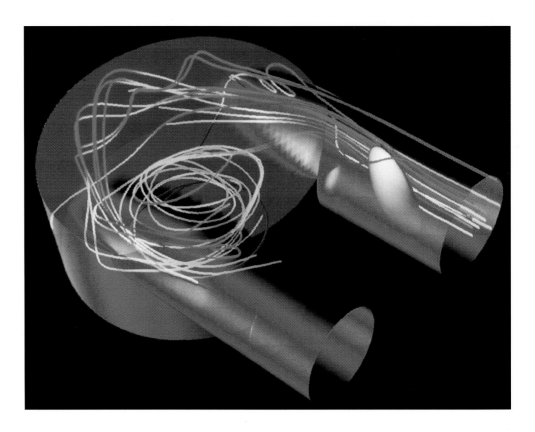

Color coding height to a particle trace helps locate its path.

Chris Gong, Cetin Kiris, Dochan Kwak, and Stuart Rogers, NASA Ames Research Center, Moffett Field, CA, USA.

[1] Cetin Kiris, Ph.D. Dissertation. Stanford University 1991/NASA Ames Highlights Video 1990.

Application (Biofluid Mechanics)

The behavior of the Penn State artificial heart is simulated. The vortex created by blood flowing through the central portion of the heart illustrates good wall washing over the entire chamber, reducing the chances that clots will form.[1] The computations were performed on a Cray Y-MP supercomputer and displayed on a Silicon Graphics IRIS workstation using NASA Ames PLOT3D, SURF, GAS, and Mrakevec.

Technique

Particle traces simulating blood flow are computed over time and colored to indicate height (blue, low; red, high) within the artificial heart. Plotting the model 50% transparent reveals internal structure and the particle traces. Highlights emphasize the 3-D nature of the model.

Hints

The colored particle trace is useful to show path of flow and value of some variable along that path. ◊ See **6-7** for a similar treatment of color paths.

2 dependent variables
3 independent variables
Relates vector and scalar
   fields
Computational Fluid
   Dynamics

**Multiple isosurfaces
relate vector and scalar
fields of a fluid flow.**

S. J. Klein, Stanford University, Stanford, CA, USA; S. K. Robinson, P. R. Spalart, NASA Ames Research Center, Moffett Field, CA, USA; submitted by Fergus J. Merritt, NASA Ames Research Center.

Application (Incompressible Fluid Flow)

A computer computation using Navier-Stokes equations for incompressible fluid flow shows that vortices embedded within the turbulent boundary are associated with production and dissipation of turbulence, fluctuations in surface pressure, and growth of a boundary layer.

Technique

On this multiple isosurface image, a perspective grid locates the bottom and back boundaries of the simulation and provides a reference while enhancing the 3-D effect. The size, shape, and position of isosurfaces help reveal relationships. Opaque orange represents low-velocity fluid; translucent purple represents high-velocity fluid. The white netlike isosurface represents low pressure; green represents high pressure.

Hints

This multiple-isosurface technique can be used to show relationships among any 3-D values, whether they are scalar or vector. ◊ This example shows that at least four flow variables (one for each color) may be simultaneously displayed and compared. ◊ Sometimes images can be simplified by omitting information already known to those who will be using the images. In this example no directional indicators are plotted because the researchers know the direction of flow.

1 dependent variable
3 independent variables
Describes vector field
Visualization

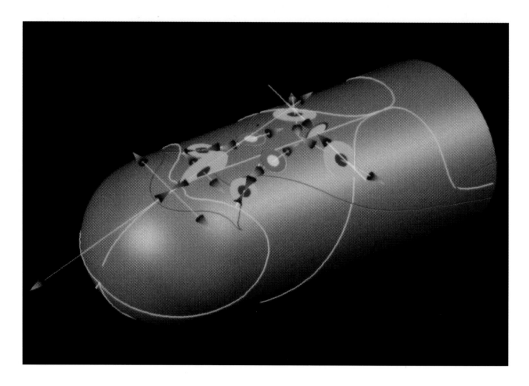

**Glyphs provide
uncluttered view of a
3-D vector field.**

James L. Helman and
Lambertus Hesselink, Stanford
University, Stanford, CA, USA.

[1] S. X. Ying, L. B. Schiff, and J.
L. Steger, "A Numerical Study
of Three-Dimensional
Separated Flow Past a
Hemisphere Cylinder," in
AIAA 19th Fluid Dynamics,
Plasma Dynamics and Lasers
Conference, Paper 87-1207,
American Institute of
Aeronautics and Astronautics
(June 1987).

[2] R. H. Abraham and C. D.
Shaw, *Dynamics: The Geometry
of Behavior* parts 1–4, (Santa
Cruz, CA: Ariel Press, 1984).

[3] James Helman and Lambertus
Hesselink, "Analysis and
Representation of Complex
Structures in Separated Flows,"
Proceedings SPIE Conference
on Extracting Meaning from
Complex Data, Vol. 1459, San
Jose, CA (February 1991).

Application (3-D Vector Fields)

Visual techniques for representing 3-D vector fields are studied; the vector field is created by simulating the fluid flow around a blunt cylindrical object.[1] The image was rendered on a Silicon Graphics 4D 220-GTX workstation with in-house software.

Technique

Topological visualization uses dynamical systems theory[2,3] to describe 3-D vector fields using glyphs and particle traces. The critical points, where the vector field vanishes, are denoted by sets of disks and arrows. The size, color, and orientation of these disks and arrows represent dynamical systems theory measures of the vector field. The blue and yellow curves are the streamlines that connect the critical points. The blunt cylindrical object is highlighted to enhance the 3-D effect.

Hints

This technique requires some knowledge of dynamical systems theory and, therefore, should be used only with selected audiences. ◊ Using glyphs to represent structures of interest in a vector field results in an uncluttered but quantitatively accurate image. ◊ See **3-9** for another application of dynamical systems theory to show vector fields.

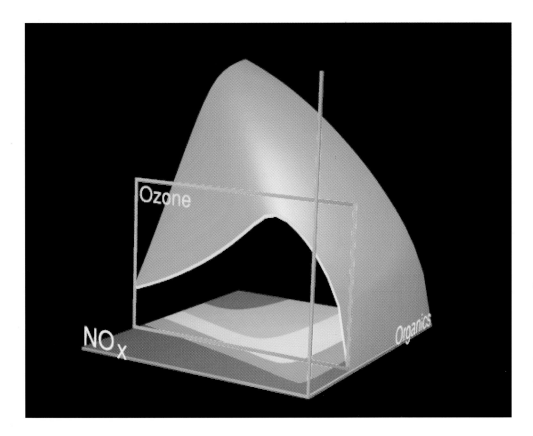

1 dependent variable
2 independent variables
Correlates scalars
Computer Graphics

**Redundant encoding
facilitates
understanding of three
related variables.**

Christopher Nuuja, Pittsburgh
Supercomputing Center,
Pittsburgh, PA, USA; Gregory
McRae and Armistead Russel,
Carnegie Mellon University,
Pittsburgh, PA, USA.

Application (Visualization)

Redundant encoding facilitates comprehension of an image that shows the relationship among three variables: amount of ozone as a function of organics and nitrogen oxides. The image was ray-traced on the Cray Y-MP supercomputer with the Cray rendering system.

Technique

This combination surface plot, isoplot, and *x-y* plot communicates more clearly the condition that the isoplot alone depicts. The image shows the variable ozone as a green surface, which is a function of two other variables: nitrogen oxides and organics. A purple rectangle sits at a fixed value of organics, cutting the surface of ozone to reveal a yellow *x-y* plot. The *x-y* plot clearly shows an ozone peak between the extremes of nitrogen oxides, whereas the isoplot gives up this information only after study.

Hints

Redundant encoding can emphasize information embedded in an image, much as an arrow or a magnified callout can direct attention to a selected region.

1 dependent variable
2 independent variables
Locates values
Mechanical Engineering

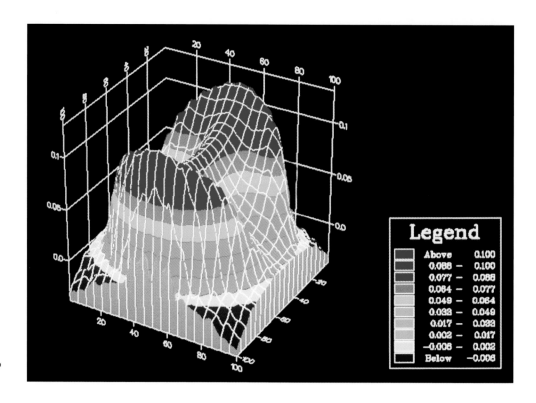

Grid lines locate values.

Fred McClurg and Hoa D.
Nguyen, Idaho National
Engineering Laboratory, Idaho
Falls, ID, USA.

Application (Heat Transfer)

Heat transfer on a droplet in an electroconvective environment is simulated. The electric field interacts with surface charge, giving rise to internal motion that results in a temperature distribution, as plotted. This visualization was created on a DECstation 5810. UNIRAS's software package, UNIGRAPH 2000, created the model.

Technique

Grid lines for the base of a cube are overlaid on a pseudocolor surface plot and labeled to help locate coordinate values. Both height and surface color are used to determine temperature across a horizontal slice of the droplet. The vertical slices taken on two axes and colored gray emphasize the variation in temperature. The legend identifies the range of values for each color.

Hints

Orthogonal grid lines and scale numbers can be added to images to provide accurate locations for coordinates. ◊ The gray vertical surface could show the relationship between two variables while holding the third variable constant. ◊ See **7-1** for use of a vertical slice to clarify the relationship between two variables.

1 dependent variable
2 independent variables
Reveals structure
Computer Graphics

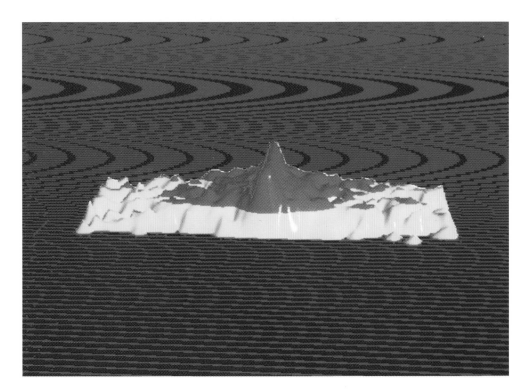

Mapping a critical value to a contrasting color reveals unexpected structure.

Verlan Gabrielson, Sandia National Laboratories, Livermore, CA, USA.

Application (Visualization)

Using the MESA package[1] on a VAX 780 to study a small 2-D field reveals this unusual moirélike pattern. Further study disclosed that the blue, patterned field that is supposed to be zero throughout is exactly zero in some places but only approximates zero in others. This accidental discovery led to the technique described here.

Technique

A pseudocolor plot helps validate a 2-D array of data. A critical value is assigned a color, and the remaining values are mapped in contrasting colors. Height also corresponds to value. Any unexplained pattern or structure revealed by color or height indicates that further analysis is needed to determine if the unexplained pattern or structure is caused by errors in the data or in the rendering tools.

Hints

Assigning a contrasting color will quickly identify erroneous, widely varying data and is particularly useful in spotting deviations from critical values, where minute differences can lead to incorrect answers. Whenever a rounding-off error is suspected, this technique can be used to test or verify critical values.

[1] Watterberg, Peter. A., "MESA: A Ray Tracing Rendering Package, Programmers Manual," Unpublished Report, Sandia National Laboratories, Albuquerque, NM, 1988.

**1 dependent variable
2 independent variables
Distinguishes classes
Flow Visualization**

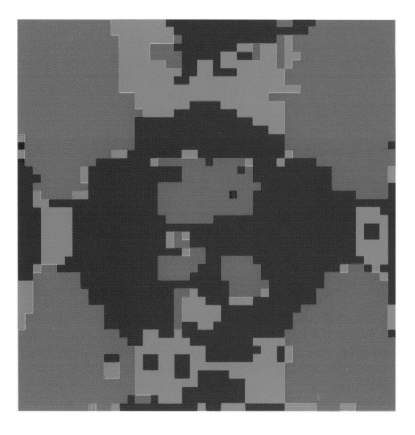

**Color distinguishes
classes of flow features.**

A. Ravishankar Rao, IBM T. J.
Watson Research Center,
Yorktown Heights, NY, USA.

[1] A. R. Rao, *Taxonomy for
Texture Description and
Identification* (New York:
Springer-Verlag, 1990).

Application (Feature Extraction)

Automatic extraction of information from fluid flow images is studied. The image was rendered on an IBM RS6000 workstation with in-house software.

Technique

An algorithm[1] based on the geometric theory of differential equations exploits the visual appearance of the flow by applying an orientation field (see **6-8**) to classify types of flow. The types are color coded red for spiral-phase portraits, blue for saddles, and green for nodes. This algorithm can also locate critical points to further clarify a fluid flow image.

Hints

Feature extraction and identification quickly focus the reader's attention, making it worthwhile to develop a computer program to scan an image highlighting areas of interest. ◊ Whereas this image instantly communicates location of flow types, **6-8**, which depicts the same data, would require time to extract the same information.

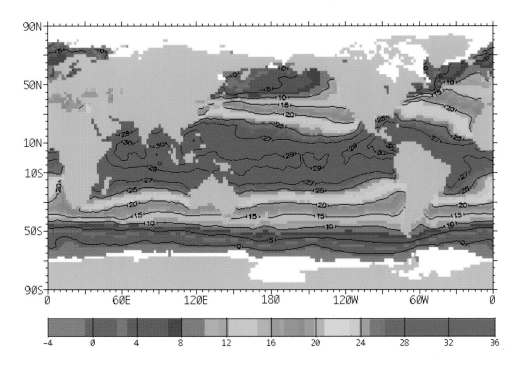

1 dependent variable
2 independent variables
Distinguishes regions
Atmospheric Science

A color region is emphasized by making competing regions white or gray.

Dean N. Williams and Robert L. Mobley, Lawrence Livermore National Laboratory, Livermore, CA, USA.

Application (Global Climate Modeling)

Sea surface temperature and location of sea ice data are brought together to compare atmospheric models. In-house software rendered the image on a Sun Microsystems workstation.

Technique

A single data array of sea surface temperatures is used to construct the pseudocolor map. The portions of the array that correspond to land and ice regions are filled with out-of-range numbers to distinguish them from the sea surface. Coloring the sea ice region white and the land gray steers the eye to the colorful sea surface temperatures. The pseudocolor also quickly verifies the data by showing warming toward the equator. Black isolines are annotated with temperature values, and labeled axes provide a geographic-coordinates reference.

Hints

Omitting data not being studied reduces visual clutter and increases communication. ◊ This example also demonstrates the psychological power of color: the eye tends to avoid the white and gray areas and focus on the color. ◊ Breaks in the isolines to accommodate the temperature values make the numbers more readable.

1 dependent variable
2 independent variables
Reveals change
Computational Physics

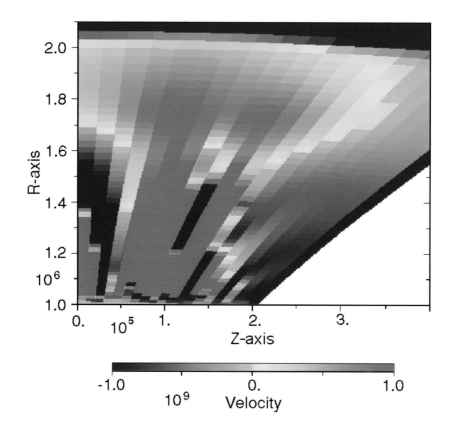

A distinct color change emphasizes the boundary.

Richard I. Klein, Lawrence Livermore National Laboratory, Livermore, CA, USA; Johnathon Arons, University of California, Berkeley, CA, USA; Raymond C. Cochran, Peter R. Keller, Lawrence Livermore National Laboratory.

[1] Richard I. Klein and Johnathon Arons, "Time-Dependent Two-Dimensional Radiation Hydrodynamics of Accreting Matter onto Highly Magnetized Neutron Stars," Proceedings of 23rd ESLAB Symposium on Two Topics in X-Ray Astronomy, Bologna, Italy, 13–20 September, 1989 (ESA SP-296, Nov. 1989).

[2] Written by the University of Illinois, National Center for Supercomputing Applications, Urbana, IL.

Application (Astrophysics)

The calculation[1] simulated accretion of matter from a star onto the surface of a companion x-ray pulsar, a highly magnetized neutron star. The data were calculated and the image was created on a Cray Y-MP supercomputer with in-house graphics libraries. The image was sent to an Apple Macintosh II for display by a modified version of IMAGE.[2]

Technique

This pseudocolor plot visualizes the velocity profile of the accreting material; negative velocity (blue) is inward toward the pulsar, and positive velocity (yellow to red) is outward* away from it. A distinct color change was made to occur at zero to emphasize that the variable being plotted changes sign at zero. The color bar correlates the colored zones of the calculational mesh to the changing velocity. See the paragraphs on color in Section I for more information on selecting color tables.

Hints

This discontinuous color technique may create misleading, apparent discontinuities where none exist; therefore, the technique should be used to emphasize only known discontinuities. ◊ In this example, visualization techniques using contouring or the color table with the visible light spectrum did not illustrate the researchers' predictions as well as the distinct color change. ◊ This technique contrasts with Figure iv, page 41, where the intent is to hide changes close to zero.

---

* The red regions of outflow are extremely low in density and may be "photon bubbles" moving through the gas. The calculation and visualization may provide observational predictions to be tested by x-ray telescopy experiments that NASA will fly in the mid-1990s.

1 dependent variable
2 independent variables
Distinguishes classes
Computational Fluid
  Dynamics

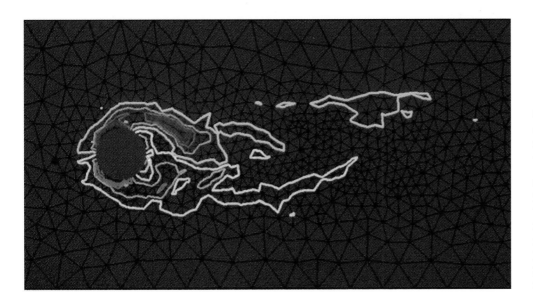

Color isolines
emphasize positive and
negative values of a
variable.

Charles A. Hall, University of
Pittsburgh, Pittsburgh, PA,
USA; George L. Mesina and
Mark J. Oliver, Idaho National
Engineering Laboratory Idaho
Falls, ID, USA; Thomas A
Porsching, University of
Pittsburgh.

Application (Incompressible Fluid Flow)

This simulation of a viscous incompressible fluid[1] flowing past a circular cylinder shows vorticity. As the fluid passes the obstruction, eddies form and are eventually shed. The data were generated on a Cray X-MP supercomputer with the in-house TRIDUAL simulator. The image was then visualized on a Silicon Graphics 4D 220-GTX workstation with the in-house visualization package TRIVIEW.

Technique

Isoplot lines are colored according to vorticity value. The positive vorticity values, which correspond to counterclockwise flow, are colored from red (large) to yellow (small). The negative vorticity values, corresponding to clockwise flow, are colored from deep blue (large) to light blue (small). No color is used for values near zero. The computational grid is drawn in black to distinguish it from the isolines. The isolines, generated with a modified version of Bloomenthal's method[2] applied to two dimensions, are made thicker than the grid lines for emphasis.

Hints

7-6 applies a similar color technique to distinguish between positive and negative values. ◊ Because of the many orders of magnitude covered in the range of data, we chose to color each zone according to its value rather than create isolines.

[1] Charles A. Hall, Thomas A. Porsching, and George L. Mesina, "On a Network Method for Unsteady Incompressible Fluid Flow on Triangular Grids," Submitted for publication.

[2] J. Bloomenthal, "Polygonalization of Implicit Surface," *Computer Aided Geometric Design* 5(1988): 341–355.

1 dependent variable
2 independent variables
Distinguishes classes
Solid State Physics

Classifying by meaningful color facilitates understanding.

Jean-François Colonna, Lactamme (CNET, École Polytechnique), France; Jean-François Gouyet, Michel Rosso, Bernard Sapoval, PMC (CNRS, École Polytechnique), France.

Application (Particle Diffusion)

Studying a computer model of a 2-D diffusion of particles on a square mesh revealed a microscopic event triggering a macroscopic event. The computation and the visualization were executed on a Silicon Graphics 4D 20 workstation with K, a machine-independent language.

Technique

In this image each particle is represented by a + sign on a square mesh. The +'s are sized to permit the particles to physically touch neighboring particles, thus visually indicating connectivity. Using the mnemonic device of a map colored according to geographic features to represent the data facilitates comprehension of the complex relationships in this display. The empty mesh points are light blue to represent lakes, and dark blue to represent the sea. The particles are green to suggest the earth, which is connected to the emitting source; red and light red to suggest islands, which are not connected to the emitting source; and yellow to suggest the shoreline, which is the boundary of the emitting source. In this study the unexpected occurrence of a particle (drawn white and as indicated by an arrow near the center of the image) caused a dramatic increase in the length of the boundary (yellow) by connecting an island to the emitting source.

Hints

Relating abstract concepts to familiar, more concrete concepts facilitates understanding of the abstract concepts.

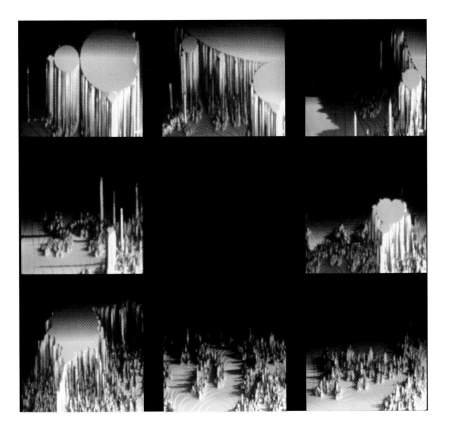

1 dependent variable
2 independent variables
Reveals structure
Mathematics

Successively magnifying an image reveals structure.

Jean-François Colonna,
Lactamme (CNET, École
Polytechnique), France.

Application (Dynamical Systems)

A Mandelbrot set is used to study dynamical systems. The computation and the visualization were executed on a Silicon Graphics 4D 20 workstation with K, a machine-independent language.

Technique

2-D scalar field values plotted as heights easily discern relative values. Communicating or examining microscopic detail is facilitated by zooming into the image by successively magnifying parts of the surface (from top left to lower right).

Hints

Successive magnification permits observation of self-similarity and helps in studying the relationship between the microscopic and macroscopic features of the data, such as the self-similarity observed in chaos. ◊ How we display 2-D scalar field values depends upon our intent. If we are discerning location, the scalar values are better displayed as colors. But if we are comparing values, the scalars are better displayed as heights. In a topological map where relative height and location both matter, we may want to use both height and color, as in **10-7**. If maintaining a relationship between the magnified picture and the original picture is important, **5-3** offers a good technique. Drawing a box around the area or using an easily recognizable shape or pattern can also orient the magnified and original pictures.

3 dependent variables
2 independent variables
Reveals differences
Visualization

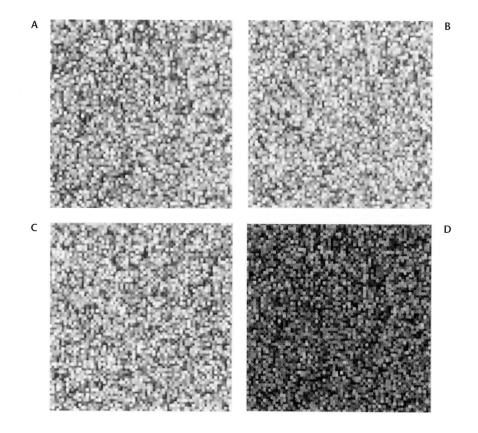

**Color reveals
differences not
apparent in black and
white.**

Haim Levkowitz, Ronald M.
Pickett, Kerry Shetline, and
Stuart Smith, University of
Massachusetts at Lowell,
Lowell, MA, USA.

[1] H. Levkowitz, "Color Icons:
Merging Color and Texture
Perception for Integrated
Visualization of Multiple
Parameters," in *Visualization
'91* (Los Alamitos, CA: IEEE
Computer Society Press,
October 22–25, 1991).
Expanded version available as
Technical Report R-91-005,
Department of Computer
Science, University of
Massachusetts at Lowell.

[2] H. Levkowitz and G. T.
Herman, "GLHS: A Generalized
Lightness, Hue, and Saturation
Color Model," (1991).
Submitted for publication.
Available as Technical Report
R-91-004, Department of
Computer Science, University
of Massachusetts at Lowell.

Application (Data Visualization)

Visual techniques for analyzing multiparameter image data are studied[1,2] with in-house software, X Window environment, and Motif.

Technique

Figures A, B, and C are specially created with known differences between the top and bottom half of each image. Figure D is constructed by coloring the pixels of Figure A red, Figure B green, and Figure C blue, and then combining the three images into one to reveal the differences between the top and bottom halves not apparent in the black-and-white images.

Hints

As many as three multiparameter graytone images, such as some combination of computed tomography (CT), positron emission tomography (PET), or magnetic resonance imaging (MRI) images, or two or three multispectral satellite images, are needed for this technique. ◊ See **1-4**, **1-9**, and **2-7**, which create multiparameter images for study and **13-9**, which uses glyphs to analyze a multiparameter image.

1 dependent variable
3 independent variables
Locates regions
Medicine

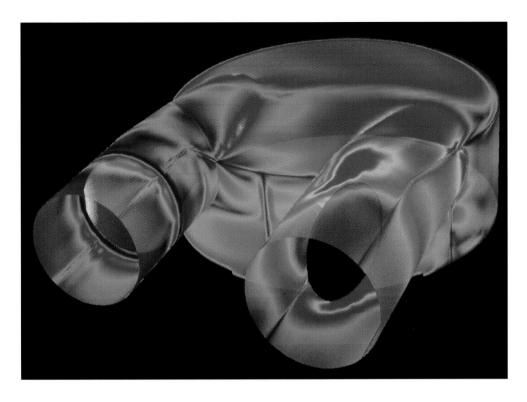

Pseudocolored surface of a 3-D model quickly locates regions of high values.

Chris Gong, Cetin Kiris, Dochan Kwak, and Stuart Rogers, NASA Ames Research Center, Moffett Field, CA, USA.

Application (Biofluid Mechanics)

The Penn State artificial heart model is studied to locate regions of high vorticity so that the internal chamber can be appropriately designed. High vorticity implies high shear stress, which may result in damage to blood cells flowing near the solid boundaries. The computation was performed on a Cray Y-MP supercomputer and rendered on a Silicon Graphics IRIS workstation using NASA Ames PLOT3D; SURF; GAS; and Mrakevec.

Technique

Pseudocoloring the model's interior surface locates maximum vorticity: blue, low; red, high. Making the model 50% transparent reveals internal mechanical structure to demonstrate how high vorticity is related to the physical features.

Hints

Making the model 50% transparent is a useful technique for relating internal structure to surface values. ◊ Although 3-D vorticity data are throughout the volume, the image is simplified by representing only the data that touch a surface.

8-2 Surface and Slice

1 dependent variable
3 independent variables
Locates maximum
Structural Engineering

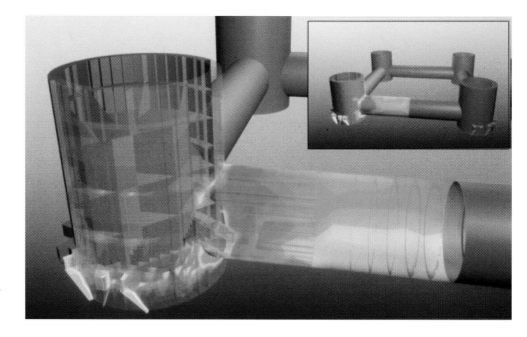

Translucent model and pseudocolor locate maximums.

Mark Smith, Cognivision, Inc., Westford, MA, USA.; submitted by Olin Lathrop.

Application (Stress Analysis)

Stress on a tension leg of an offshore oil-drilling platform is computed on a VAX 11/785 and rendered on an Apollo DN10000 with the Cognivision, Inc., FOTO visualization program.

Technique

The computed stress for one portion of the tension leg is pseudocolored transparent blue to opaque red to represent low to high stress. The geometric model is cut away to show internal stress and to provide a reference scheme for locating the stress. Lighting and perspective help to show 3-D. The inset (upper right), with only surface stress indicated, gives the complete configuration of the oil platform's lower hull.

Hints

Insets, models, or cutaway models provide a reference for locating features. ◊ Compare with **9-1**, which uses a cutaway technique only, and **8-1**, which uses a translucent model only. Each of these three techniques is effective. ◊ Translucency becomes especially powerful in stereoscopic images or a slowly rotating animation. The added depth perception makes details understandable that would otherwise appear to be visual clutter.

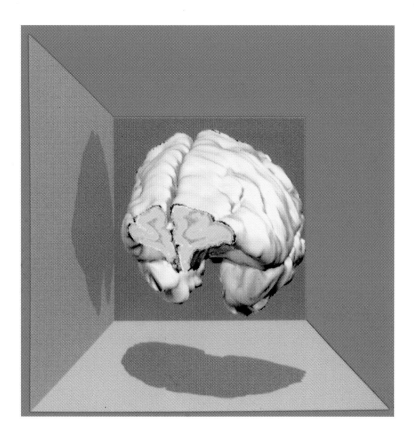

1 dependent variable
3 independent variables
Depicts shape
Medicine

Size and shape of a 3-D model are better understood by showing the model and its 2-D projections.

Arthur W. Toga, University of California Los Angeles School of Medicine, Los Angeles, CA, USA.

Application (Medical Imaging)

Approximately 40 coronal sections of a brain are assembled in this 3-D reconstruction of autoradiographic data. The images were computed with in-house software on a VAX 8530 computer and displayed on a Gould Image Processing system.

Technique

A model's 2-D size and shape are illustrated by casting shadows onto the walls of a box. Perspective, shading, and specular reflection help identify 3-D surface geometry. Colors of the planar surface (determined by a cutting plane) display the glucose utilization rate.

Hints

Casting shadows is a seldom-used but helpful technique for showing the shape and size of an object's largest cross-section. The object that is to cast a shadow must be carefully positioned to make meaningful shadows on the bounding box. If, as in **12-7**, we treat the walls as mirrors, we can also see the surface features of the unseen sides. ◊ See **5-6** for a similar shadow-cast example.

1 dependent variable
3 independent variables
Locates extremum
Computational Fluid
    Dynamics

**Overlaying a 3-D model
on a pseudocolor plot
locates extremum.**

A. Globus, D. Kerlick,
Computer Sciences Corpora-
tion, NASA Ames Research
Center, Moffett Field, CA,
USA; G. Bancroft, P. Kelaita, R.
McCabe, Fergus J. Merritt, T.
Plessel, Y. M. Rizk, Sterling
Software, NASA Ames Research
Center; P. G. Buning, NASA
Ames Research Center; I. T.
Chiu, Iowa State University,
NASA Ames Research Center; J.
L. Steger, University of
California Davis, Davis, CA, USA.

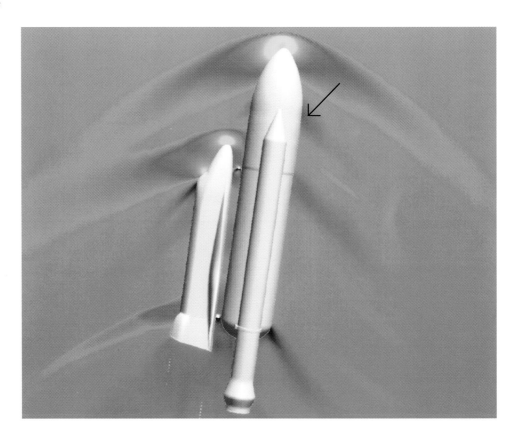

[1] P. G. Buning, I. T. Chiu, S.
Obayashi. Y. M. Rizk, and J. L.
Steger, "Numerical Simulation
of the Integrated Space Shuttle
Vehicle in Ascent," *Proceedings
AIAA Atmospheric Flight Mechanics
Conference* (Minneapolis: American
Institute of Aeronautics and
Astronautics, 1988).

[2] G. Bancroft, F. Merritt, T.
Plessel, P. Kelaita, R. McCabe,
and A. Globus, "FAST: A Multi-
Processing Environment for
Visualization of CFD," in
Visualization '90 (Los
Alamitos, CA: IEEE Computer
Society Press, 1990).

[3] G. D. Kerlick, "ISOLEV: A
Level Surface Cutting Plane
Program for CFD Data," Report
RNR-89-006, NAS Applied
Research Office, MS T045-1,
NASA Ames Research Center,
Moffett Field, CA, 94035.

Application (Aerodynamics)

A calculation[1] approximating steady flow around the NASA shuttle in launch configuration shortly after liftoff demonstrates that computational fluid dynamics can simulate some of the major shocks and expansions in the flow around a complex aerodynamic body. Pressure data were calculated on a Cray 2 supercomputer and rendered on a Silicon Graphics IRIS 4D 320-VGX workstation using FAST.[2]

Technique

The Marching Cubes algorithm[3] generates a 2-D slice through the 3-D pressure field. The color mapped to the pressure at each vertex is chosen according to the visible light spectrum (red, high; blue, low). The resultant slice is Gouraud shaded. The shuttle model is then combined with the slice to show the relationship between geometry and pressure. The shuttle's geometry is displayed as lighted, shaded surfaces to improve 3-D perception.

Hints

Several slices must be examined to understand all the important features in a 3-D field. ◊ At some angles or locations, slices may give misleading impressions. For example, the dark blue expansion near the top of the external tank (indicated by arrow) is caused not by the tank, but probably by the nose of the solid rocket booster, which is not intersected by the slice. ◊ Placing a model on a volume's slice provides a reference, but may be misleading for the uninitiated. The object may not be touching the slice at all, but is merely a reference. Combining a reference object with a volume slice must be done with care.

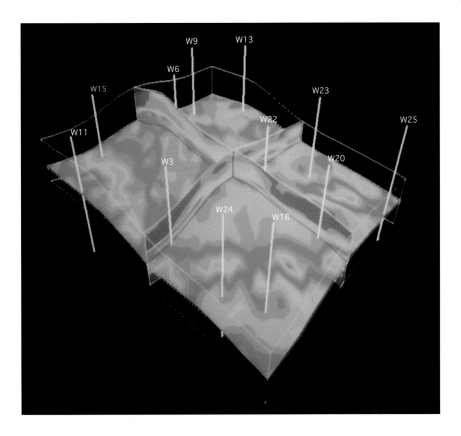

Logical slice planes reveal structure in fluid flow.

Van Bui-Tran, Chakib Bennis, Jean-Louis Pajon, Claude Lallemand, and Gisèle Legendre, Institut Français du Pétrole; Rueil-Malmaison, France; Jean-Marc Chautru, BEICIP.

Application (Oil Exploration)

Permeability values of oil reservoirs computed with HERESIM™[1] are interactively visualized on a Silicon Graphics IRIS workstation to understand fluid flow in the reservoir.

Technique

Data are constructed on a 3-D logically rectangular grid.* Three slices of the data following the terrain are constructed. The slices that define the permeability values are pseudocolored according to the visible light spectrum (blue, low; red, high). A white bounding box and removal of hidden surfaces help enhance 3-D understanding. The distorted shapes of the box and the slice planes follow the contour of the terrain to relate permeability structure to depth. The labeled white vertical lines representing existing oil wells provide a reference for the structures. Thin lines mark the slice plane's intersection.

Hints

This distortion technique is useful for revealing structure relative to some underlying contour, such as terrain. ◊ The logical slice plane technique is used to quickly scan 3-D data because of its low computational cost.

[1] HERESIM™, developed by Institut Français du Pétrole and École des Mines de Paris, Centre de Géostatistiques, marketed by BEICIP–France.

---

* Mathematically, the vertices of the rectangles are defined by $x(i, j, k)$, $y(i, j, k)$, $z(i, j, k)$. Each of the three logical slices is constructed by holding one of the i, j, k parameters constant.

1 dependent variable
3 independent variables
Reveals structure
Geology

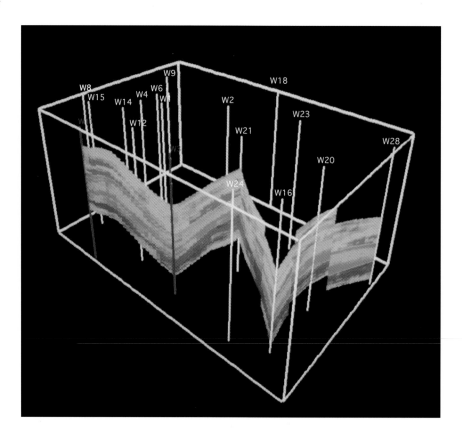

Connected partial 2-D slice planes reveal structure.

Van Bui-Tran, Chakib Bennis, Jean-Louis Pajon, Claude Lallemand, and Gisèle Legendre, Institut Français du Pétrole; Rueil-Malmaison, France; Jean-Marc Chautru, BEICIP.

[1] HERESIM™, developed by Institut Français du Pétrole and École des Mines de Paris, Centre de Géostatistiques, marketed by BEICIP–France.

Application (Oil Exploration)

The lithofacies structure of an oil reservoir is studied. Notice the dislocation toward the right side of the image indicating vertical earth movement along a fault line. Data were computed with HERESIM™[1] and interactively visualized on a Silicon Graphics IRIS workstation.

Technique

Following a connected line segment, truncated vertical slice planes are pieced together like a folding screen to show vertical cross-sections of lithofacies. Labeled red and white vertical lines locate oil wells particularly interesting to the researcher and provide reference for the lithofacies structures. The folding screen, pseudocolored to distinguish lithofacies of different materials, reveals the fault line. Perspective applied to the white bounding volume enhances 3-D.

Hints

Naming this technique "folding screen" invokes a familiar mental image to help viewers understand how the data are represented.

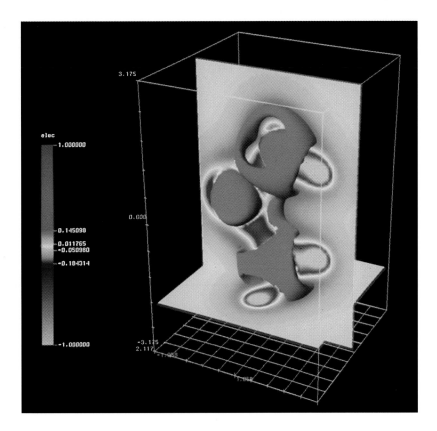

1 dependent variable
3 independent variables
Relates structure and shape
Computational Chemistry

A pseudocolored slice and isosurface reveal an object's internal structure relative to its shape.

Steven Chin, IBM T. J. Watson Research Center, Yorktown Heights, NY, USA; Contributed by Catriona Gaeta and Mike Wilson, Wavefront Technologies, Santa Barbara, CA, USA.

Application (Molecular Modeling)

The electron density of a dimethyl sulfide molecule is analyzed on a regular 3-D grid of 102,000 points and rendered with Wavefront Technologies' Data Visualizer.

Technique

A combined isosurface and pseudocolor plot locates an isosurface shape relative to the internal shape of the object of which it is a part. The isosurface constructed from the 3-D electron density is plotted in red. The slice planes defining the pseudocolor plots are also constructed from the electron density. Images are interactively created by moving the slice planes to various locations and adjusting the color table until the molecule's shape and internal structure are revealed. The scale numbers, axes, and grid help quantify location and shape. The labeled color key helps identify electron density values.

Hints

This technique can be used to represent shape and internal structure of an object represented in a 3-D scalar field. ◊ A nonlinear color key is needed to bring out the structure. See **9-2** and **9-8** for a different representation of similar data.

1 dependent variable
3 independent variables
Locates regions
Marine Science

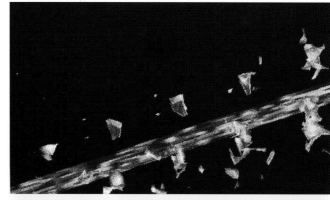

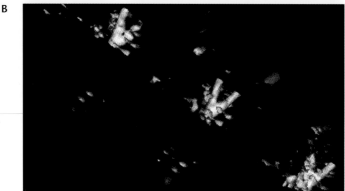

**Pseudocolor locates
regions of interest.**

Margarida A. Karahalios, Alade
O. Tokuda, University of
South Florida, Tampa, FL,
USA.

[1] KRAKENC, written by
Richard Heitmeyer, Naval
Research Laboratory, Washington, DC, USA.

[2] Margarida A. Karahalios,
"Underwater Source Localization Using Scientific Visualization," M.S. Thesis, University
of South Florida, Tampa, FL,
USA. (1991).

[3] James D. Foley, Andries van
Dam, Steven K. Feiner, and
John F. Hughes, *Computer
Graphics: Principles and Practice*
(Reading, Mass.: Addison-
Wesley, 1990).

Application (Underwater-Source Localization)

The probability of locating underwater sounds is simulated.[1] Visual techniques[2] are studied to determine if sounds can be located quickly and accurately. The resulting discovery that 3-D structures in the probability field are related to underwater sounds may lead to more efficient locating. The simulation executed on a Stardent computer, and the image was rendered with AVS, also on a Stardent.

Technique

A probability value ranging from 0 to 1 is simulated at each cube in a $256 \times 256 \times 256$ volume. An arbitrary slice through the volume is pseudocolored according to the visible light spectrum (blue, low; red, high). Regions of interest are revealed by using the isosurface tiler[3] to locate surfaces of value 100 or greater and to color them gray. The gray surfaces represent a probability that a source of sound is located at that position. The overlapping red and gray areas (Figure A) reveal the most likely locations of the sound. Rotating and magnifying the image further revealed unusual structure (Figure B) in the probability field.

Hints

The discovery of unusual structures or relationships is facilitated by the visual exploration of data; see also **3-7** and **7-3**, where unusual structures were observed.

1 dependent variable
3 independent variables
Reveals surface values
Visualization

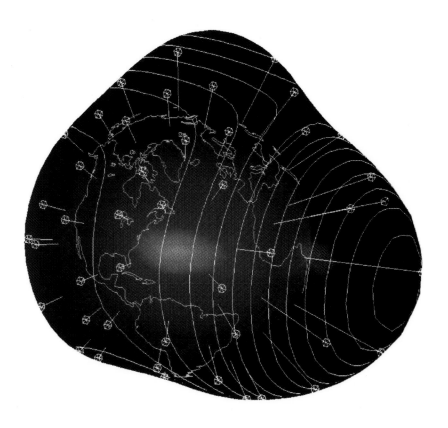

A translucent surface and "stickpins" depict data measured on a sphere.

Gregory M. Nielson and Thomas A. Foley, Arizona State University, Tempe, AZ, USA; David Lane, NASA Ames Research Center, Moffett Field, CA, USA; Ramamani Ramaraj, Tennessee Technical University, Cokeville, TN, USA.

Application (Surface-Value Visualization)

Techniques for representing data measured on a sphere are studied.[1-4] An interactive C program using the Silicon Graphics GL library was run on a Silicon Graphics 4D 320 workstation.

Technique

A translucent surface depicts data measured at various locations on a red sphere that is highlighted and has yellow reference lines (the continents) drawn in perspective to emphasize 3-D. The points of the white stickpins indicate measurement locations. The heights of the stickpins show relative data values. The heads of the stickpins indicate a 3-D location and are used to determine the shape of a black translucent surface. White isolines are then drawn on the black surface to help indicate surface shape and relative data values.

Hints

Stickpins are effective for viewing scalars measured on a surface. ◊ Stickpin length shows relative value more accurately than a 2-D pseudocolor image; however, when used in 3-D with perspective, additional cues such as isolines are needed.

[1] Thomas A. Foley, "Interpolation of Scattered Data on a Spherical Domain," in *Algorithms for Approximation* II, M. Cox and J. Mason, eds. (London, Eng.: Chapman and Hall), pp. 303–310.

[2] Thomas A. Foley, Gregory M. Nielson, David Lane, and Ramamani Ramaraj, "Visualizing Functions over a Sphere," *Computer Graphics and Applications* 10, 1 (January 1990): 32–40.

[3] David A. Lane, "Representation and Visualization of Scattered Multivariate Data," Ph.D. Thesis, Arizona State University, Tempe, AZ, (1991).

[4] See additional references at the end of Section II, p. 182.

8-10 Surface and Slice

1 dependent variable
3 independent variables
Reveals surface values
Visualization

Surface values are visualized as a surface above the surface.

Gregory M. Nielson and Thomas A. Foley, Arizona State University, Tempe, AZ, USA; David Lane, NASA Ames Research Center, Moffett Field, CA, USA; Bernd Hamann, Mississippi State University, Jackson, MS, USA; Ramamani Ramaraj, Tennessee Technical University, Cokeville, TN, USA; Hans Hagen, University of Kaiserlautern, Kaiserlautern, Germany; Richard Franke, Naval Postgraduate School, Monterey, CA, USA.

[1] Thomas A. Foley, Gregory M. Nielson, David Lane, Richard Franke, and Hans Hagen, "Interpolation of Scattered Data on Closed Surfaces," *Computer Aided Geometric Design* 7, 1–4 (January 1990): 303–312.

[2] Richard Franke and Gregory M. Nielson, "Scattered Data Interpolation and Applications: A Tutorial and Survey," in *Geometric Modelling: Methods and Their Applications*, H. Hagen and D. Roller, eds. (New York: Springer-Verlag, 1991), pp. 131–160.

[3] Gregory M. Nielson, Thomas Foley, Bernd Hamann, and David Lane, "Visualization and Modelling of Scattered Multivariate Data," *Computer Graphics and Applications* 11, 3 (May 1991): 47–55.

A   B

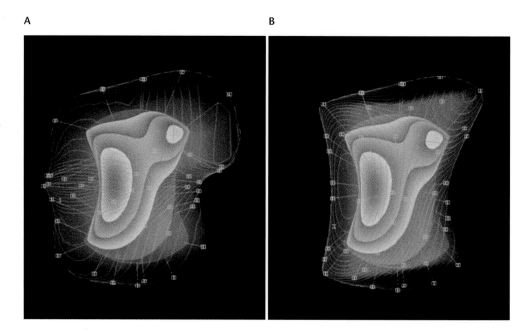

Application (Surface-Value Visualization)

A visualization technique[1-3] for interpreting the meaning of values measured on an irregular surface is studied on a Silicon Graphics 4D 320 workstation with in-house software using the Silicon Graphics GL graphics library.

Technique

At each point measured on an irregular surface, a "stickpin" is placed. In Figure A, the stickpin is positioned perpendicular to the measurement position. In Figure B, the stickpin is oriented on a radial from the center of the domain. In both images the length of the stickpin is proportional to the value measured. A translucent surface is then constructed through the heads of the stickpins. The surface colors also indicate the surface values.

Hints

The main advantage in creating a surface above a surface is that it allows measured values to be represented as a height. Small changes in height are easier to discern than small changes in color. See **7-2**, **7-3**, and **7-9** where surface height is relative to measurements on a plane. ◊ Creating a surface above a surface may be especially effective when the variable being measured on the surface, such as temperature, has an effect above the surface. ◊ See **8-11** for another technique for visualizing values measured on a surface as a surface. ◊ In Figure A, the surface-above-a-surface technique may not work in concave regions of the irregular surface where the stickpins cross. This technique could also be ineffective if the irregular surface were rough.

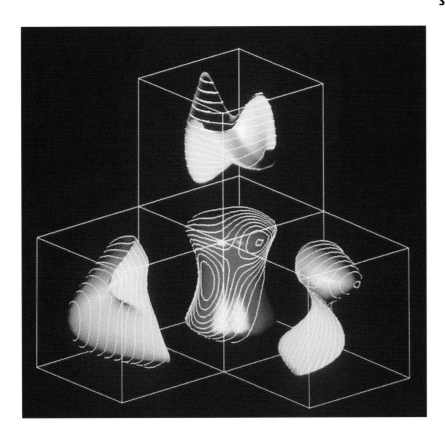

1 dependent variable
3 independent variables
Reveals surface values
Visualization

Surface values are visualized as surfaces with isolines.

Gregory M. Nielson and Thomas A. Foley, Arizona State University, Tempe, AZ, USA; David Lane, NASA Ames Research Center, Moffett Field, CA, USA; Bernd Hamann, Mississippi State University, Jackson, MS, USA; Ramamani Ramaraj, Tennessee Technical University, Cokeville, TN, USA; Hans Hagen, University of Kaiserlautern, Kaiserlautern, Germany; Richard Franke, Naval Postgraduate School, Monterey, CA, USA.

Application (Surface-Value Visualization)

A visualization technique for interpreting the meaning of values measured on an irregular surface[1-4] is studied on a Silicon Graphics 4D 320 workstation with in-house software using the Silicon Graphics GL graphics library.

Technique

The surface values of an irregular red surface are projected to planes in adjacent boxes. The values on each projection plane are used to construct a blue surface through the points created by treating the point values as a height perpendicular to this plane. Corresponding isolines are drawn in white on each surface. The surfaces are oriented by placing them in stacked cubes indicated by the light blue lines.

Hints

The gray lines representing stacked cubes are necessary to orient the viewer. ◊ Projecting the red surface onto the face of the cube will not work when the projection leads to multivalues. ◊ See **8-10** for other techniques for visualizing values measured on a surface as a surface.

[1] Thomas A. Foley and David A. Lane, "Visualization of Irregular Multivariate Data," in *Visualization '90* (Los Alamitos, CA: IEEE Computer Society Press, 1990), pp. 247–254.

[2] Richard Franke and Gregory M. Nielson, "Scattered Data Interpolation and Applications: A Tutorial and Survey," in *Geometric Modelling: Methods and Their Applications*, H. Hagen and D. Roller, eds. (New York: Springer-Verlag, 1991), pp. 131–160.

[3] David A. Lane, "Representation and Visualization of Scattered Multivariate Data," Ph.D. Thesis, Arizona State University, Tempe, AZ (1991).

[4] See additional references at the end of Section II, p. 182.

9-1 Volume

1 dependent variable
3 independent variables
Reveals structure
Biology

Cutaway technique reveals internal structure.

Julie Newdoll, Hans Chen, Michael McCarthy, and Alok Mitra, University of California San Francisco, San Francisco, CA, USA.

[1] Alok Mitra, Michael P. McCarthy, and Robert M. Stroud, "Three-Dimensional Structure of the Nicotinic Acetylcholine Receptor and Location of the Major Associated 43-kD Cytoskeletal Protein, Determined at 22 Ångstroms by Low Dose Electron Microscopy and X-Ray Diffraction to 12.5 Ångstroms," *Journal of Cell Biology* 109 (1989).

[2] PRESOLID written by Hans Chen and David Agard, University of California San Francisco, San Francisco, CA, USA.

[3] RENDACH written by Hans Chin and Julie Newdoll, University of California San Francisco, San Francisco, CA, USA.

Application (Structural Biology)

The acetylcholine receptor protein structure is studied[1] to learn how nerve cells interact. In-house codes PRESOLID[2] and RENDACH[3] using the DORÉ graphics package on the Stardent Titan computer created the image.

Technique

Experimental data are combined with a theoretical model to better understand protein structure. Crystallographic and microscopic sectioning data are combined to produce volume density data. Two isosurfaces are derived from the experimental volume data: purple represents protein density and blue represents membrane density. Brown cylinders represent the theoretical model, a helical protein bundle. The cylinders are drawn smooth in contrast to the experimental "lumpy" data. Different colors represent different biological functions to aid understanding. A lighting model enhances 3-D understanding. Part of the volumetric data is cut away to reveal the internal protein structure.

Hints

The cutaway in this image reveals the internal structure, but **8-2** is an example of how transparency is used to reveal internal structure.

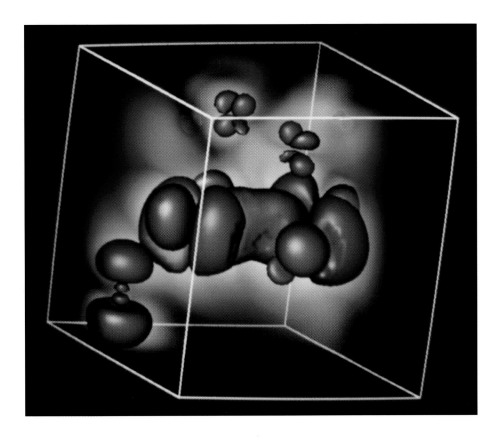

1 dependent variable
3 independent variables
Reveals shape
Chemistry

**Colored isosurfaces
reveal shape and
colored haze indicates
region of field effects.**

Wolfgang Krueger, GMD-
HLRZ, Bonn, Germany.

Application (Molecule Visualization)

A solution of the Schrödinger equation is used to generate the 3-D data for the psi-function of an iron protein molecule.[1] The simulation to create the data was run on a supercomputer. The image was rendered on a Silicon Graphics IRIS workstation with in-house volume-rendering software, which is based on transport theory.*

Technique

This image is created using a transport theory[2,3] approach to reveal shape and field effects. Spatial decay of the field is indicated by the colored haze; the isodensity surfaces are created opaque with highlights and shading; and the sign of the field is indicated by color. The colored, realistically lighted isosurfaces reveal shape, and the colored haze indicates the area of field effects.

Hints

This technique can be used to model any 3-D scalar field where it is important to visualize spatial decay of some variable relative to an isosurface of the variable.

[1] Data provided by L. Noodleman and D. Green, Scripps Clinic, La Jolla, CA.

[2] Wolfgang Krueger, "The Application of Transport Theory to Visualization of 3-D Scalar Data Fields," *Computers in Physics* 4, 4 (July/August 1991): 397–406.

[3] Wolfgang Krueger, "Volume Rendering and Data Feature Enhancement," *Computer Graphics* 24, 5 (November 1990): 21.

* The visualization approach is based on the linear transport theory for the transfer of particles in inhomogeneous amorphous media. The advantages of this approach are its rigorous mathematical formulation, applicability to data from different disciplines, and wide variety of contextual cues.

1 dependent variable
3 independent variables
Locates class
Geology

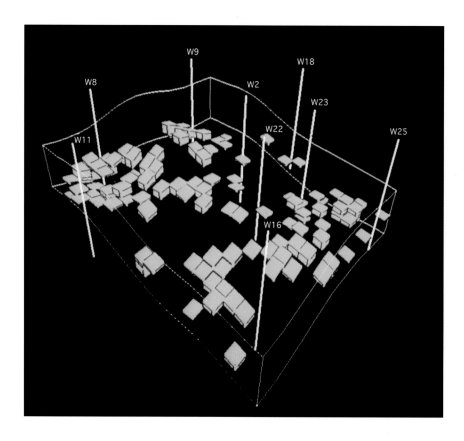

An isosurfacelike plot locates a specific class by making other classes transparent.

Van Bui-Tran, Chakib Bennis, Jean-Louis Pajon, Claude Lallemand, and Gisèle Legendre, Institut Français du Pétrole; Rueil-Malmaison, France; Jean-Marc Chautru, BEICIP.

[1] HERESIM™, developed by Institut Français du Pétrole and École des Mines de Paris, Centre de Géostatistiques, marketed by BEICIP–France.

Application (Oil Exploration)
Data derived from a geostatistical simulation are used to study fluid flow in an oil reservoir. The image is rendered on a Silicon Graphics IRIS workstation using HERESIM™.[1]

Technique
An oil reservoir is divided into logical cubes called lithofacies. An isosurfacelike plot is constructed by discretely coloring facies according to their geological class (clay or sandstone). Facies edges are drawn black to identify each facies. Each class is independently studied by making the other classes transparent. The volume of study, outlined in white, follows the contour of the land. Each labeled white vertical line locates an oil well and provides a reference point to locate the lithofacies class.

Hints
Volume density data are generally treated as a continuous variable; however, in this case the facies represent a specific geological formation and are discrete. Therefore, no smoothing or interpolation is performed. ◊ See **3-6** for an example of using transparency to allow comparison of two structures within a continuous volume.

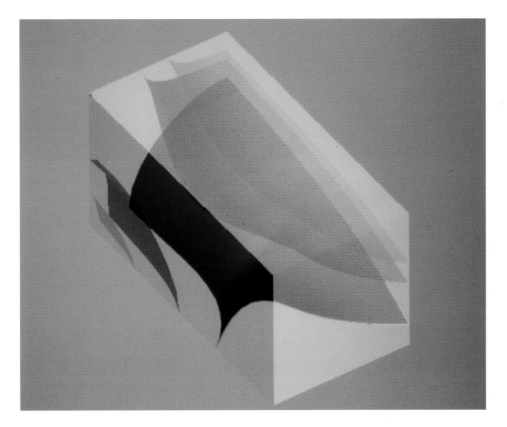

1 dependent variable
3 independent variables
Depicts shape
Mechanical Engineering

Translucent isosurfaces
depict the shape of a
3-D scalar field.

Richard S. Gallagher, Swanson
Analysis Systems, Houston,
PA, USA; Joop C. Nagtegaal,
Hibbitt, Karlsson & Sorensen,
Inc., Providence, RI, USA.

Application (Finite Element Analysis)

This study of stress distribution within a solid model was computed on a VAX 8600 and rendered on a Tektronix 4336 workstation with hardware Gouraud shading and translucency.

Technique

A surface plot shows isosurfaces of stress values throughout a solid. At the vertices of a coarse volume grid, bicubic surfaces are constructed[1] from the stress values and gradients of these values. A separate bicubic interpolation of surface geometry and surface normals is performed to guarantee visual continuity between surfaces generated from adjacent volume elements. The image is rendered with a surface-based extension to the Marching Cubes algorithm.[2] The degree of translucency is varied with the magnitude of the scalar value: isosurfaces of higher values are more opaque. The exterior visible surfaces of the volume are shown with translucency to provide a physical frame of reference without occluding the data.

Hints

Rotating the image to allow different vantage points helps us see the actual shapes of the isosurfaces. Just as isolines show the shape of a 2-D scalar field, the isosurface shows the shape of a 3-D scalar field. ◊ See also **9-5** for the use of color to represent the shape of a 3-D scalar field. ◊ Comparing this example with **9-5** suggests that interactively adjusting the number of surfaces and the viewing orientation will help optimize the image's information content.

[1] Richard S. Gallagher and Joop C. Nagtegaal, "An Efficient 3D Visualization Technique for Finite Element Models and Other Coarse Volumes," Proceedings of SIGGRAPH '89, in *Computer Graphics* 23, 3 (August 1989).

[2] William E. Lorensen and Harvey E. Cline, "Marching Cubes: A High Resolution 3-D Surface Construction Algorithm," Proceedings of SIGGRAPH '87, in *Computer Graphics* 21, 4 (July 1987).

9-5 Volume

1 dependent variable
3 independent variables
Depicts shape
Computational Fluid
  Dynamics

Isosurfaces depict shape of a 3-D scalar field.

Alexander Gelman, Vincent A. Mousseau, and Mark J. Oliver, Idaho National Engineering Laboratory, Idaho Falls, ID, USA.

[1] J. Bloomenthal, "Polygonalization of Implicit Surface," *Computer Aided Geometric Design* 5 (1988): 341–355.

Application (Heat Convection)

A simulation describes a gas-filled room with a heat source (red edges) and a heat sink (blue edges). The data were computed on a Cray X-MP supercomputer using the in-house HOTFLO gas simulation code. The image was then visualized on a Silicon Graphics 4D 220-GTX workstation with in-house visualization software.

Technique

Approximately 15 isosurfaces are generated with a modified Marching Cubes algorithm adapted from Bloomenthal's method.[1] Isosurfaces are colored according to the visible light spectrum (blue, cold; red-orange, hot) to accentuate the distribution of temperature within the volume. Rendering the isosurfaces inside a transparent volume delineated by edges gives the feeling of dimensionality. Volume edges are colored to indicate the boundary temperature conditions.

Hints

Bloomenthal's method rapidly generates surfaces suitable for real-time interactive animation. ◊ Users of the method should be aware that in some geometries the method breaks down, resulting in "holes" in objects. These holes, which may not be seen in animations at 30 frames per second, can be very obvious and therefore misleading when analyzing a single image. ◊ See **9-4** for another example of representing the shape of a 3-D scalar field, but using fewer surfaces and just one color.

1 dependent variable
3 independent variables
Reveals structure
Chemistry

Isosurfaces composed of tiny spheres reveal structure.

Daniel J. Sandin and Fred Dech, Electronic Visualization Laboratory, University of Illinois, Chicago, IL, USA.

Application (Molecular Modeling)

In AIDS drug design, electron densities of eight molecular orbitals of the AZT molecule[1] are studied. The image was computed on an AT&T Pixel Machine.

Technique

Each cell on a computational lattice contains the value of the AZT molecule's electron density. Small spheres are drawn in the cells intersected by the electron density isosurface. Different-colored spheres represent different isosurface values. Spheres are used instead of points so that a lighting model can be applied, enabling us to better see the shape of the implied surfaces. Both internal and external structure are revealed.

Hints

See **8-7**, **9-2**, and **9-8** for other examples of isosurface modeling (also used for electron density). ◊ Interactively rotating the image affords a better understanding of the structure.

[1] Data Coordinates, T. J. O'Donnell, Cambridge Crystallographic Data Bank.

9-7 Volume

1 dependent variable
3 independent variables
Locates extremes
Meteorology

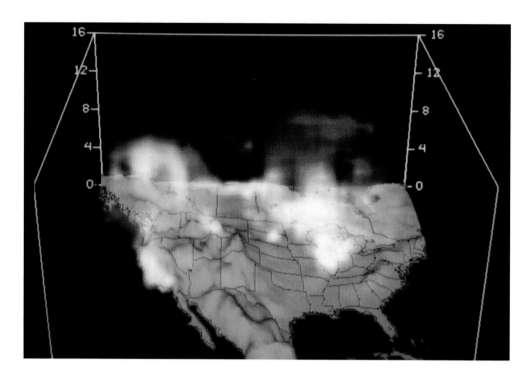

Opacity locates extremes.

William L. Hibbard, University of Wisconsin, Madison, WI, USA.

[1] W. Hibbard and D. Santek, "Interactivity Is the Key," Chapel Hill Workshop on Volume Visualization, University of North Carolina, Chapel Hill (1989), pp. 39–43.

Application (Weather Simulation)

Data were generated from an atmospheric simulation with the limited-area mesoscale prediction system to gain insight into cloud cover and its role in global heating and cooling. The simulation was executed on a Cray X-MP supercomputer, and the image was rendered on an IBM 4381 with the in-house 4-D McIDAS software.

Technique

Cloud water density is volume-rendered as a translucent "fog" with opacity proportional to density.[1] Shading, highlights, and a perspective cube (white lines) that encloses the terrain map enhance 3-D understanding. Locating the terrain map beneath the clouds provides a reference. A height scale helps indicate the height of the clouds.

Hints

Performing interactive adjustments in opacity until the water vapor appears cloudlike facilitates comparing actual cloud appearance to the simulated appearance. ◊ Opacity locates extremes in this image, whereas **11-4**, Figure A, uses color. ◊ Fog or cloudlike features are created and used in many ways; see **5-7**, **5-9**, **5-10**, **6-6**, **9-2**, **10-4**, **12-1**, **12-2**, **12-7**, and **12-8**.

1 dependent variable
3 independent variables
Reveals shape
Computational (Physical)
   Chemistry

**Isosurfaces reveal
shape.**

Stephan R. Keith, Sterling
Software, Palo Alto, CA, USA;
Harry Partridge, NASA Ames
Research, Moffett Field, CA,
USA.

Application (Molecular Bonds)

Schrödinger equations are solved on a Cray supercomputer to obtain a 3-D electron probability density volume. The electron density was visualized on an Ardent Titan running SURMAP[1] calling the DORÉ graphics package to help understand how molecular bonds form.

Technique

Isolines, constructed on regularly spaced slices through the volume, are connected to form polygons. The polygons are flat-shaded and form isosurfaces that are colored to represent different electron density values. Lighting creates light and dark regions to enhance the 3-D effect of the structure.

Hints

A common 2-D contouring algorithm can be used to construct the isolines, which are then connected to form the polygons of the isosurfaces. ◊ See **8-7** and **9-2** for different visual techniques for revealing a 3-D shape.

[1] Software written by Gary Villere, Sterling Software, Palo Alto, CA, USA.

**3-D Model
Reveals structure
Solid State Physics**

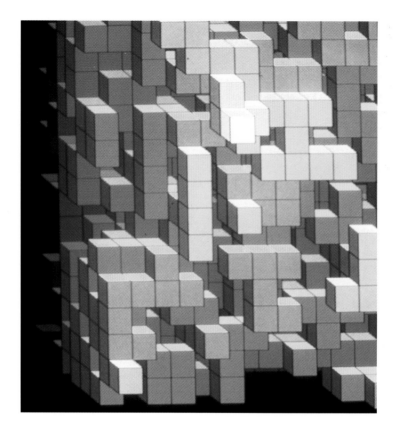

**Connected cubes reveal
the structure of porous
material.**

Jean-François Colonna,
Lactamme (CNET, École
Polytechnique), France.

Application (Fractal Aggregates)

The 3-D diffusion process of a material through a fractal aggregate, approximating a porous substance, is studied. The computation and the visualization were executed on a Silicon Graphics 4D 20 workstation with K, a machine-independent language.

Technique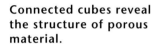

The 3-D diffusion process is modeled on a cubic mesh, representing each piece of the fractal aggregate as a cube to emphasize connectivity—that is, touching cubes are connected. Open spaces between the cubes help reveal the edges of internal cubes, permitting understanding of the porous interior structure. Shading enhances the 3-D effect. Using one hue emphasizes that only one type of physical material is being modeled.

Hints

Rotating the model to view it from different vantage points reveals more internal structure.

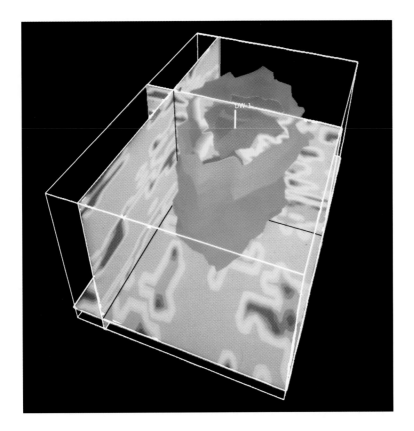

1 dependent variable
3 independent variables
Locates shape
Geology

Isosurfaces and cutting planes locate shapes.

Van Bui-Tran, Chakib Bennis, Jean-Louis Pajon, Claude Lallemand, Gisèle Legendre, Dominique Guerillot, and Pierre Lemouzy, Institut Français du Pétrole, Rueil-Malmaison, France.

Application (Oil Exploration)

The fluid flow saturation pattern created by injecting water into the region of producing oil wells is studied. HERESIM™[1] and SCORE™[2] simulate the data. The image was rendered on a Silicon Graphics workstation.

Technique

Two isosurfaces of water saturation created by the Marching Cubes algorithm[3] and shown in green and brown locate the region where water has been injected. Three cutting planes are colored according to the visible light spectrum to indicate the amount of water (blue, low; red, high). The cutting planes show distribution of water in the surrounding area and permit comparison with distribution of water near the injection point, represented by a labeled vertical line. The isosurfaces reveal the saturation pattern of the injected water, and the cutting planes help locate the shape. The white perspective-bounding box enhances the 3-D effect and locates the cutting planes. Thin black lines mark the intersection of the slice planes.

Hints

This technique helps to locate isosurfaces in a volume or to relate isosurfaces to surrounding features. ◊ See **8-7**, which uses isosurfaces and cutting planes to determine shape.

[1] HERESIM™, developed by Institut Français du Pétrole and École des Mines de Paris, Centre de Géostatistiques, marketed by BEICIP–France.

[2] SCORE™, developed by Elf Aquitaine, Gaz de France, Institut Français du Pétrole.

[3] W. Lorensen and H. Cline, "Marching Cubes: A High Resolution 3D Surface Construction Algorithm," *Computer Graphics* 21, 24 (1987).

1 dependent variable
3 independent variables
Reveals surface complexity
Medicine

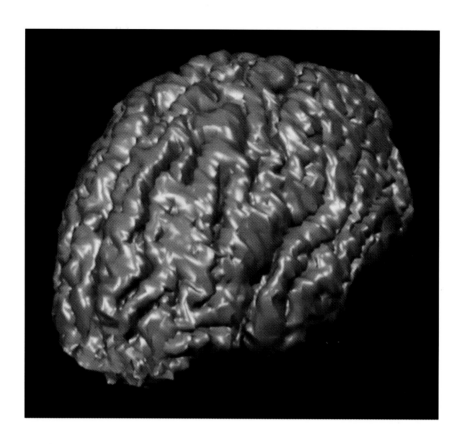

Shading, specular reflection, and color emphasize surface geometry.

Arthur W. Toga, University of California Los Angeles School of Medicine, Los Angeles, CA, USA.

Application (Medical Imaging)

A 3-D reconstruction of a brain from approximately 45 axial magnetic resonance imaging (MRI) slices is studied. The images were computed with in-house software on a VAX 8530 computer and displayed on a Gould Image Processing system.

Technique

A wire-frame model is constructed from the detected edges of each axial MRI slice of the brain. Shading, specular reflection, and color are applied to the model to emphasize the brain's surface geometry and to suggest realism. Perspective enhances 3-D appearance.

Hints

Distorted surfaces result if too few slices are used to reconstruct the solid. The necessary number is a judgment call: the rougher or more complex the surface, the more slices needed. ◊ Specular and shading coefficients of the rendering algorithm must be adjusted carefully so that depth cueing is not obstructed and surface complexity remains obvious. ◊ This technique is useful for constructing 3-D models from 2-D slices and for emphasizing the surface geometry of a 3-D model.

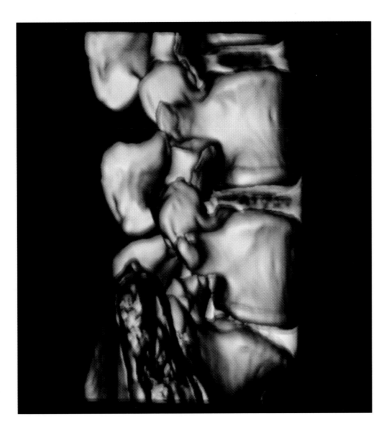

1 dependent variable
3 independent variables
Reveals structure
Medicine

Colored isosurfaces and translucent volume density reveal structure.

Wolfgang Krueger, GMD-HLRZ, Bonn, Germany.

Application (Medical Imaging)

A transport theory* approach[1] to visualization is used to plan medical surgery. The raw computed tomography (CT) image data[2] were converted and filtered with in-house software and then rendered on a Silicon Graphics IRIS workstation.

Technique

CT slices are stacked to form a volume. The transport theory approach reveals detailed structure and sharp demarcation between scalar values; a parameter, the surface scattering term,[†] controls the level of detail. Two different thresholds identify materials of different densities and are colored differently by a surface and volume source term[†] to distinguish them from each other.

Hints

This technique can be used to render 3-D scalar fields where sharp differences or detail must be shown.

[1] Wolfgang Krueger, "The Application of Transport Theory to Visualization of 3-D Scalar Data Fields," *Computers in Physics* 4, 4 (July/August 1991): 397–406.

[2] Data provided by A. Kern, Radiological Institute of the University of Berlin.

---

* The visualization approach is based on the linear transport theory for the transfer of particles in inhomogeneous amorphous media. The advantages of this approach are its rigorous mathematical formulation, application to data from different disciplines, and wide variety of contextual cues.

† See description in reference 1.

10-3 Models

3-D Model
Depicts context
Architecture

**Secondary information
aids analysis.**

Michael Stephen Zdepski and
Michael Hoon, School of
Architecture of the New Jersey
Institute of Technology,
Newark, NJ, USA.

[1] Michael Stephen Zdepski and
Glenn Goldman, "Reality and
Virtual Reality," Association
for Computer Aided Design in
Architecture, Los Angeles, CA
(October 1991).

[2] Michael Stephen Zdepski and
Glenn Goldman,
"Previsualization," National
Computer Graphics Associa-
tion (April 1989).

[3] Michael Stephen Zdepski,
"Image and Reality," ACM:
SIGGRAPH (August 1991).

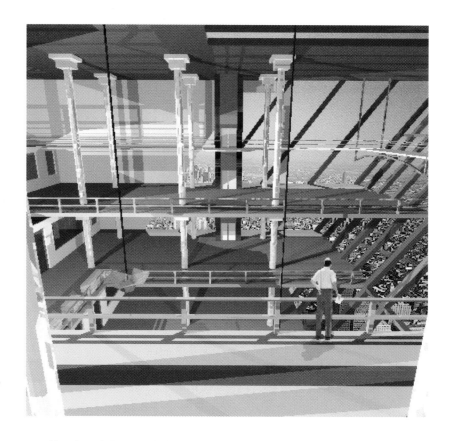

Application (Site Modeling)
Contextual clues are used to help evaluate proposed architectural designs.[1-3] The model was created with Design Futures' MEGACADD, Mathematica's Tempra, and Graphic Software's Big D running on a PC386/25 with a Targa 16 graphics card.

Technique
A realistic architectural model is created with surface attributes (colors, reflectances, transparencies, specular or diffuse surfaces, and textures) and natural and artificial lighting (point-source or parallel-ray lighting, and light color). A human figure is positioned in the model to indicate relative size. Architectural site photographs are scanned, scaled, and placed behind the architectural model. The final image is created by rendering the architectural image and describing nonmodel surfaces as transparent to reveal the underlying site photograph.

Hints
Placing a model (or data) in its proper context aids analysis and interpretation. In this example, the human figure and the site photograph convey an understanding of size and show how all the elements are related. ◊ See also **5-2**, where a model (context) is necessary to understand the data, and **12-5**, which uses background context to create a mood.

3-D Model
Enhances realism
Computer Graphics

Placing an object in a familiar context enhances realism.

David S. Ebert, Ohio State University, Columbus, OH, USA.

Application (Photorealism)

A turbulent gas computer model is used to create realistic-appearing steam. The gas flow model uses the EDGE graphics library developed at Ohio State University. The image was rendered on a Hewlett-Packard HP 9000 series 370 TSRX workstation.

Technique

Computed gas flow is combined with surface-defined, polygonal objects. The steam is rendered with self-shadowing as well as with shadowing of the steam onto the teacup[1] and wall using a table-based shadowing technique.[2] The surfaces are rendered with a scanline A-buffer technique.[3]

Hints

In some images, appropriate context can be a valuable interpretive tool. The white smudge in this image is interpreted as steam because it is placed in context with a cup and saucer. If the context were a graffiti-marked wall, the viewer could mistakenly interpret the smudge as spray paint. ◊ The rendering system that produced this image allows efficient combination of volume-rendered objects with surface-rendered objects. ◊ See **12-5** for an example of using secondary information to create a mood. ◊ See **5-7**, **5-9**, **5-10**, **5-12**, **6-6**, **9-2**, **9-7**, **10-4**, **12-1**, **12-2**, **12-7**, and **12-8** for other ways to handle fog or cloudlike features.

[1] Teacup data supplied by Stephen F. May, Ohio State University, Columbus, OH, USA.

[2] David S. Ebert, "Solid Spaces: A Unified Approach to Describing Object Attributes," Ph.D. Dissertation, Ohio State University, Columbus, OH (1991).

[3] David S. Ebert and Richard E. Parent, "Rendering and Animation of Gaseous Phenomena by Combining Fast Volume and Scanline A-Buffer Techniques," Proceedings of SIGGRAPH '90, in *Computer Graphics* 24, 4 (August 1990): 357–366.

10-5 Models

1 dependent variable
2 independent variables
Reveals shape
Computer Graphics

Selecting polygons based on surface detail optimizes computing speed while retaining shape.

Lori L. Scarlatos, Grumman Data Systems, Woodbury, NY, USA; Theo Pavlidis, State University of New York at Stony Brook, NY, USA.

[1] Lori Scarlatos and Theo Pavlidis, "Hierarchical Triangulation Using Cartographic Coherence," *CVGIP: Graphical Models and Image Processing* 54, 2 (March 1992): 147–161.

[2] Lori L. Scarlatos, "A Refined Triangulation Hierarchy for Multiple Levels of Terrain Detail," *Proceedings Image V Conference*, Phoenix, AZ (June 19–22, 1990), pp. 115–122.

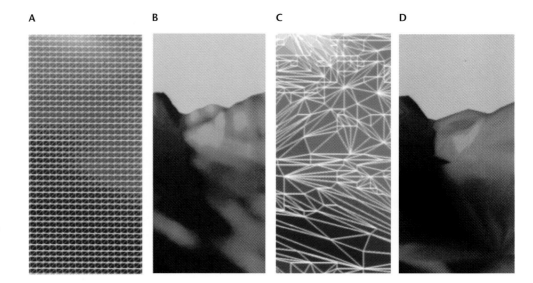

A   B   C   D

Application (Surface Modeling)

Techniques for representing data that will reduce rendering time for animation and interactive data analysis are studied. Digital terrain elevation data are used to illustrate the technique. The surface model was run on a VAX 8530 and rendered on a Silicon Graphics IRIS 4D 370 workstation with in-house software.

Technique

Figure A shows a common approach for creating a 3-D surface. A 2-D array of data, represented by color (blue, low; yellow, high), is overlaid with a regular grid of many rectangles. These 2-D rectangles are rendered as a 3-D surface by changing the (x, y) vertex definitions to (x, y, z) locations, where z is the value of the data at the vertex. The rectangles are then colored, lighted, and shaded, as in Figure B. Figure C, with the same data as Figure A, creates a hierarchy of triangulations[1, 2] that correlates to different levels of data detail. This more time-efficient technique applies larger triangles to overlay data in regions where the data values are unchanging and smaller triangles to overlay regions of change. The resultant Figure D, similar to Figure B, uses just enough triangles to render the scene accurately and is four times faster.

Hints

Although terrain data are modeled (complete with blue background for sky and shades of yellow for the terrain to enhance realism), this technique can be used to quickly render any surface. ◊ This hierarchy is useful for zooming in and out of a scene, allowing one to render areas of greater importance in greater detail. This surface-definition technique, which allows one to pay for computer processing time only when it is needed, can be especially effective when visually scanning large data sets.

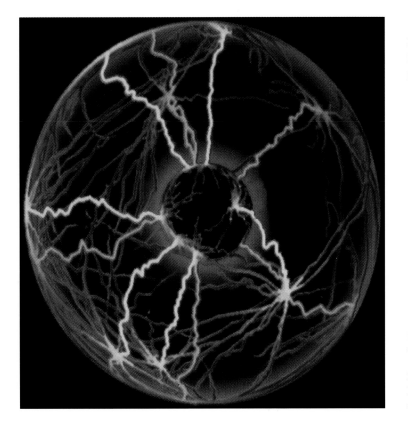

1 dependent variable
3 independent variables
Reveals structure
Electrical Engineering

Front-to-back order and brightness emphasize the important structure.

Daniel Carr, Precision Visuals, Inc., Boulder, CO, USA; submitted by Lew Harstead.

Application (Electrical Discharge Modeling)

Discharge data from a plasma globe simulation are rendered on a Sun Microsystems workstation with Precision Visual's PV-WAVE.

Technique

The dark-colored lines, which have the weakest discharge, are plotted first; the brightly colored lines, which have the strongest discharge, are plotted last. This ordering ensures that a weak discharge will not blot out a strong one. The final image is processed with an image-smoothing technique called boxcar averaging, which enhances the realism of the electrical discharge.

Hints

This image illustrates an important design consideration. The viewer's attention is drawn to the important information by making the strong discharge brighter and placing it on top. ◊ **4-4** also uses this technique.

10-7 Models

1 dependent variable
3 independent variables
Identifies shapes
Geography

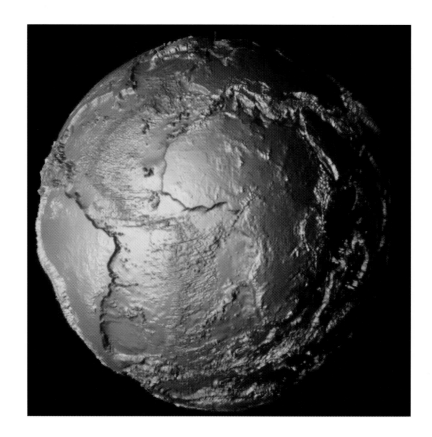

**Redundant encoding
aids shape recognition.**

Lloyd A. Treinish, IBM T. J.
Watson Research Center,
Yorktown Heights, NY, USA.

[1] National Space Science Data
Center, Greenbelt, MD, USA.

[2] IBM, *Data Explorer User's
Guide*, to be published.

[3] Lloyd A. Treinish and Craig
Goettsche, "Correlative
Visualization Techniques for
Multidimensional Data," *IBM
Journal of Research and
Development* 35, 1/2 (January/
March 1991).

[4] Frederick Pearson, II, *Map
Projections: Theory and
Applications* (Boca Raton, FL:
CRC Press, 1990).

Application (Terrain Visualization)

Topography and bathymetry (topography of the ocean floor) elevation data[1] from minus 9877 to 7220 meters relative to sea level are studied. The data are averaged to 10 arc-minute resolution, implying more than 2,000,000 polygons. The image was rendered on the IBM Power Visualization System with the IBM Data Explorer.[2, 3]

Technique

A hemisphere of the earth is mapped[4] to a sphere. Height and depth measurements texture the map by creating bumps proportional to height at the location of each height measurement; color redundantly encodes height (blue, low; red, high). This texture is further visually enhanced by modeling light and shadows. The physiology of the eye is more responsive to changes in texture than to changes in color, making the topographical shape stand out.

Hints

Textures are a useful redundant cue for enhancing shape discrimination. ◊ See **2-8** and **5-4** for other examples of using the bump-map technique.

Computerized techniques from photography enhance realism.

John Prusinski, CyberGrafix, Warwick, NY, USA; Peter Lulleman, Philadelphia Video Lab, Inc., Merion, PA, USA.

Application (Photorealism)

This United States Geological Survey image of Mars was rendered from Digital Elevation Map data as a test frame for an animation. The image was rendered on an Amiga 2000 with VISTApro.[1]

Technique

A photorealistic, pseudocolored view of Mars topography is created by using techniques similar to those of the professional photographer. From several low-resolution views that offer slight changes in camera angle, lighting intensity, and direction, the best view is selected. Making a prominent foreground feature slightly out of focus and using that indistinct feature to frame the sharply focused, more distant features emphasizes 3-D. A smoothing algorithm and Gouraud shading minimize image artifacts caused by extensive errors in the data. The color and lighting also enhance realism.

Hints

Contrast this technique for creating a sense of depth with **12-1** and **12-2**, which focus on the foreground and use atmospheric haze to enhance depth.

[1] Virtual Reality Laboratories, Inc., San Luis Obispo, CA, USA.

10-9 Models

1 dependent variable
3 independent variables
Reveals shape
Medicine

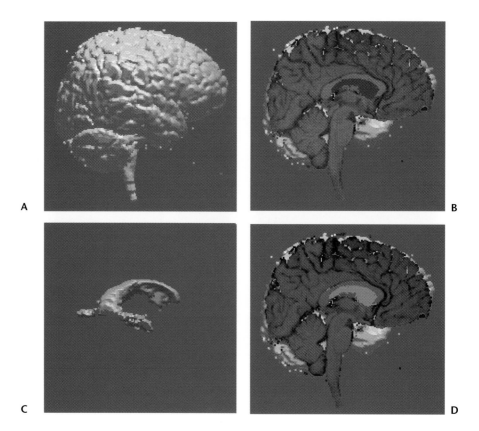

A

B

C

D

A scan-line algorithm and color reveal the shape of objects within a volume.

Don Stredney and Steven F. May, Advanced Computing Center for the Arts and Design, Ohio State University, Columbus, OH, USA; Michael W. Torello, Ohio Sleep Medicine Institute and Riverside Methodist Hospitals, Dublin, OH, USA.

[1] D. L. Stredney, "3-D Brain Visualization for Biomedical Education," *Visions: A Publication of the Ohio Supercomputer Center*, 3.1 (Winter 1990).

[2] M. W. Torello, "Cray Research System Carries Brainstorm to Reality," *Cray Channels: A Cray Research, Inc. Publication* (Summer 1990).

[3] C. A. Csuri, S.'Dyer, J. Faust, and R. Marshall, "A Flexible Integrated Graphics Environment for Supercomputers and Workstations," *Science and Engineering on Cray Supercomputers*, Cray Research, Inc. (1987), pp. 533–548.

[4] See additional references at the end of Section II, p. 182.

Application (Medical Imaging)

This research is an attempt to develop tools[1-3] for enhancing the spatial and color resolution of magnetic resonance imaging (MRI) data for surgical planning, teaching, and research. Current tools include a Sun Microsystems 4/110 workstation for manipulating data and images. A Cray Y-MP supercomputer processes data and images. Software tools include in-house software developed by the Advanced Computing Center for the Arts and Design and the apE (animation production Environment) visualization toolkit developed at the Ohio Supercomputer Center.

Technique

Fifty-five MRI intensity slices consisting of 256×256 data points are joined to form a volume. A scan-line algorithm[4] tests voxel (volume element) visibility by checking whether a voxel intensity value lies within a specified range. The voxels within that range are determined as visible and are used to describe surfaces that are illuminated and colored. Figures A through D show surfaces described by selecting one or more intensity values. Figures B and D show internal structure by applying the technique to one-half the volume.

Hints

Identifying voxels with a specific intensity value and using them to describe a surface provides a fairly realistic representation. ◊ Artifacts can be caused by similarities in pixel intensity values for different types of tissue. Different MRI slices for the same brain have different baseline pixel intensity values and must be normalized. ◊ MRI slices that do not line up with the previous slice require interpolation, which may introduce spatial errors. ◊ See **8-3** and **10-1** for related MRI techniques.

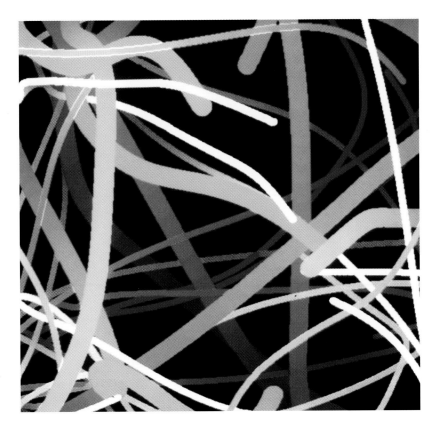

3 dependent variables
3 independent variables
Identifies shape
Polymer Chemistry

Color, size, and rigidity identify shapes.

Jean-François Colonna,
Lactamme (CNET, École
Polytechnique), France.

Application (Computation of Chains)

Polymer chains are simulated with a 3-D random walk with parameters of rigidity, length, and the smallest distance between any two chains. The image reveals how the chains avoid each other and validate the physical model. The computation and the visualization were executed on a Silicon Graphics 4D 20 workstation with K, a machine-independent language.

Technique

Different components of a structure are depicted and located relative to each other. Color, length, width, and rigidity distinguish components. Showing objects in front of or behind other objects and shading help to achieve 3-D effect and to reveal collisions.

Hints

These modeling techniques can be used to show or to compare structure and relationships of stringy substances. ◊ Rotating the image interactively allows us to see the image better.

3-D Model
Locates shape
Computational Materials
    Science

Colored spheres depict
type or environment of
an atom.

Verlan K. Gabrielson and M. I.
Baskes, Sandia National Laboratories, Livermore, CA, USA.

[1] M. I. Baskes, M. S. Daw, and
S. M. Foiles, "The Embedded
Atom Method: Theory and
Application," SAND 88-8851,
Sandia National Laboratories,
Livermore, CA, USA (January
1989).

Application (Molecular Dynamics)

The image shows results of molecular dynamic dislocation mobility near a helium bubble in nickel. The embedded-atom method, which performs atomistic calculations at surfaces and interfaces,[1] is used for analysis. ATOMS, an in-house code, was run on a Cray supercomputer and the image was rendered on a Raster Technology terminal.

Technique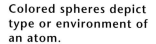

A 3-D arrangement of spheres illustrates the mechanical properties of a nickel lattice with a helium bubble. Yellow spheres represent nickel atoms; green spheres, helium atoms; and red spheres, dislocation cores. Drawing the spheres as a planar set of concentric circles develops a 3-D effect by assigning the atom's color intensity as a cosine function of the radius of each circle. Perspective is applied to enhance 3-D. The interior of the lattice at a given row can be seen by rotating the upper spheres up about the *x*-axis and the lower spheres down about the *x*-axis.

Hints

This "3-D sphere" drawing technique is extremely fast and suitable for real-time animation of models composed of spheres, especially if one can take advantage of hardware-drawn circles.

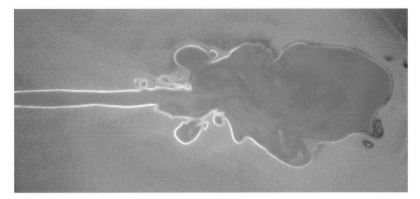

A

1 dependent variable
2 independent variables
Reveals structure
Astronomy

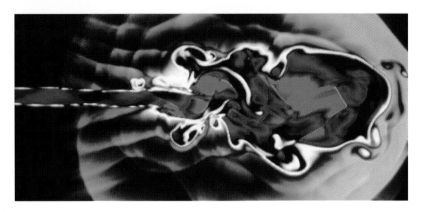

B

Proper choice of color reveals structure.

Donna J. Cox, National Center for Supercomputing Applications, School of Art & Design, University of Illinois, Urbana, IL, USA; Michael Norman, National Center for Supercomputing Applications.

Application (Computational Astrophysics)

This simulation using a magnetohydrodynamics code shows the density of matter in an astrophysical jet in intergalactic space. Complex flow patterns and vortices are modeled. Images were rendered on a Silicon Graphics Workstation with data from an in-house application code on a Cray supercomputer.

Technique

Before-and-after pseudocolor maps constructed from the same data illustrate the dramatic change in meaning communicated by changing the color table. Changing the color that a data point receives reveals hidden structure in Figure B by creating color contrasts that the eye is better able to discern.[1-3]

Hints

A color key as in Figure iv, page 41, that illustrates the color table should be included if it is important to correlate color to the variable's value. ◊ Another technique, histogram equalization, used in **11-3**, could automatically bring out detail. A more reliable way of discovering patterns, however, is to manually and interactively step through a collection of color tables.

[1] D. Cox, "Using the Supercomputer to Visualize Higher Dimensions: An Artist's Contribution to Scientific Visualization," *Leonardo: Journal of Art, Science and Technology* 21 (1988): 233–242.

[2] D. Cox, "The Art of Scientific Visualization," *Academic Computing* (March 1990): 20–40; references at end of journal.

[3] G. Meyer and D. Greenberg, "Perceptual Color Spaces for Computer Graphics," Proceedings of SIGGRAPH '80, in *Computer Graphics* (July 14–18, 1980).

1 dependent variable
3 independent variables
Reveals structure
Computer Graphics

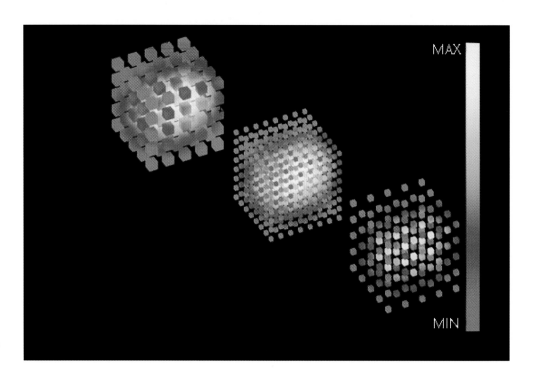

Small cubes reveal 3-D structure.

Gregory M. Nielson, Arizona State University, Tempe, AZ, USA; Bernd Hamann, Mississippi State University, Jackson, MS, USA.

[1] Bernd Hamann, "Visualization and Modeling Contours of Trivariate Functions," Ph.D. Thesis, Arizona State University, Tempe, AZ (1991).

[2] Gregory M. Nielson, Thomas A. Foley, Bernd Hamann, and David Lane, "Visualization and Modeling of Scattered Multivariate Data," *Computer Graphics and Applications* 11, 3 (May 1991): 47–55.

[3] Gregory M. Nielson and Bernd Hamann, "Techniques for the Interactive Visualization of Volumetric Data," in *Visualization '90*, (Los Alamitos, CA: IEEE Computer Society Press, October 1990), pp. 45–50.

Application (Visualization)

Invented data are used to demonstrate an interactive technique for visualizing volume. In-house software and the Silicon Graphics GL library rendered the image on the Silicon Graphics 4D 320 workstation.

Technique

Three cubic volumes illustrate three examples of the "tiny-cubes" technique for visualizing regularly spaced, coarse data throughout a cube.[1-3] The data value at each location determines the color of the vertices of the tiny cube drawn there. The tiny cubes are color coded according to the color key at right. A hidden-surface algorithm enhances the 3-D effect. Internal or external structure is best revealed by interactively adjusting three parameters of the code: number of cubes in each direction, size of cubes, and spacing between cubes.

Hints

Rotating the cubic volume provides different views through the volume and significantly enhances understanding of the data. ◊ To use this technique effectively, one must keep the number of tiny cubes relatively small. It is difficult to see "inside" when the number of cubes in each direction is greater than twelve. Relatively large cubes tend to emphasize external features, but small cubes allow one to see internal structure. ◊ See also **9-6**, which uses small spheres to reveal 3-D structure.

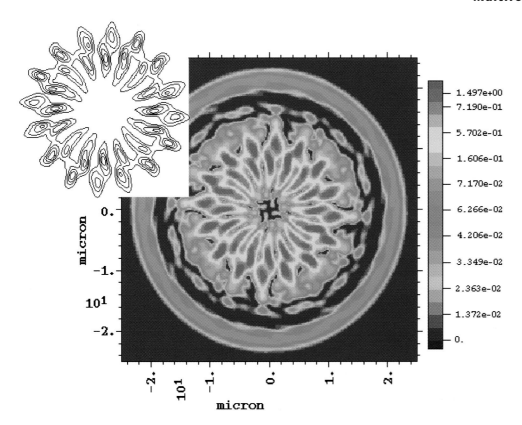

1 dependent variable
2 independent variables
Reveals structure
Computational Physics

**Histogram equalization
of color values reveals
complex structure.**

M. D. Feit, J. A. Fleck, Jr., and
P. P. Weidhaas, Lawrence
Livermore National Labora-
tory, Livermore, CA, USA.

Application (Lasers)

A computer application[1] simulates the propagation of a laser beam through a
nonlinear medium. The image shows a self-focusing intensity pattern that develops
after the laser traverses the medium. Such self-focusing is of practical importance
because the high intensities formed can damage optical media such as glass lenses.
The data were calculated by an optical propagation code, and the image was
computed by a postprocessor with in-house graphics libraries on a Cray X-MP
supercomputer. The image was plotted on a color Versatec printer for analysis.

Technique

On a pseudocolor scalar field, colors are assigned to pixels according to intensity
values and correlated to a color key to identify regions of effective intensity (red).
In addition to color, we use histogram equalization[2] to help reveal the complex
structure. Histogram equalization assigns an equal number of pixels to each color
to bring out otherwise hidden meaning. The black-and-white isoplot of the scalar
field, inset at the upper left corner of the image, graphically demonstrates the value
of using color and histogram equalization to reveal complex structure.

Hints

The visible light spectrum is a reasonable first step in analyzing 2-D scalar fields
because it spreads the data over a large number of colors. ◊ Histogram equalization,
which spreads the data equally over the color range, is especially helpful in
revealing small disturbances over a large constant background or in revealing very
sharp peaks. We have choices in our way of representing the color key. In this image
the colors appear to change smoothly, but the reference numbers are not linear; in **6-1**,
though, the colors appear to change irregularly but the reference numbers are linear.

[1] M. D. Feit and J. A. Fleck, Jr.,
"Beam Nonparallaxity,
Filament Formation and Beam
Breakup in the Self-Focusing
of Optical Beams" *J. Opt. Soc.
Am.* B 5 (1988): 633.

[2] Azriel Rosenfeld and Avinash
C. Kak, *Digital Picture
Processing* (San Diego:
Academic Press, 1982), pp.
231–237.

1 dependent variable
2 independent variables
Locates extremes
Computational Physics

Contouring quickly reveals gradients and shapes, and color quickly locates extremes.

Scott T. Brandon and Kathleen M. Dyer, Lawrence Livermore National Laboratory, Livermore, CA, USA.

A   B

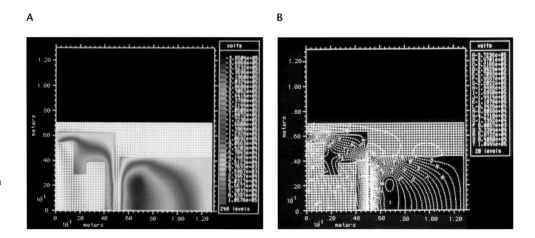

Application (Electromagnetism)

Electrostatic potential of a virtual cathode oscillator is simulated. The data were generated and the picture was computed with a Cray 1 supercomputer. The computed image was sent to a Tektronix 4125 high-resolution color terminal for display and analysis.

Technique

On the pseudocolored scalar field (Figure A) color locates the extremum and is indexed to a key to show approximate values. The black-and-white image (Figure B) clearly shows the location and shape of isolines and is indexed to a key that gives exact values. The spacing of the isolines represents gradients. Dotted isolines indicate negative values; solid isolines are positive values. In both images, small squares identify the boundaries of the experiment, providing a reference framework for the viewer.

Hints

The meaning to be communicated determines whether we show one or both images. Isolines could also be plotted on the color image, but including them would risk making the image complex and hard to understand.

1 dependent variable
3 independent variables
Shows surface values
Architecture

A

B

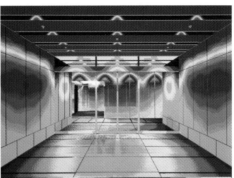

Ray tracing simulates illumination and shows surface values.

Shinichi Kasahara and Hideaki Iwaida, Kajima Corporation, Tokyo, Japan.

Application (Building Illumination)

Lighting requirements for an architectural design are studied. The images were rendered with REALS, an in-house tracing program, and modeled with CATIA, a 3-D computer-aided design (CAD) system by Dassault Systems for modeling on an IBM 3090.

Technique

Figure A is produced with a ray-tracing technique[1] to render a geometric model. Modeling individual light sources provides a realistic view of the combined illumination to evaluate the appearance. Figure B, a pseudocolor image made by the same ray-tracing technique, uses discrete color bands to locate equal brightness values. The bands are correlated to the color key at the bottom of the image. Figure B is used to understand the brightness values in each portion of the room and to help design the lighting.

[1] Turner Whitted, "An Improved Illumination Model for Shaded Display," *Communications of ACM 23,* 6 (June 1980): 343–349.

Hints

Selecting the proper color table is vital for bringing out the desired information. The table for these images was chosen for realism and for brightness analysis. ◊ **11-1** also illustrates how selection of color key influences the type of information that is revealed. ◊ See **8-1** for yet another color table to show data values on a surface.

1 dependent variable
3 independent variables
Identifies shape
Computer Science

A

B

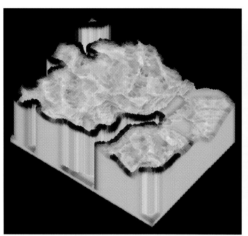 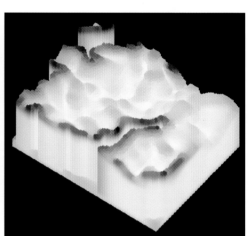

Diffusion algorithm identifies shape of 3-D scalar field.

Yaser Yacoob, University of Maryland, College Park, MD, USA.

[1] Y. Yacoob and Y. I. Gold, "3-D Object Recognition via Simulated Particles Diffusion," *Proceedings IEEE Conference on Computer Vision and Pattern Recognition (CVPR)*, San Diego (June 1989), pp. 442–449.

[2] Y. Yacoob, "Displaying Voxel-Based Objects According to Their Qualitative Shape Synthesis," in *Visualization '90* (Los Alamitos, CA: IEEE Computer Society Press, October 1990), pp. 51–58.

Application (Computer Vision)

This research investigates qualitative shape description of any kind of a 3-D scalar field. The image was produced using in-house software running on Thinking Machines Corporation Connection Machine (CM-2) 8K processors configuration.

Technique

A 3-D shape is revealed by applying a diffusion algorithm[1,2] to a $128 \times 128 \times 128$ 3-D scalar field that is a voxel array. The process simulates the diffusion of particles from the boundary voxels to the interior of the volume. Twenty time-steps of the diffusion algorithm reveal detailed shapes (Figure A). Two hundred time-steps reveal only large scale features (Figure B). In both figures, the boundary voxels are shaded according to the density of particles in the voxel. The darker the shade, the more dense the particles, the more convex the shape.

Hints

This diffusion technique for shape identification does not work for thin objects or sparse 3-D data because the particles have no space into which they can move. ◊ The choice of a color table achieves different visualization effects. Using two colors emphasizes convexities and concavities while reducing the smoothness of the image. ◊ Distinct colors can be used to segment the image for shape recognition. ◊ See **4-1** for different techniques for determining shape.

A

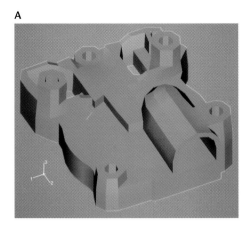

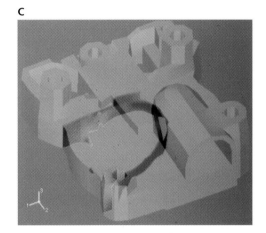

B

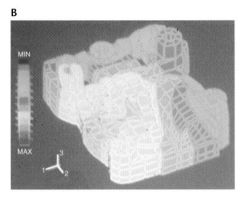

C

1 dependent variable
3 independent variables
Correlates scalars and
   shape
Mechanical Engineering

Combination plot shows internal and external values relative to external shape.

Richard S. Gallagher, Swanson Analysis Systems, Houston, PA, USA; Todd Gerhardt, Kohler Company, Kohler, WI, USA; Joop C. Nagtegaal, Hibbitt, Karlsson & Sorensen Inc, Providence, RI, USA.

Application (Finite Element Analysis)

This simulation models the temperature of a small-engine cylinder head.[1] The image was computed on a VAX 8600 and rendered on a Tektronix 4336 workstation with hardware Gouraud shading and translucency.

Technique

This combination plot uses three techniques to provide a more thorough understanding of temperature distribution. A solid model (Figure A), constructed from a bicubic interpolation of surface geometry and surface normals to ensure visual continuity, illustrates external geometry. A color-coded model (Figure B), keyed to the color bar at left, shows relative surface temperature. A grid structure of light blue polygonal lines shows the refinement level of the calculation. The translucent model (Figure C), which reveals an isosurface location of temperature, is rendered with a surface-based extension to the Marching Cubes algorithm.[2, 3]

Hints

Multiple techniques often provide fuller understanding of the data. The resultant image is best used, however, by one researcher or by an audience with time to study the different views. ◊ See **2-3** and **2-6** for other multiple-technique images.

[1] Todd Gerhardt, Cylinder Head Data, Kohler Company, Kohler, WI, USA.

[2] William E. Lorensen and Harvey E. Cline, "Marching Cubes: A High Resolution 3-D Surface Construction Algorithm," Proceedings of SIGGRAPH '87, in *Computer Graphics* 21, 4 (July 1987).

[3] Richard S. Gallagher and Joop C. Nagtegaal, "An Efficient 3D Visualization Technique for Finite Element Models and Other Coarse Volumes," Proceedings of SIGGRAPH '89, in *Computer Graphics* 23, 3 (August 1989).

11-8 Multiform Visualization

A

B

1 dependent variable
3 independent variables
Reveals structure
Computational Fluid
   Dynamics

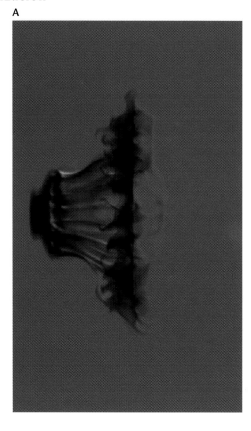

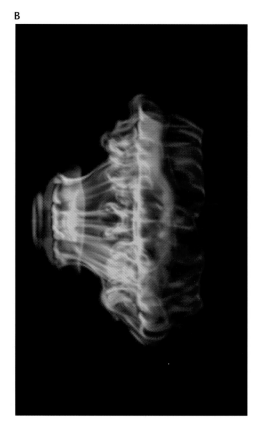

Minute adjustments in opacity and background reveal structure.

Richard I. Klein, Michael J. Allison, and Thomas M. Kelleher, Lawrence Livermore National Laboratory, Livermore, CA, USA.

[1] Andrew Barlow, "New Workstation Graphics for Engineers," *Computer-Aided Engineering* 9, 9 (September 1990): 40.

[2] K. Akeley and T. Jermoluk, "High-Performance Polygon Rendering," *Computer Graphics* 22, 4 (August 1988): 239–246.

Application (Turbulent Fluid Flow)

The structure of fluid flow is studied by modeling the changes that occur when a spherical, interstellar cloud is subjected to a strong shock from a supernova explosion. The computational model was executed on a Cray Y-MP supercomputer and rendered on a Stardent computer with in-house software.

Technique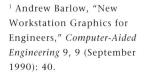

The computational model's 3-D adaptive mesh is first converted to a rectilinear mesh and volume rendered with the compositing alpha-blend algorithm[1,2] with the low-density and high-density values opaque. From the many images of the same data set rendered, two are shown here. Figure A shows the data with the very low-density fluid omitted so that structure occluded by that fluid can be observed. Figure B shows the very low-density fluid but uses a black background to enhance contrast to reveal complex, connected, very low-density structures.

Hints

Rotating the image, removing data, and changing opacities sometimes reveals more than one expects. Researchers originally thought the data had very little structure. Rotating the image, however, provided vantage points suggesting an intricate structure hidden by cloud material; that matter was then removed by selectively plotting data and adjusting opacity.

3-D Model
Identifies classes of objects
Biomedical

A

B

Color coding identifies objects and reveals physical relationships.

Chris Gong, Rei Cheng, Muriel D. Ross, and Joseph Varelas, Biocomputation Center, NASA Ames Research Center, Moffett Field, CA, USA.

Application (3-D Reconstruction)

This image, derived from electron micrographs, was created to show the physical relationships between neural elements in a gravity-sensing organ in the mammalian inner ear. This image revealed to the researchers for the first time that the neural elements are morphologically organized for weighted, parallel-distributed processing of information. The image was rendered on a Silicon Graphics IRIS 4D-GT workstation executing the ROSS[1] software.

Technique

A 3-D model is constructed[2, 3] from an ordered set of many 2-D images. The 2-D images are created by tracing elements of interest from thin slices of the gravity-sensing organ and assigning the elements an arbitrary value. The reconstructed 3-D model has the same relative size, position, and connectivities as the actual organ. Elements are selected by value and are colored to discriminate among and to enhance recognition of the separate parts. Smooth shading is applied for visual interest as well as to emphasize the 3-D nature of the image. In Figure A, the model is created with opaque surfaces to reveal the external shape. In Figure B, one of the elements is made translucent and the model is rotated slightly for better understanding of its interior shape.

Hints

Image orientation is important in this case: gravitational biologists are interested in the directional sensitivity of an element's location. ◊ Using the same colors for the elements facilitates comparison from reconstruction to reconstruction.

[1] Muriel Ross, Rei Cheng, Tony Lam, and Glenn Meyer, "ROSS 2.2. Reconstruction of Serial Sections," 1991. Documentation available upon request.

[2] Muriel Ross, Lynn Cutler, Glenn Meyer, Tony Lam, and Parshaw Vaziri, "3-D Components of a Biological Neural Network Visualized in Computer Generated Imagery. I. Macular Receptive Field Organization," *Acta Otolaryngologica* (Stockholm: 1990): 83.

[3] Muriel Ross, Glenn Meyer, Tony Lam, Lynn Cutler, and Parshaw Vaziri, "3-D Components of a Biological Neural Network Visualized in Computer Generated Imagery. II. Macular Neural Network Organization," *Acta Otolaryngologica* (Stockholm: 1990): 235.

1 dependent variable
3 independent variables
Reveals structure
Combustion Engineering

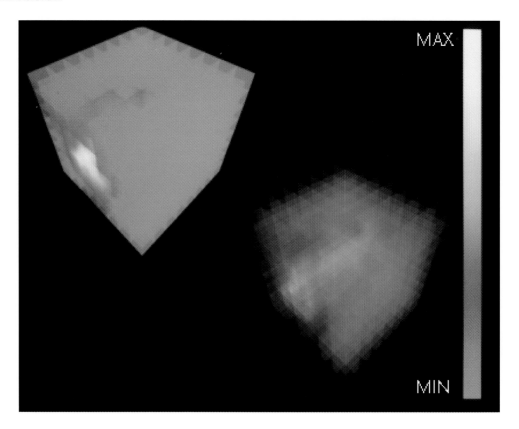

Translucency reveals structure within a volume.

Gregory M. Nielson, Arizona State University, Tempe, AZ, USA; Bernd Hamann, Mississippi State University, Jackson, MS, USA; Marshall Long, Yale University, New Haven, CT, USA.

[1] Marshall B. Long, Kevin Lyons, and Joseph K. Lam, "Acquisition and Representation of 2D and 3D Data from Turbulent Flows and Flames," in *Scientific Visualization*, G. Nielson and G. Shriver, eds. (Los Alamitos, CA: IEEE Computer Society Press, 1990), pp. 132–139.

[2] Bernd Hamann, "Visualization and Modeling Contours of Trivariate Functions," Ph.D. Thesis, Arizona State University, Tempe, AZ (1991).

[3] Gregory M. Nielson, Thomas A. Foley, Bernd Hamann, and David Lane, "Visualization and Modeling of Scattered Multivariate Data," *Computer Graphics and Applications* 11, 3 (May 1991): 47–55.

[4] See additional references at the end of Section II, p. 182.

Application (Computational Fluid Dynamics)

The distribution and concentration of gas in a region containing a flame is studied.[1] In-house software with the Silicon Graphics GL library was run on a Silicon Graphics 4D 320 workstation.

Technique

In this volumetric technique for visualizing 3-D data and functions, the domain is decomposed into a number of voxels; then each voxel face is treated as translucent. The parameter that controls the level of transparency can be changed, allowing the user to look deeper and deeper into the data.[2-4] The left-hand image shows the transparency variable set to *opaque*, and the right-hand image shows the parameter set to *more transparent* to reveal internal structure. The color key at right correlates the highs and lows in the data.

Hints

If the domain is decomposed into a large number of voxels, the rendering time becomes extremely long and the effectiveness of interactive analysis is reduced. ◊ Rotating the cubic volume provides different perspectives to help understand the structure. ◊ Different color tables may bring out other information, as in **11-1**.

A

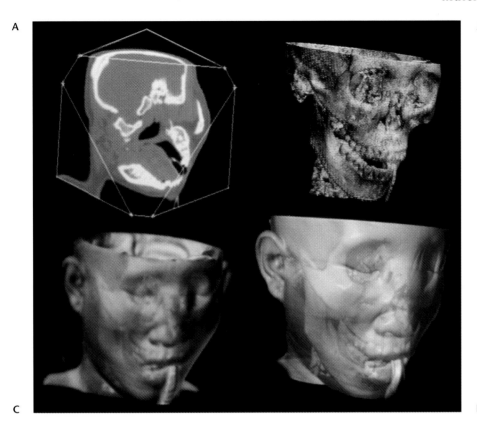

C   D

B   **1 dependent variable**
3 independent variables
Reveals structure
Medicine

**Different volume-
rendering techniques
on the same data set
reveal different
structure.**

E. Ruth Johnson and Charles
E. Mosher, Jr.; submitted by
Donna McMillan, Sun
Microsystems, Research
Triangle Park, NC, USA.

Application (Medical Imaging)

Volume visualization of computed tomography (CT) data provides insight into the location and condition of tissues, muscles, tumors, and other internal structures. The CT data were rendered with the SunVision SunVoxel software on Sun Microsystems workstations.

Technique

Three techniques are used to render a $256 \times 256 \times 256$ array.[1] The multiplanar projection (Figure A) is useful for exploring volumetric data. One or more slice planes are moved through the volume to render pseudocolored voxel values, which represent relative density. The wire frame shows the positions of the cutting plane, and color and intensity help distinguish relative values. In Figure B, the point cloud rendering[2] is useful for showing the shape described by a collection of voxels having the same value. In this case, the voxel value equals the density of bone. In ray casting (Figures C and D) different shading algorithms are used. Color and opacity values are assigned to density ranges in the volume. In Figure D, the external values have semitransparent opacity value, so that the underlying structure can be seen.

Hints

Large data sets are not always needed to reveal the relevant information. See **1-5**, which uses a $133 \times 122 \times 68$ volume; **10-9**, which uses $256 \times 256 \times 55$ volume; and **11-6**, which uses a $128 \times 128 \times 128$ volume.

[1] E. Ruth Johnson and Charles E. Mosher, Jr., "Integration of Volume Rendering and Geometric Graphics," Proceedings of the Chapel Hill Workshop on Volume Visualization, Chapel Hill, NC (May 18–19, 1989).

[2] J. S. Prothero and J. W. Prothero, "A Software Package in C for Interactive 3-D Reconstruction and Display of Anatomical Objects from Serial Section Data," National Computer Graphics Association Conference Proceedings, Vol. 1 (1989), pp. 187–192.

1 dependent variable
3 independent variables
Locates scalars
Environmental Protection

Volume rendering with surface reference cues locates distribution of values.

Andrea J. S. Hin and Edwin Boender, Delft University of Technology, Delft, The Netherlands; Johan Dijkzeul Dutch State Agency for Public Works, The Hague, The Netherlands; Frits H. Post, Delft University of Technology; Tjark van den Heuvel, Dutch State Agency for Public Works; Theo van Walsum, and Jack Versloot, Delft University of Technology.

[1] Andrea J. S. Hin, Edwin Boender, and Frits H. Post, "Visualization of 3D Scalar Fields Using Ray Casting," presented at the *First Eurographics Workshop on Visualization in Scientific Computing*, Clamart, France (April 23–24, 1990), to be published.

[2] Theo Van Walsum, Andrea J. S. Hin, Jack Versloot, and Frits H. Post, "Efficient Hybrid Rendering of Volume Data and Polygons," *Advances in Scientific Visualization* (New York: Springer-Verlag, 1992, to be published).

A

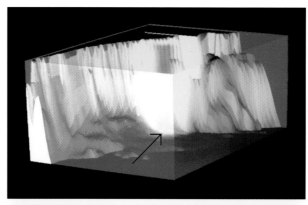

B

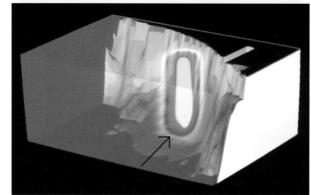

Application (Ocean Pollution)

A 3-D computer model of fluid flow simulates dispersion of pollutants from a source on the North Sea bottom along the Dutch coast. The in-house program AQUA rendered the image on a Hewlett-Packard HP 9000 series 375 workstation.

Technique

Diffuse plumes of pollution, indicated by an arrow in each figure, are rendered with a technique[1,2] that models light absorption in translucent media according to data on concentration of pollution. Opacity of the plume increases as the concentration along the line of sight increases. In Figure A, the plume is mapped to one color, red in this case. In Figure B, which is rotated 90 degrees, the hue of the plume varies with the amount of pollution, revealing location of maxima and density variation within the plume. In both figures the mountainlike surface results from scaling the terrain height of the nearly flat North Sea bottom, making it appear opaque, and flat-shading it to give the surfaces an angular appearance. The boundary of the modeled volume is translucent and light-reflecting to create a glasslike appearance.

Hints

Diffuse features, such as these constructed with translucency, are difficult to locate in space. Therefore we need information on depth, such as terrain features and volume bounds. ◊ The flat shading also distinguishes the terrain from the smooth-appearing pollution. ◊ Viewpoint animation, shading, shadows, or stereoscopy can also enhance 3-D interpretation. The volume model visualized here is named Aquarium Model, evoking a familiar mental image to help understand the data.

3-D Model
Depicts organic objects
Computer Art

3-D modeling techniques create realistic organic objects.

Ned Greene, Paul Heckbert, and Jules Bloomenthal, NYIT Computer Graphics Lab, Old Westbury, NY, USA.

Application (Entertainment)

Techniques for modeling organic objects are developed for a sixty-image sequence for the SIGGRAPH '84 Omnimax film[1] *The Magic Egg.*[2] The animation is a repeating sequence of 60 images in which the viewer appears to move down a "corridor" in a lattice.[3] Images were rendered on a VAX 780 using Ikonas frame buffers.

Technique

The vines are modeled as polygonal tubes swept along splines and rendered with bump mapping to give the impression of relief. The texture map for the bark is created by x-raying a plaster cast of real tree bark. Leaves and flower petals are meshes of triangles with associated color and texture information. Leaves are texture mapped with a digital painting of leaves. Haze is simulated by attenuating contrast as an exponential function of depth.

Hints

Without the haze provided by the attenuating contrast, this 3-D image would be practically incomprehensible. ◊ The technique of using real tree bark and digital painting demonstrates that textures need not be computer generated but can be modeled in the laboratory as needed.

[1] Ned Greene and Paul Heckbert, *Creating Raster Omnimax Frames from Multiple Perspective Views with the Elliptical Weighted Average Filter*, IEEE Computer Graphics and Applications (June 1986).

[2] Paul Heckbert, *Making the Magic Egg: A Personal Account*, IEEE Computer Graphics and Applications (June 1986).

[3] Ned Greene, *Animating Escher with Computer Graphics*, Proceedings of the International Congress on M. C. Escher, Rome, Italy (March 1985).

3-D Model
Creates natural scenes
Computer Graphics

2-D fractal scalar fields displayed as 3-D surfaces portray natural scenes.

Jean-François Colonna, Lactamme (CNET, École Polytechnique), France.

[1] Benoit B. Mandelbrot, *The Fractal Geometry of Nature* (New York: W. H. Freeman, 1983).

[2] Jean-François Colonna, "Animation of Fractal Objects," Canadian Information Processing Society and Canadian Man-Computer Communications Society Proceedings: Computer Graphics Interface, London, Ontario, Canada (June 19–23, 1989).

Application (Picture Synthesis)

Fractal geometry[1, 2] is used to model a mountainous scene. The computation and visualization were executed on a Silicon Graphics 4D 20 workstation with K, a machine-independent language.

Technique

Fractal geometry creates a 2-D fractal scalar field. Treating the scalars as heights creates a 3-D surface that resembles a mountainous landscape. A uniform 2-D scalar field is mapped onto the surface to create the uniform texture, and the haze is added with Z-buffering. Colors and highlights also help establish realism.

Hints

In the hands of a computer artist, fractals become the malleable clay for creating real or imaginary worlds. With fractal geometry we can construct such objects as trees, snowflakes, and ferns. See **7-9** for an example of an imaginary landscape. ◊ Fog is used in this image for realism, but fog and cloudlike features are created and used in many ways. See **5-7**, **5-9**, **5-10**, **6-6**, **9-2**, **9-7**, **10-4**, **12-1**, **12-7**, and **12-8**.

3-D Model
Models natural terrain
Computer Graphics

Scene-generation technique facilitates creation of natural textures.

Ken-ichi Anjyo, Hitachi Research Laboratory, Hitachi Ltd., Ibaraki-ken 319-12, Japan.

Application (Picture Synthesis)

Research in generating scenes has led to techniques for producing natural-appearing land, water, and clouds at low computational costs. The images were created with the HITAC M-680H computer.

Technique

The modeling technique Semi-Globalized Spectral Synthesis[1-3] forms fractal textures for natural scenes by generating different irregular surfaces of triangles that correspond to different geographic features in the scene. The scene is built up by creating a collection of different irregular surfaces. A 3-D model is then created by rendering the triangles with a Z-buffer algorithm.

Hints

Low computation cost makes this modeling technique useful for applications where computation speed is important, as in animation. This technique is also helpful in quickly generating panoramic landscapes.

[1] K. Anjyo, "A Simple Spectral Approach to Stochastic Modeling for Natural Objects," *Proceedings in Eurographics* (1988), pp. 285–296.

[2] K. Anjyo, Semi-Globalized Spectral Synthesis, in B. E. Brown, ed., SIGGRAPH '89 Technical Slide Set Credits, *Computer Graphics* 24, 1 (1990): 8.

[3] K. Anjyo, "Semi-Globalization of Stochastic Spectral Synthesis," *The Visual Computer* 7, 1 (1991):1–12.

3-D Model
Depicts 3-D
Computer Art

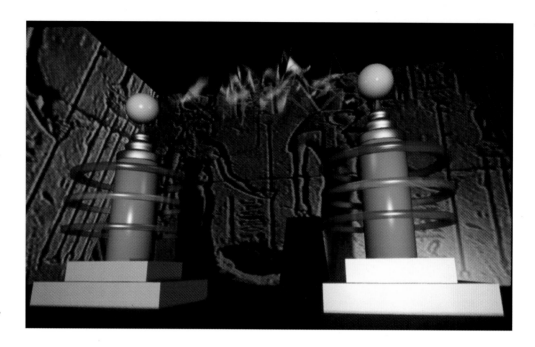

Light and dark colors
make 2-D objects
appear 3-D.

Gregory MacNicol, Santa Cruz,
CA, USA.

Application (Art)

This artistic experiment used Crystal Graphics's Crystal 3D software running on a Micronics 486 with a Targa graphics board.

Technique

The artistic use of dark and light colors and perspective causes all the surfaces, which are actually 2-D, to look like 3-D surfaces. Lightning-shaped polygons and nearly transparent shapes of blue, pink, and white convey arcing high voltage. Adding to the sense of arcing are the spheres atop supporting cylinders, which evoke memories of high school science experiments with Leyden jars and Tesla coils.

Hints

As this 2-D example shows, computationally intensive 3-D graphics are not always needed to convey 3-D. See **2-9**, which constructs 3-D with 2-D objects. ◊ Context can be important. Here splashes of color model static discharge; in other contexts, the same splashes could be understood as, say, particle beams or spray paint.

**Placing a model in a
context adds meaning
and enhances
understanding.**

Bob Shillito and Tim Duke,
Shillito & Company, Bristol,
England.

Application (Entertainment)

This whimsical scene is a still frame from a short movie. Silver Tree, a high-resolution paint system, was used to create this scene on a Sun Microsystems SPARCstation.

Technique

Placing a model in a context provides secondary information about the model. The plant-covered building, lighting and shadows, rich vegetation, and the duck motif on the model suggest an English country garden. The asterisk on the neck of the spoon suggests sunlight glinting through the trees. Sizing the model as the dominant object focuses attention on it and shows detail. The darker colors and blurring effect of distance also cause the viewer to focus on the model. In the movie, the flags under the handle and the triangles and quadrilaterals accentuate the outside garden scene by blowing around.

Hints

Using a context that provides secondary information can be particularly valuable to create a subtle impression or to illustrate how the model is used.

3-D Model
Depicts motion
Computer Art

Position of familiar shapes depicts motion.

Kenneth G. Hamilton, Computervision, Bedford, MA, USA.

[1] J. M. Lane, L. C. Carpenter, T. Whitted, and J. F. Blinn, "Scan Line Methods for Displaying Parametrically Defined Surfaces," *Communications of the ACM* 23, 1 (January 1980): 23–34.

Application (Entertainment)

A visual ploy is created for the SIGGRAPH conference with the teapot data base so often used to test visual algorithms. The image was created on a Sun Microsystems SPARCstation 1+ using Wavefront.

Technique

A 3-D model is created with highlights and shadows.[1]

Hints

This image is interesting because it demonstrates that experiential cues rather than artificial contextual cues can convey the sense of motion. The bullet and its placement, the missing part of the teapot, the jagged objects suspended in midair relative to the teapot collectively "tell the story." These experiential cues eliminate the need for contextual cues, such as motion blur, arrows, particle traces, and comet tails, which can clutter an image rather than clarify it.

**Reflective surface
reveals hidden side.**

Tullia Redaelli Spreafico, RGB,
Computer Graphics, Milan,
Italy.

Application (Commercial Art)

The image, which appears on the cover of a company brochure, was generated with
Time Art's Lumena and Crystal Graphics's Crystal 3D software on a PC compatible.

Technique

Two digitized and retouched photos and one computer-generated reflective grid are
combined to form this image. Reflecting the main object on the shiny grid cleverly
reveals the object's hidden side and also shows that the object is slightly raised at
one end. The reflection, lighting, shadows, and the receding-square grid create the
3-D effect. The clouds contribute a context, convey secondary information, create
eye appeal, and set a mood.

Hints

Using a reflection to reveal a hidden side can eliminate the need for additional
images to show details of an object. ◊ **5-6** and **8-3** show another format for revealing
hidden information using shadows. ◊ The sides of the box in **8-3** could also be
changed to reflective surfaces to reveal the hidden sides.

3-D Model
Depicts 3-D
Computer Art

Shape, surface reflection, and context depict 3-D transparent object.

Tullia Redaelli Spreafico, RGB, Computer Graphics, Milan, Italy.

Application (Commercial Art)
Designed for the cover of a brochure for a gas and water distributor, this image was generated with Time Art's Lumena and Crystal Graphics's Crystal 3D software on a PC compatible.

Technique
Reflections from a digitized photograph on a shiny, drop-shaped solid object are highlighted with Gouraud shading and then electronically pasted on top of the digitized photograph to create the impression of 3-D transparency.

Hints
Combining these rather simple techniques to form this very effective image demonstrates that techniques do not have to be complex to make a powerful impression. Using a reflection algorithm to accurately represent a transparent object is a clever artistic trick. ◊ Artists, trained to communicate visually, may be able to offer suggestions to help represent scientific data effectively.

**3-D Model
Describes 3-D
Computer Art**

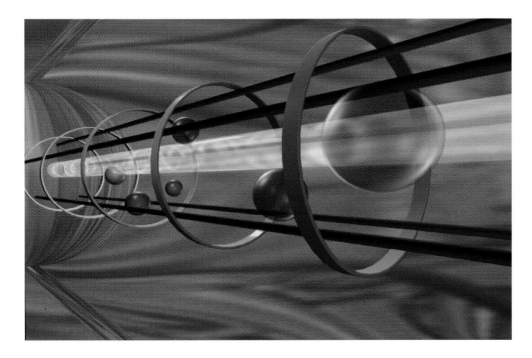

**Artistic depth cues
achieve a 3-D
impression.**

Gregory MacNicol, Santa Cruz,
CA, USA.

Application (Artistic Exploration)

This imaginary scene was created to evaluate the rendering options and output quality of Crystal Graphics's Crystal 3D software running on a Micronics 486 with a Targa graphics board.

Technique

Perspective, opacity, color, and reflection are combined to give the 3-D effect. Objects converge and shrink, spheres become more opaque, and the color striations in the reflection narrow as they recede.

Hints

Unlike some techniques that require powerful computers, tools for creating and enhancing 3-D images such as this one are readily available on small desktop computers. ◊ Artistically manipulated, desktop tools can create effective representations, such as the light beam in this image, which varies colors to suggest fluctuations in beam intensity. (This same "beam" technique can be used to convey the motion of a high-velocity object, such as a comet or particle beams, or to convey electromagnetic radiation.) ◊ By selecting eye-pleasing, coordinated colors that unify the image, the artist attracts viewer attention while improving comprehension and retention of information. Such unifying elements make any image more effective and help communicate.

3-D Model
Compares effectiveness
Computer Art

Contextual cues
compare effectiveness.

Tullia Redaelli Spreafico, RGB,
Computer Graphics, Milan,
Italy.

Application (Pharmaceutical Advertising)

This artistic portrayal of the effectiveness of three drugs interacting with a cellular membrane was created with Time Art's Lumena and Crystal Graphics's Crystal 3D software on a PC compatible.

Technique

Three drugs represented as green, orange, and pink spheres are shown passing or not passing through membrane barriers, the blue spheres. Additional contextual cues distinguish the drugs: triangle, black line, and white halo. The position of the larger spheres and the disarray of the small blue spheres suggest degrees of effectiveness. The small green spheres indicate that drug is breaking up as it fails to penetrate the first membrane. The lengths of the cometlike tails on the spheres suggest speed of penetration. Highlights on the spheres, the shadow cast by the orange sphere, the successively narrower and fainter horizontal lines, and the darker colors for more distant features all suggest 3-D.

Hints

We portray the behavior of objects interacting with their environment to learn more about those objects. Conversely, **5-6** depicts how objects behave as they interact with their environment so that we can learn more about that environment. See **12-6** for another way of illustrating motion and interaction but without using artificial cues to convey motion.

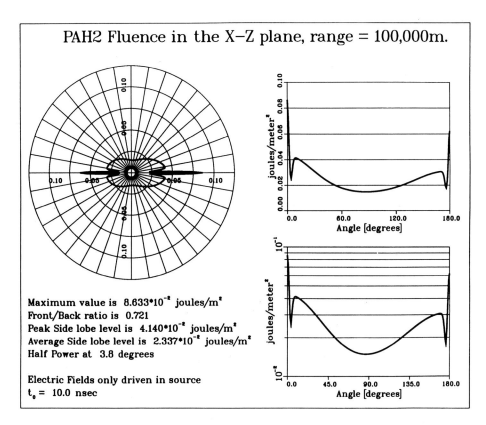

PAH2 Fluence in the X–Z plane, range = 100,000m.

Maximum value is 8.633•10⁻² joules/m²
Front/Back ratio is 0.721
Peak Side lobe level is 4.140•10⁻² joules/m²
Average Side lobe level is 2.337•10⁻² joules/m²
Half Power at 3.8 degrees

Electric Fields only driven in source
t_0 = 10.0 nsec

1 dependent variable
2 independent variables
Correlates scalars
Electrical Engineering

Different representations of the same data communicate different information.

Ronald F. Schmucker, Lawrence Livermore National Laboratory, Livermore, CA, USA.

Application (Antenna Design)

Angular position versus total energy delivered by an antenna is studied.[1,2] The data were calculated on a supercomputer and the image was plotted on a VAX VMS system with in-house software using DISSPLA graphics library.[3]

Technique

Data can usually be presented in more than one format, as shown by these four different representations of the same data. The polar plot (upper left) emphasizes the shape of the electrical field; the linear plot (upper right) emphasizes minor variations in that field; the semilog plot (lower right) emphasizes dramatic changes in the field; annotations (lower left) call out important information that could be derived by more detailed analysis of the data as represented.

Hints

This simple example illustrates a vital point: the way of representing data can influence the information derived. Therefore, knowing the visualization goal of an image is crucial to selecting the appropriate representation. ◊ **11-1**, **11-4**, and **13-12** are other examples of making the same data reveal different information by choosing different representations. ◊ Displaying quantities as text on a graph relieves the viewer of having to read values off the graphs or having to calculate a quantity by hand. ◊ The speed with which information is perceived also depends on how the data are represented. For example, to emphasize symmetry, we should rotate Figure A 90 degrees because left–right symmetry is easier to perceive than top–bottom symmetry. ◊ Presenting unfamiliar information in several ways helps communicate a more comprehensive view of the data.

[1] Ronald F. Schmucker, John A. Futterman, and Richard W. Ziolkowski, Lawrence Livermore National Laboratory, Livermore, CA, USA, private communications (1986–1989).

[2] R. F. Schmucker and R. W. Ziolkowski, "Modeling Large Pulsed Antenna Arrays," *Engineering Research and Development Thrust Area Report FY88*, UCRL-53868-88 (June 1988).

[3] CA-DISSPLA User Manual, Computer Associates International, Inc., 711 Stewart Ave., Garden City, NY, 11530.

3-D Model
Identifies direction
Computer Graphics

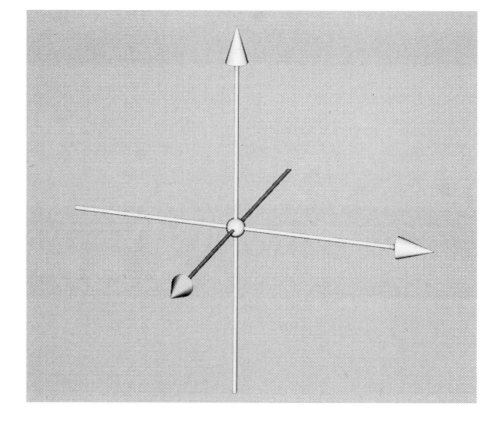

Shaded 3-D arrows provide an unambiguous orientation reference.

Fred R. McClurg, Idaho National Engineering Laboratory, Idaho Falls, ID, USA.

Application (Visualization)

The reference axis is one of the solid models constructed to teach Boolean set operators as part of a computer-aided mechanical engineering class. The models were created with Control Data Corporation's software package ICEM Solid Modeler running on their CYBER 170/855 mainframe.

Technique

Shading, highlights, and the use of geometric cones for arrowheads, cylinders for axes, and a sphere for the origin create an unambiguous 3-D reference axis. Shading one axis uniquely defines the other two. The cone yields an arrowhead shape for all 2-D projections except when the axis is pointed directly out of or into the page.

Hints

Modeling arrows with cylinders and cones may help visualize a 3-D vector field. ◊ Colored arrows could visually describe yet another variable. ◊ Many of the new 3-D or volumetric tools create objects without giving cues to orientation, which sometimes makes interpretation difficult; this 3-D reference axis would help. See also **2-3** and **6-2**, Figure A, for other examples of 3-D reference axes.

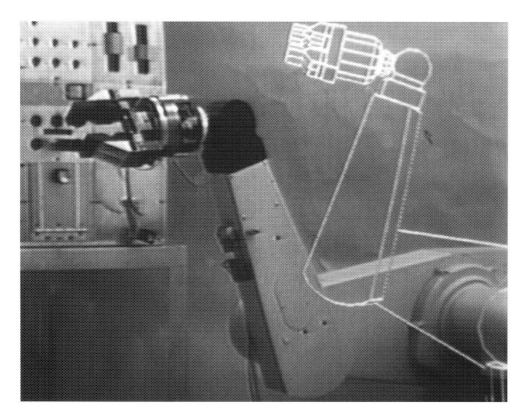

**3-D model
Reveals location
Mechanical Engineering**

**Wire-frame model
predicts location of
actual object.**

Won S. Kim and Antal K. Bejczy, Jet Propulsion Laboratory, Pasadena, CA, USA; Steven Venema, University of Washington, Seattle, WA, USA.

Application (Telerobotics)

Visual feedback techniques to improve the operator's control of a robot located on a distant earth satellite are studied.[1-3] A wire-frame model was computed and rendered on a Silicon Graphics IRIS 4D-GT70 workstation; a Gen-Lock board and real-time camera were used to overlay the arm's actual position.

Technique

A computer-generated wire-frame model instantly depicts an operator-controlled change in position of a remotely located PUMA robot arm. This instantaneous feedback helps the earthbound operator of the robot to overcome the mental confusion caused by the 2- to 3-second delay between initiation of the command and the visual feedback from the arm's actual movement. The image shows a wire-frame model predicting the position into which a withdrawal command will put the PUMA arm before the arm has responded. The operator receives visual confirmation of the actual change in position when the PUMA arm moves to the position of the wire-frame arm 2 to 3 seconds later.

Hints

Merging images from experiment and simulation can help validate a simulation. ◊ With a wire-frame model we could distinguish where features were located in a simulated image from their placement in an actual image.

[1] A. K. Bejczy, W. S. Kim, and S. Venema, "The Phantom Robot: Predictive Displays for Teleoperation with Time Delay," *Proceedings of IEEE International Conference of Robotics and Automation*, Cincinnati, OH (May 1990), pp. 546–551.

[2] W. S. Kim, "Graphics Overlay and Camera Calibration for Predictive Displays," Jet Propulsion Laboratory Internal Document Engineering Memorandum 347-89-273 (December 1989).

[3] W. S. Kim and A. K. Bejczy, "A Graphics Display for Operator Aid in Tele–manipulation," *Proceedings of IEEE Conference on Systems, Man, and Cybernetics*, Charlottesville, VA (October 1991).

**2-D model
Shows structure
Experimental Physics**

**Coarse digitization
allows qualitative
analysis of structure.**

Milton Van Dyke, Stanford
University, Stanford, CA, USA;
submitted by A. Ravishankar
Rao, IBM T. J. Watson
Research Center, Yorktown
Heights, NY, USA.

[1] W. Yang, *Proceedings of the
Third International Symposium
on Flow Visualization* (1983),
pp. 681–685.

[2] K. Imaichi and K. Ohmi,
"Numerical Processing of Flow
Visualization Pictures—
Measurement of Two-
Dimensional Vortex Flow,"
Journal of Fluid Mechanics 129,
(1983): 283–311.

[3] Milton Van Dyke, *An Album
of Fluid Motion* (Stanford, CA:
Parabolic Press, 1982).

Application (Fluid Dynamics)

An experimental visualization technique adds glass beads to a fluid, illuminates the beads stroboscopically, and then photographs the beads to permit observation of complex fluid motion.[1,2] Vortices and other flow patterns resulting from the side-to-side motion of fluid in a cylinder are readily apparent.

Technique

An image[3] was digitized with a Javelin CCD camera and Matrox digitizer board to a 480×480 grid of pixels, each having an intensity value ranging from 0 to 255. This rather simple technique demonstrates that a coarse image can retain the gross structure of fluid motion.

Hints

A costly high-resolution image is not always needed to communicate pertinent information. **6-8** and **7-4** show how coarse images can be analyzed by the computer to abstract and classify information. ◊ See also **9-6**, which also uses light reflecting from tiny spheres to visualize shape.

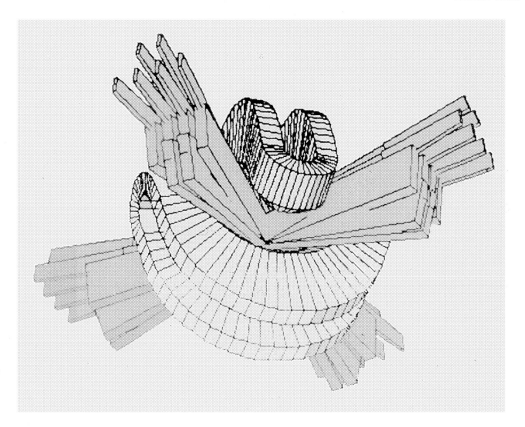

3-D model
Analyzes feasibility
Fusion Engineering

**Computerized model
building demonstrates
viable configuration.**

John A. Horvath, Lawrence
Livermore Laboratory,
Livermore, CA, USA.

Application (Design Analysis)

Computer modeling of the Yin-Yang magnet is used to evaluate which proposed locations for neutral beam injectors and aim points are feasible. A Control Data Corporation CDC 7600 executed SAMPP,[1] a finite element postprocessor used for polygon display and for manipulating models.

Technique

A polygonal computer model verifies that an actual model can be built. Polygons represent magnet surfaces or surfaces of constant neutral beam flux intensity. Polygon edges serve as fiducials for locating points on the magnet.[2,3] A significant feature of this technique is the use of the error-detection mechanism of the visualization algorithm to detect intersecting polygons that signal impossible locations for beam injectors.

Hints

Views without perspective could also determine viable orientations for the beam injectors. ◊ Cross-sections can provide visual evidence, if necessary, of interference between parts. ◊ The error-detection capability of the graphics can be used to verify that objects touch as well as to detect unwanted intersections.

[1] E. B. Brown, "Structural Analysis Movie Post-Processor (SAMPP) User's Manual," Lawrence Livermore National Laboratory, Report UCID-30097 (1975).

[2] J. Horvath, "Using Computer Graphics to Analyze the Placement of Neutral Beam Injectors for the Mirror Fusion Test Facility," Lawrence Livermore National Laboratory, Report UCRL-80106 (1977).

[3] R. C. Ling, et al., "Ion Trajectories of the MFTF Unshielded 80-keV Neutral Beam Sources," Lawrence Livermore National Laboratory, Report UCRL-81086 (1978).

1 dependent variable
1 independent variable
Classifies results
Electrical Engineering

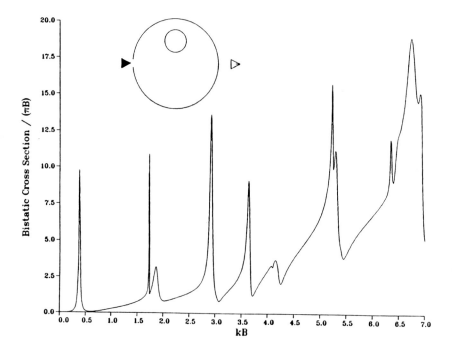

$A=0.25$ $B=1.00$ $C=0.50$ $\theta=175.0$ $\Phi=90.0$
$\varphi inc=180.0$ $\varphi=0.0$ $z=(0., 0.)$

A stylized model of the computational configuration classifies results.

Ronald F. Schmucker, Lawrence Livermore National Laboratory, Livermore, CA, USA.

[1] Ronald F. Schmucker and Richard W. Ziolkowski, Lawrence Livermore National Laboratory, Livermore, CA, USA, private communications (1986–1989).

[2] "Computational Issues in Electromagnetic Coupling to a Slit Cylinder Enclosing an Off-Set Cylinder," *Proceedings of the 1987 ARRAY Conference,* Montreal, Canada (April 1987). This work was also published as UCRL-95835 (January 1987).

[3] "Numerical Calculations of Solutions to Canonical Aperture Coupling Problems," *Seventh Biennial CUBE Symposium,* Pleasanton, CA (October 1986).

[4, 5] See additional references at the end of Section II, p. 182.

Application (Scattering and Coupling of Electromagnetic Energy)

A computer model determines the scattering and coupling of electromagnetic energy received by a slit cylinder surrounding a closed cylinder.[1-4] The data were calculated on a supercomputer and then plotted on a VAX VMS system with in-house software using DISSPLA graphics library.[5]

Technique

A simple technique for drawing a stylized model of a computational experiment on an *x-y* plot quickly relates computed results to the model configuration. The black triangle depicts direction of incident energy; the open triangle depicts the viewing angle. Numerical values at the top identify parameter values in the computation.

Hints

The stylized model must be positioned after displaying the computed results so that those results are not obscured. ◊ See **13-7** for a stylized model that can be used not only to classify results but also to provide a frame of reference for the data.

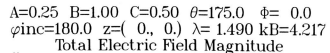

A=0.25 B=1.00 C=0.50 θ=175.0 Φ= 0.0
φinc=180.0 z=(0., 0.) λ= 1.490 kB=4.217
Total Electric Field Magnitude

1 dependent variable
2 independent variables
Locates values
Electrical Engineering

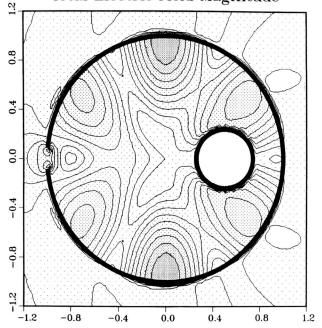

The maximum field magnitude is 7.748 at location (0.000, 0.935)

A stylized model locates values.

Ronald F. Schmucker, Lawrence Livermore National Laboratory, Livermore, CA, USA.

Application (Scattering and Coupling of Electromagnetic Energy)

A computer model determines the scattering and coupling of electromagnetic energy received by a slit cylinder surrounding a closed cylinder.[1–4] The data were calculated on a supercomputer and then plotted on a VAX VMS system with in-house software using DISSPLA graphics library.[5]

Technique

An isoplot reveals the shape of an electromagnetic field. Density of dots in the isoplot increase as the field strength increases, revealing extremes. A stylized model drawing of the computer experiment is superimposed on the plot, helping to locate values relative to the model. Numerical values at the top of the plot identify parameter values of the experiment. For ease of interpretation, the maximum value and its location are given at the bottom of the image.

Hints

The dot patterns, an inexpensive substitute for color, may be necessary for some publications. ◊ Because dots do not provide precise values, important values should be listed on the image. ◊ Unlike other shading (cross-hatching and stripes), dots provide a smooth transition and prevent the appearance of discontinuities. ◊ Drawing models of the objects involved with the computed values can give convenient points of reference as users zoom or pan through the data.

[1] Ronald F. Schmucker and Richard W. Ziolkowski, Lawrence Livermore National Laboratory, Livermore, CA, USA, private communications (1986–1989).

[2] "Computational Issues in Electromagnetic Coupling to a Slit Cylinder Enclosing an Off-set Cylinder," *Proceedings of the 1987 ARRAY Conference*, Montreal, Canada (April 1987). This work was also published as UCRL-95835 (January 1987).

[3] "Numerical Calculations of Solutions to Canonical Aperture Coupling Problems," *Seventh Biennial CUBE Symposium*, Pleasanton, CA (October 1986).

[4, 5] See additional references at the end of Section II, p. 182.

3-D Model
Shows orientation
Computer Art

**A humanlike figure
shows orientation.**

Kenneth G. Hamilton,
Computervision, Bedford, MA,
USA.

[1] G. Farin, *Curves and Surfaces
for Computer Aided Geometric
Design: A Practical Guide,* 2nd
ed. (New York: Academic
Press, 1990).

[2] G. Elber and E. Cohen,
"Hidden Curve Removal for
Free Form Surfaces," Proceed-
ings of SIGGRAPH '90, in
Computer Graphics 24, 4
(August 1990): 95–104.

Application (Art)

Experimental visual effects are evaluated. The image was rendered on a Sun Microsystems SPARCstation 1+ using Computervision CADDS4X Solidesign software.

Technique

The Nurb-based modeling system[1] for solids and composite ("sewn"-together), trimmed surfaces creates an imaginary landscape, which is rendered by displaying visible curves.[2] The placement of a humanlike figure, in the form of a waiter carrying a tray with bottle and glasses, clarifies the orientation of the image.

Hints

Many 3-D visualizations are difficult to relate to the original data set because orientation cues are often omitted. Among this book's many examples of images with orientation cues are **6-2**, Figure A, **8-6**, **8-11**, **9-10**, **13-2**, and **13-5**. Orientation cues that help correlate a 3-D visualization to the original data set should be an integral part of any 3-D visualization, especially when the visualization is to be shown to others. ◊ See **10-3** for an example of using a human figure for both size and orientation.

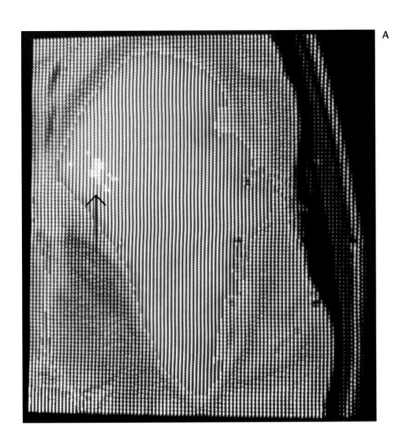

A

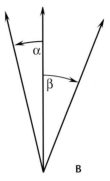

B

2 dependent variables
2 independent variables
Locates cluster
Medicine

Glyphs create visual patterns that reveal hidden information.

Stuart Smith, University of Massachusetts at Lowell, Lowell, MA, USA.

Application (Medical Imaging)

Two different gray-scale images (not shown) from a magnetic resonance imaging (MRI) machine are analyzed to locate a hot spot (metabolic center) in a tumor not seen in either image. An in-house visualization program was executed on Thinking Machine's massively parallel Connection Machine to compute these images. The image was rendered onto the CM Frame Buffer and displayed on the high-resolution CM display.

Technique

A textured image is formed (Figure A) by glyphs,[1] which are geometric shapes that represent data points. A glyph's shape is determined by the values of the variables being analyzed. In this example two identical-looking MRI images (not shown) are mapped to a simple glyph consisting of two line segments joined into a V shape (Figure B). The grayscale value at each pixel position in one MRI image controls both angle α and the length of the left line segment; the grayscale value at each pixel position in the other MRI image controls both angle β and the length of the right line segment. Regions of similar texture in the resulting plot identify like data. The single brightened region, indicated by an arrow at the left of Figure A, identifies a hot spot. It is important to note that neither MRI image by itself revealed this hot spot.

[1] Richard J. Littlefield, "Using the Glyph Concept to Create User-Definable Display Formats," *Proceedings of the Fourth Annual Conference and Exposition of the National Computer Graphics Association* (1983).

Hints

Multiline glyphs, whose shapes are determined by multidimensional data bases, have been successfully used with as many as 30 variables. ◊ Using glyphs and combining two or more views of the same data into one image accentuates minor differences that may not be seen when using only one view. Once the area of commonality is found, the researcher must use other techniques to understand the relationship.

12 dependent variables
4 independent variables
Identifies relationships
Experimental Physics

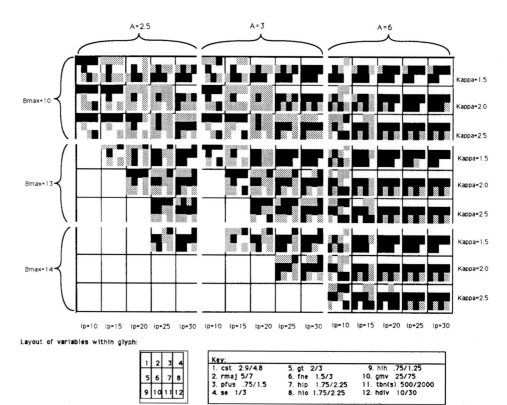

Layout of variables within glyph:

1	2	3	4
5	6	7	8
9	10	11	12

Key:

1. cst 2.9/4.8	5. gt 2/3	9. hlh .75/1.25
2. rmaj 5/7	6. fne 1.5/3	10. gmv 25/75
3. pfus .75/1.5	7. hip 1.75/2.25	11. tbn(s) 500/2000
4. se 1/3	8. hlo 1.75/2.25	12. hdiv 10/30

**Graytone locations
identify relationships in
multivariate data.**

Jeff Beddow, Microsimulations
Research, Minneapolis, MN, USA.

[1] Jeff Beddow, "Shape Coding
of Multidimensional Data on a
Microcomputer Display," in
Visualization '90, (Los
Alamitos, CA: IEEE Computer
Society Press, October 1990).

[2] L. J. Perkins, J. D. Galambos,
and J. L. Beddow, "Formalisms
for Evaluating ITER System
Studies and Operational
Performance Analyses," ITER
Meeting on Physics and
Design, San Diego, CA (July
10, 1991).

Application (Fusion Reactor Design)

The diagram[1] represents data compiled to study optimal reactor design.[2] A Cray
supercomputer simulating the operation of the tokamak fusion reactor produced
the data. The diagram was rendered on an Apple Macintosh II, executing Datapix,
an in-house program.

Technique

Each glyph, representing a tokamak design, uses the ability of the human eye to
recognize rectilinear patterns and groupings. The glyph is built of 12 small rectangles: 4 across, 3 down. Labels of the axes and locations of the glyph indicate the
four input values. Lines and spacing between glyphs help locate the glyphs in the
4-D space. Each small rectangle is shaded according to the desirability of the
variable's value: black is desirable, unshaded is undesirable, and gray is neutral.
Dominant visual codes encode the desirable values to quickly locate areas of
interest. The legend at the bottom identifies the output variables used and the
numeric range studied. Repeating patterns among the glyphs help to understand
correlations among the variables. The white glyphs at the lower left side of the
image clearly show input values that should be avoided. The comb-shaped glyphs
in the right half of the image suggest possible correlation among the eight black
variables.

Hints

Interactive arrangement of independent variables may be needed to reveal relationships. ◊ This glyph technique is particularly useful for finding relationships when
many variables are involved. ◊ Because the technique requires time to study, it is not
a good format for group presentation.

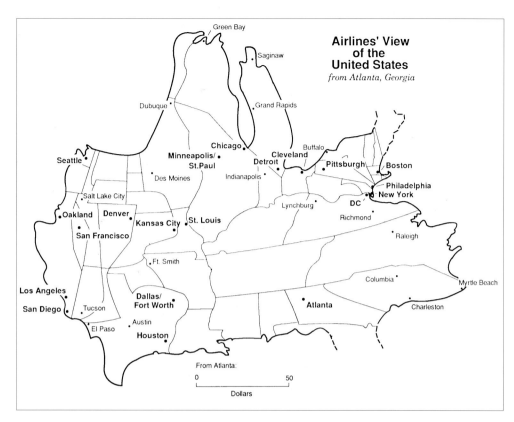

Airlines' View
of the
United States
from Atlanta, Georgia

From Atlanta:
0   50
Dollars

1 dependent variable
2 independent variables
Reveals patterns
Business

Measuring physical space using a parameter of interest reveals patterns.

Borden D. Dent, Georgia State University, Atlanta, GA, USA.

Application (Cartography)

Irregularities in the airline rate structure from Atlanta, Georgia, to various other cities in the United States are studied. The data were imported into Micrografx Designer software on a Zenith 386 IBM-compatible microcomputer for processing and then rendered on a 300-dpi QMS laser printer.

Technique

A map of the United States is distorted[1-3] to show distance in dollars rather than in miles. A rough sketch of a map is hand drawn by scaling the map in terms of dollars. North–south distances are held nearly true with respect to Atlanta to help maintain some similarity in shape to the original map. The rough sketch is then scanned by a Hewlett-Packard scanjet and used as a guide in creating the final map. The spatial transformation reveals a pattern: it is relatively more expensive to travel to nearby cities.

Hints

Scaling maps or data in nontraditional ways can reveal unseen relationships. ◊ This technique works best if the scalar used to distort the maps or data is a function of distance.

[1] Borden D. Dent, "Communication Aspects of Value-by-Area Cartograms," *American Cartographer*, Vol. 2 (1975), pp. 154–168.

[2] T. L. C. Griffin, "Cartographic Transformation of the Thematic Map Base," *Cartography*, Vol. 11 (1980), pp. 163–174.

[3] Waldo Tobler, "A Continuous Transformation Useful for Districting," *Annals of the New York Academy of Sciences* 219 (1973): 215–220.

3 dependent variables
3 independent variables
Shows 3-D position and
   velocity
Aircraft Navigation

Two representations of the same data illustrate the importance of designing the image to needs of the viewer.

Stephen R. Ellis, NASA Ames Research Center, Moffett Field, and University of California Berkeley School of Optometry, Berkeley, CA, USA; Michael W. McGreevy, NASA Ames Research Center, Moffett Field, CA, USA.

[1] Stephen R. Ellis, "Pictorial Communication: Pictures and the Synthetic Universe," in Stephen R. Ellis, ed., *Pictorial Communication* (London: Taylor and Francis, 1991).

[2] Michael W. McGreevy and Stephen R. Ellis, "Format and Basic Geometry of a Perspective Display of Air Traffic for the Cockpit," NASA TM 86680, Ames Research Center, Moffett Field, CA (1990).

[3] Stephen R. Ellis, Michael W. McGreevy, and Robert Hitchcock, "Perspective Traffic Display Format and Airline Pilot Traffic Avoidance," *Human Factors* 29 (1987): 371–382.

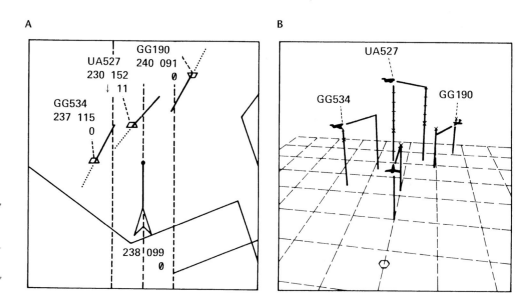

A   B

Application (Cockpit Display)

Air traffic displays designed to prevent aircraft collisions are studied. A Pascal program on a DEC 11/70 renders the image on an Evans and Sutherland PS II display device.

Technique

The images use different techniques to display the same data. In both images, alphanumeric codes identify aircraft relative to the pilot's aircraft. In Figure A, the flight path of each aircraft is further described by three groups of numbers: the first number indicates current altitude; the second, projected altitude some delta-time later; and the third, the rate of change in altitude (direction indicated by small arrow beneath numerical data for UA527, the only aircraft changing altitude). An arrowhead indicates each aircraft's current position and direction. Ten small dots, whose spacing indicates relative speed, represent an aircraft's previous position. In Figure B, each aircraft's flight path is described by contextual cues[1-3] instead of numbers. A perspective grid reference plane helps locate the aircraft. Vertical lines connecting the beginning and ending points of an aircraft's path show the relative altitude change and also help locate the aircraft. In this study, where collision avoidance is the purpose, measures of performance indicate that Figure B is interpreted faster than Figure A. If knowing aircraft altitude is the purpose, however, then Figure A conveys that information more quickly.

Hints

We cannot assume that the viewer can quickly understand information simply because it is in the image. These two images reveal the same information about aircraft altitude, speed, and position. However, the technique in Figure A, which emphasizes properties of objects, makes it easier to read aircraft altitude and the technique in Figure B, which emphasizes relationships among objects, makes it easier to see spatial relationships.

A

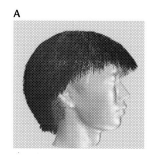

**3-D Model
Depicts textures
Computer Graphics**

B

**Attention to detail
results in realistic
textures.**

Yasuhiko Watanabe and
Yasuhito Suenaga, Nippon
Telephone and Telegraph
Corporation Human Interface
Laboratories, Yokosuka,
Kanagawa 238-03 JAPAN.

Application (Photorealism)

This photorealistic rendering of human hair was produced with the trigonal prism-based wisp model.[1] Hair was modeled and rendered on a Silicon Graphics IRIS 4D workstation with a hardware Z-buffer.

Technique

Hair texture (Figure A) is realistically rendered by individual trigonal prisms. The shape of the hair becomes the shape of a bundle of trigonal prisms. Smooth hair texture is produced by adding a small amount of randomness to the direction vector of the trigonal prisms. Varied hair types can be achieved by modifying the trigonal parameters of direction, thickness, density, length, and color. Two examples are shown in Figure B.

Hints

A large number of polygons is generated to produce detail; therefore, we recommend a hardware geometry engine for rendering speed. ◊ The trigonal prism-based wisp model can also render woolly or furry objects as well as textile surfaces that have a nap. ◊ Placing the trigonal prism on a model, as in Figure A, provides a context that enhances photorealism. ◊ See **10-4** for another use of context to enhance photorealism. ◊ Attention to detail (using many variables) makes the hair look more realistic. See **5-11** for similar attention to detail.

[1] Y. Watanabe and Y. Suenaga, "Drawing Human Hair Using Wisp Model," Proceedings of Computer Graphics International '89, Leeds, UK, June 27–30, 1989.

Additional References

2-7

[4] D. Cox, "Scientific Visualization: Mapping Information," *Ausgraph '90 Proceedings*, ed. Michael Gigante, Technical Program Chairman, Australia Computer Graphics Association, Inc., Melbourne, Australia (September 10–14, 1990): pp. 101-106.

[5] D. Cox, "Scientific Visualization: Collaborating to Predict the Future," *EDUCOM Review* 25, 4 (Winter 1990): 38–42.

[6] H. T. Fisher, *Mapping Information: The Graphic Display of Quantitative Information* (Cambridge, Mass.: Abt Books, 1982).

[7] G. Meyer and D. Greenberg, "Perceptual Color Spaces for Computer Graphics," Proceedings of SIGGRAPH '80, in *Computer Graphics* (July 14–18, 1980).

4-4

[4] Richard A. Becker, Stephen G. Eick, Eileen O. Miller, and Allan R. Wilks, "Network Visualization," *Fourth International Symposium on Spatial Data Handling Proceedings*, Zurich, Switzerland (July 1990), pp. 285–294.

[5] Richard A. Becker, Stephen G. Eick, Eileen O. Miller, and Allan R. Wilks, "Dynamic Graphical Analysis of Network Data," *Interface '90 Proceedings*, East Lansing, MI (May 1990).

[6] Richard A. Becker, Stephen G. Eick, Eileen O. Miller, and Allan R. Wilks, "Network Visualization," *American Statistical Association '90 Conference Proceedings*, Anaheim, CA (August 1990).

4-7

[4] Richard A. Becker, Stephen G. Eick, and Allan R. Wilks, "Basics of Network Visualization," *IEEE Computer Graphics and Applications* 11, 3 (May 1991): 12.

[5] Richard A. Becker, Stephen G. Eick, Eileen O. Miller, and Allan R. Wilks, "Network Visualization: User Interface Issues," *Proceedings SPIE Conference on Extracting Meaning from Complex Data*, San Jose, CA (February 1991).

[6] Richard A. Becker, Stephen G. Eick, Eileen O. Miller, and Allan R. Wilks, "Dynamic Graphics for Network Visualization," in *Visualization '90* (Los Alamitos, CA: IEEE Computer Society Press, October 1990).

8-9

[4] Gregory M. Nielson and Ramamani Ramaraj, "Interpolation over a Sphere," *Computer Aided Geometric Design* 4 (1987): 41–57.

[5] Gregory M. Nielson, Thomas A. Foley, Bernd Hamann, and David Lane, "Visualization and Modeling of Scattered Multivariate Data," *Computer Graphics and Applications* 11, 3 (May 1991): 47–55.

[6] Ramamani Ramaraj, "Interpolation and Display of Scattered Data over a Sphere," M.S. Thesis, Arizona State University, Tempe, AZ (1986).

8-11

[4] Gregory M. Nielson, Thomas Foley, Bernd Hamann, and David Lane, "Visualization and Modelling of Scattered Multivariate Data," *Computer Graphics and Applications* 11, 3 (May 1991): 47–55.

10-9

[4] W. K. Shieh, M. W. Torello, and D. L. Stredney, "A Distributed Three-Dimensional Brain Visualization System," *Proceedings of the 12th Annual International Conference, IEEE Engineering in Medicine and Biology Society,* Philadelphia, PA (November 1, 1990).

11-10

[4] Gregory M. Nielson and Bernd Hamann, "Techniques for the Interactive Visualization of Volumetric Data," in *Visualization '90* (Los Alamitos, CA: IEEE Computer Society Press, October 1990), pp. 45–50.

[5] Gregory M. Nielson and Tim Dierks, "Modelling and Visualization of Scattered Volumetric Data," SPIE Conference Proceedings 1459, San Jose, CA (February 1991).

13-6

[4] "Scattering from a Slit Cylinder Enclosing an Off-Set Impedance Surface," *Proceedings National Radio Science Meeting,* U.R.S.I. B8-8, Boulder, CO (January 1986) and Philadelphia, PA (June 1986).

[5] CA-DISSPLA User Manual, Computer Associates International, Inc., 711 Stewart Ave., Garden City, NY, 11530.

13-7

[4] "Scattering from a Slit Cylinder Enclosing an Off-set Impedance Surface," *Proceedings National Radio Science Meeting,* U.R.S.I. B8-8, Boulder, CO (January 1986) and Philadelphia, PA (June 1986).

[5] CA-DISSPLA User Manual, Computer Associates International, Inc., 711 Stewart Ave., Garden City, NY, 11530.

Appendix A
Choosing Visualization Techniques

As noted in other places, we have found it easier to select appropriate visualization techniques if we first identify our goal for visualizing data. For those who may want to try this approach, we indicate here seven very broad categories of visualization goals and list techniques used in images in Section II that can accomplish these goals. If you have only a general idea of what you want to accomplish with your data, this appendix may provide a means to focus on a specific visualization goal.

The seven categories of visualization goals and examples of their utility are:

Comparing: images, positions, data sets, subsets of data.

Distinguishing: importance, objects, activities, range of value.

Indicating directions: orientation, order, direction of flow.

Locating: position relative to axis, object, map.

Relating: concepts, e.g., value and direction, position and shape, temperature and velocity, object type and value.

Representing values: numeric value of data.

Revealing objects: exposing, highlighting, bringing to the front, making visible, enhancing visibility.

Comparing   Ordered layout of shaded rectangles within a rectangle permits
                  comparison **13-10**
              Ordered placement of successively magnified images permits comparison **7-9**
              Quantity represented as distance permits comparison **13-11**
              Grid permits comparison of position **13-12**, Figure B
              Multiple stacked images permit comparison of changes over time **5-5**
              Diagonal arrangement of images and arrow permits sequential comparison **4-5**
              Displaying time data as 2-D image permits temporal comparisons **2-2**
              Superimposed wire frame permits comparison **13-3**
              Bar-chart colors permit comparison of events **3-1**
              Animated sequence permits comparison of scalars **5-7**
              Stacked, time-ordered 1-D slices permit comparison over time **3-3**

Distinguishing

Gray shade distinguishes quality **13-10**

Dotted and solid lines distinguish negative and positive values **11-4,** Figure B

Colored lines and labels distinguish type of object **8-6**

Saturation levels of hues distinguish subclasses of object **7-8**

Discontinuity in the color table distinguishes type of object **5-12**

Color distinguishes type of object **11-9**

Shading distinguishes type **4-2**

Color distinguishes type of flow **7-4**

Letters distinguish type **2-13**

Textured appearance of glyphs distinguishes clusters **13-9**

Indicating directions

Comet tail indicates direction **6-3**

Pointed glyphs indicate direction **2-10**

A texture field indicates direction **2-8**

Light to dark color indicates direction **5-3**

Ribbons indicate direction **6-1**

Distinct color ranges indicate direction **7-7**

Stylized figure indicates direction **13-8**

Context indicates direction **12-6**

Particle traces indicate direction **5-9**

Color indicates direction **3-8**

Directed line segments indicate direction **6-4**

Axis color and labels indicate direction **6-2**

Pointed glyphs indicate direction **6-2**

Regularly spaced, equal-length arrows indicate direction **6-5**

Line segments indicate orientation **6-8**

Triangle indicates direction **13-6**

Locating

Colored isosurface intersected by 2-D slice planes locates shape **9-10**

Bright symbol locates object **7-8**

Reference map locates objects **13-11**

Colored arrow points to location of maximum **2-4**

White diamond placed on reference map shows location **4-4**

Dots extending a line indicate prior position **13-12**, Figure A

Vertical line connecting map to object locates object **13-12**, Figure B

Line represents position over time **5-8**

Height locates maximum temperature **5-8**

Color of particle trace indicates height **6-9**

Glyphs locate critical points **6-11**

Vertical, colored line on *x-y* plot locates current time **3-8**

Gray regions represent likely location of object **8-8**

3-D wire frame identifies position **13-3**

Point of stickpin identifies measurement location **8-9**

Dark vertical lines locate objects **2-6**

Labeled grid lines overlaid on surface locate coordinate values **7-2**

White grids locate objects **1-7**

Gray isosurface locates object **5-7**

Relating

Labeled vertical lines relate location and object **9-3**

Color and textured vectors relate value and direction **2-8**

Ribbon color and translucent object relate airspeed and object **6-1**

Relating (continued)   Color-coded surface relates position and temperature   **11-7**

Particle traces and translucent object relate position and shape   **6-9**

Translucent object relates position and internal colored vorticity   **8-1**

Vector field within a translucent isosurface relates scalar and direction   **6-6**

Translucent isosurface and particle traces relate scalar value and direction   **5-9**

Color relates object's location and brightness   **11-5**

Labels on circumference relate position and time of day   **3-4**

Map with color and vector field relates location, temperature, and velocity   **6-4**

Stickpin and its height relate data position and value   **8-9**

Object representation and size relate type and value of object   **2-13**

Translucent, colored grid overlaid on a map relates position and density   **1-6**

Stylized image and other plots relate network and data values   **4-3**

Color of trace relates safe or unsafe states and positions   **1-3**

Representing values   Dotted lines represent negative values   **11-4,** Figure B

Color on slice planes represents values   **8-5**

Length of comet tail represents velocity   **6-3**

Glyph height represents depth   **2-10**

Intensity of hue represents amount   **1-9**

Texture represents velocity   **5-4**

Distance between points represents amount   **13-11**

Brightness represents level of activity   **5-10**

Tightness of spiral represents turbulence   **5-11**

Distinct color ranges represent scalar ranges   **7-7**

Size, color, and orientation of arrows and discs represent values   **6-11**

Length of rectangle represents duration   **4-8**

Depth and perspective represent time   **4-8**

Color represents probability   **8-8**

Gray shade represents sign of value   **4-6**

Filled or transparent isosurfaces represent values   **6-10**

Grid size indicates amount   **1-7**

Line length indicates degree of coherence   **6-8**

Letter height represents amount of substance   **2-13**

Glyph length and angle represent values   **13-9**

Space between squares represents relative rate of change   **3-2**

Surface slice represents values   **7-1**

Clock icon represents time   **5-7**

Revealing objects   Cross-hatched area reveals boundaries   **11-4,** Figure A

3-D mesh of cubes reveals structure   **9-9**

Parallel lines reveal structure of solution space   **2-1,** Figure B

Bright, distinctly colored tetrahedrons reveal objects of interest   **5-10**

Histogram equalization of color reveals structure   **11-3**

Arrangement of spheres reveals structure   **10-11**

Opacity and color reveal area of interest   **11-12**

3-D image with selected portions opaque reveals object's structure   **11-8**

Colored haze reveals shape of region   **9-2**

Cutaway of portion of 3-D object reveals internal structure   **9-1**

Sparsely spaced color-coded cubes reveal internal and external structure   **11-2**

Small, translucent, colored spheres reveal internal and external structure   **9-6**

Revealing objects (continued)   Reflection of hidden side of image reveals object **12-7**

External voxels reveal object's shape **10-9**

Shadows reveal 2-D object's shape **8-3**

Color and degree of distortion reveal temporal behavior **5-6**

Diffusion density of 3-D scalar field reveals shape **11-6**

Appendix B
Taxonomy of Visualization Goals

The research supporting the taxonomy was done at the University of Colorado, Boulder, CO, USA, by Stephen Wehrend for an M.S. thesis with Clayton Lewis, Advisor. Stephen also identified the images in Section II that use techniques that demonstrate the visualization goals in this taxonomy.

We introduce a method for quickly determining appropriate techniques to reveal meaning in data. The method asserts that identifying the visualization goal—the information you expect to learn and communicate about your data—subsequently suggests appropriate techniques to use in achieving that goal. The visualization goal may be a suspected hidden meaning within the data or the meaning you want to communicate to others.

To use this taxonomy, you must formulate your visualization goal by pairing words from two specific vocabulary lists. One list designates nine actions you might apply to your data: identify, locate, distinguish, categorize, cluster, rank, compare, associate, and correlate. The other list names seven types of data (how you think about your data): scalar (or scalar field), nominal, direction (or direction field), shape, position, spatially extended region or object, and structure. An example of a visualization goal based on this method is "locate shape."

If a single image has several visualization goals, you should first identify and rank all of the goals to ensure that they are displayed in the image according to their importance. A pairing of action/data type should be made for each goal and any conflicts resolved by considering the more important visualization goal first.

Definitions   In the following paragraphs we define and illustrate with line art the formal vocabulary this method uses. To further illustrate the vocabulary, we also reference an example in Section II. After the definitions, we list goals described by pairing words from the two vocabulary lists, and we point to techniques in images in Section II that accomplish the goals.

Types of Action

A geometric representation of a thermometer identifies a value as temperature.

A United States map locates Colorado by shading.

Distinct fill patterns as well as shape distinguish objects.

A key to the shading assigned to the states categorizes alliances during the Civil War.

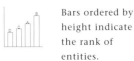

A scatterplot reveals the clustering of points in a line.

Bars ordered by height indicate the rank of entities.

Identify. To identify is to establish the collective characteristics by which an object is distinctly recognizable. Identification is the finest level of detail when an individual object is being considered. **7-8** identifies both the type and position of different particles with color. **3-4** shows labeled isolines identifying temperature values.

Locate. To locate is to determine specific position. This position may be either absolute or relative. *Locate* is frequently associated with a spatially extended region or object. In these cases, there are two properties to consider: position and boundaries with respect to the spatially extended region or object. Boundaries include the magnitude, range, or distance over which it extends. **13-9**, Figure A, demonstrates *locate* for a spatially extended region or object. Both the extent of a tumor, represented by a dark outline, and the hot spot of a tumor, seen as a bright spot, are shown. *Locate* does not always have to be associated with a spatially extended region or object: you may want to locate a particular scalar on a histogram. **6-11** locates critical points with glyphs.

Distinguish. To distinguish is to recognize as different or distinct. This depth of detail necessitates only that objects be recognized as different; no identification is necessary. **7-6** uses a discontinuous color change on a pseudocolor scalar plot to distinguish positive from negative values of a variable. **5-5** chooses hue to distinguish two materials in a volume visualization.

Categorize. To categorize is to place in specifically defined divisions in a classification. Categorization is often considered when multiple objects are to be studied and some organization is desired. In **7-8**, color identifies distinct classes of objects. **13-12**, Figure A, categorizes positions with dotted lines, object, and solid lines.

Cluster. To cluster is to join into groups of the same, similar, or related type. Clustering is intended to be used for putting together things that need to be either conceptually or physically grouped. Whereas *categorizing* places objects into preexisting categories or groups, *clustering* creates the groups as the objects are placed in them. **2-1** demonstrates clustering by magnifying a scatterplot that reveals parallel jets leading from the base to the upper right. **13-9**, Figure A, reveals clusters by differences in texture.

Rank. To rank a data type is to give it an order or position with respect to other objects of like type. Ranking is intended to be used when an absolute or a relative ranking is to be given to some series of objects. For instance, it may be important to know that the maximum and minimum elements in a group are based on some type of ordering system. Ranking also implies some type of comparison, at least in a relative sense. Stating that one object is greater or smaller than another requires comparison. Objects can be ranked according to many criteria: alphabetical, numerical, or chronological. **2-13** ranks the horizontal axis of an extended bar chart by type of substance, and the letters representing amounts of each substance are ordered by size, indicating relative quantities. **1-1** indicates rank by size.

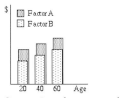

Comparison between values is facilitated with a dual-variable bar chart.

The value of a variable indicated by bar height is placed at city locations to associate the value with the city.

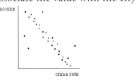

A 2-D scatterplot shows the correlation between two variables.

A scalar value is indicated by the bar height and scale.

A 2-D array of scalar values is represented by an isoplot.

The entity *book* is represented in its familiar form.

Compare. To compare is to examine so as to notice similarities and differences. Comparing is important when two or more objects need to be looked at and no rank is implied for them. As we stated in discussing rank, comparison is similar to ranking, except that you may want to compare without explicitly ordering: you may want to compare two faces in order to see how they differ. **7-9** depicts the *compare* operation with multiple images at varying magnifications placed close to one another. **1-8** compares images by subtracting one from the other and plotting differences.

Associate. To associate is to link or join in a relationship. Association is used when a relationship is drawn between two or more objects that may be otherwise unrelated. These objects or attributes need not be of the same type and often are not. **3-4** and **6-4** associate temperatures or velocities with locations on a map by placing a scalar field of temperatures over a map of the northern hemisphere.

Correlate. To correlate is to establish a direct connection. The connection may be causal, complementary, parallel, or reciprocal. Correlation is used when the relationship between two or more objects is connected in a manner that is important, if not obvious. **5-3** uses thin black lines to relate a magnified portion of an image to the whole image. **5-4** applies color and texture to examine the correlation between temperature and velocity.

Types of Data

Scalar (or **scalar field**). A scalar is a quantity that is completely specified by one number on an appropriate scale. Examples of scalars include, but are not limited to, size, temperature, density, mass, percentage, and probability. A scalar field is similar to a scalar, except that a large number of scalars is always displayed, and often the value of individual scalars is not identifiable. Scalar fields emphasize large-scale trends and boundaries. Rather than denote an exact value, the scalars typically represent some finite number of ranges, each of which is given some visual attribute, such as color or length. An example of the use of scalars can be seen in **3-4**, which depicts temperatures in the Northern Hemisphere in color. **4-7** uses the length and width of rectangles to represent scalar values.

Nominal. A nominal is an object or property distinguished from other objects or properties by its traits or characteristics. An animal or computer is an object. A property could be a texture or the state of an object, such as opened or closed. **7-8** includes several nominals; each type of particle in the image is represented by a different-colored plus sign (+).

The compass points to (direction) north.

A 2-D array of directions is represented by arrows.

A shape is determined by its outline.

The position of Denver, Colorado is indicated by an "X."

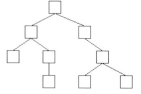
The spatially extended region of earth and country boundaries is represented by a shaded 2-D projection.

Direction (or direction field). A direction is a position to which motion or another position is referred. A direction can refer to points on the compass, hands of a clock, relative direction, or an indication, such as left, right, up, or down. **13-2** uses attached, perpendicular arrows in 3-D space to represent a right-hand coordinate system. A direction field is an associated grouping of directions. It is analogous to scalar field. **6-4** employs a number of arrows to show wind velocity throughout the earth. **6-6** indicates direction in a volume with comet tails.

Shape. A shape is a real or abstract object distinguished by its outline or surface configuration. **8-7** combines a 3-D isosurface with intersecting 2-D pseudocolor slices to reveal the shape of a field. **9-6** reveals shape with tiny colored spheres.

Position. A position is the specific location of an object. Position may be either relative to an object, such as a shape, or relative to a representation of a physical region, such as a map. For example, the position of a dog's ear could be said to be at the top of its head, the position of a storm front could be said to be at a specified latitude and longitude, or over the northwest corner of the state of Colorado. Position of course does not imply extent. For instance, the position of the Mediterranean Sea can be described as between Europe and Africa or at some central latitude and longitude. Neither of these examples of position gives any information about magnitude, range, or distance over which the sea extends. **13-9**, Figure A, identifies the location of the hot spot of a tumor by representing it as a bright spot on the monochrome image of the tumor. **1-3** distinguishes safe and unsafe positions with colors.

Spatially extended region or object (SERO). A spatially extended region or object is a continuous portion of a surface or space that satisfies specific geometric postulates, essentially a representation in which both relative and absolute measurements have meaning. That is, the distance between any two points on a region or object can be quantified and compared to any two other points on this region or object. An example of a spatially extended region is a physical map of the United States. An example of a spatially extended object is a 3-D representation of a human torso, possibly with the skin invisible and the organs assigned various colors.

A spatially extended region or object is often not the sole type of data to be displayed in an image. It is typically the context or environment in which other data types, such as positions, nominals, or scalars, are displayed. In fact, these other types of data may have meaning only within the context of the spatially extended region or object. Selecting a 2-D projection of the coastlines as a background for a direction field in **6-4** exemplifies such a region. In **10-1**, the 3-D representation of a human brain is a spatially extended object.

Structure. A structure is an arrangement from any one of the previous types of data that can be considered a single object. Structure implies connectedness. Examples of structure may be ordered, cyclic, or hierarchical. In **9-9**, single-hued cubes indicate the structure of porous material. **11-8** reveals structure by combining transparency and opacity.

A hierarchical relationship is shown as a tree (structure.)

associate direction	Vector field of arrows associates directions **6-4**
	Vector field of cometlike objects associates directions **6-6**
	Vector field of glyphs associates directions **6-2**
associate nominal and scalar	Color associates object to brightness **11-5**
	Object representation associates type of object to value **2-13**
	Stylized representation of experiment associates data set to isolines **13-7**
associate position and nominal	Color of trace associates positions with safe and unsafe states **1-3**
	Labeled vertical lines associate location with type of object **9-3**
	Position of parallel jets is associated with solution space **2-1**
associate position and scalar	Body and bar chart associate position of body to values **1-3**
	Circumference labels associate time of day to position **3-4**
	Colored isolines on map associate position to temperature **6-4**
	Opaque object within colored translucent object associate position to temperature **11-7**
	Pin location and height associate position of data to value **8-9**
	Translucent, colored grid overlaid on a map associates position to density **1-6**
	Vector field on map associates position to velocity **6-4**
associate position and shape	Particle traces and translucent object associate position to shape **6-9**
associate position, scalar, and direction	Map with color and vector field associates location, temperature, and velocity **6-4**
associate position	Dotted line, object, and solid line associate past, present, and future positions **13-12**
	Wire frame overlaid on image associates locations **13-3**
associate scalar	Bars within bars associate subgroup values to group values **2-5**
	Color and position associate density and time **3-7**
	Hue and saturation associate two values **1-4**
	Stacked *x-y* plots associate scalar values **3-8**
associate scalars and direction	Streamlines and glyphs associate direction with critical points **6-11**
associate SERO and nominal	Exaggerated height of area is associated with type of object **11-12**
associate SERO and scalar	Map and opacity associate area with density **9-7**
	Stylized image and other plots associate system to data values **4-3**
associate SERO	Inset image associates magnified portion to whole **8-2**
	Placement of images associates one to the next **7-9**
	Translucent surface overlaid on solid surface associates surfaces **1-7**
associate shape	Original adjacent to a magnified portion associates shapes **2-1**
	Successive magnification of images associates detail to overall image **7-9**

associate structure   Stepwise position and arrows associate structures   **4-5**
Translucent, colored, and connected objects associate structures   **9-6**

categorize direction   Color of line categorizes direction   **7-7**

categorize nominal   Color categorizes type of object   **4-7**
Color categorizes type of flow   **7-4**
Colored lines and labels categorize type of object   **8-6**

categorize position   Dotted line, object, and solid line categorize positions   **13-12**

categorize scalar   Dotted and solid lines categorize negative and positive values   **11-4**
Gray shade categorizes level of desirability   **13-10**
Object's color categorizes type of variable   **2-4**

categorize SERO   Colored and white regions categorize types of region   **5-4**
White grid regions on colored topological map categorize types of object   **1-7**

categorize structure   Single hue with varying intensities categorizes structure   **9-9**

cluster direction   Vector field of arrows on map clusters direction   **6-4**
Vector field of cometlike objects clusters direction   **6-6**

cluster nominal   Colors reveal clusters   **7-8**
Opacity reveals cluster of objects   **9-3**
Size and color of sphere reveal a cluster   **12-10**

cluster position   Colored objects among transparent objects cluster visible objects   **9-3**

cluster scalar   Color reveals clusters   **1-9**
Magnification reveals clusters of dots   **2-1**
Particle color reveals clusters   **6-3**
Similar patterns in ordered layout reveal clusters   **13-10**
Textured appearance of glyphs reveals clusters   **13-9**, Figure A

cluster SERO   Colored objects among transparent objects cluster visible objects   **9-3**

cluster shape   Black-and-white glyphs cluster shapes   **13-10**

cluster structure   Black-and-white glyphs cluster structures   **13-10**
Translucent, colored, and connected objects cluster structure   **9-6**

compare direction   Red orientation lines permit regional comparisons   **6-8**

compare nominal   Bar-chart colors permit comparison of events   **3-1**
Colored textual identifiers permit comparison   **2-12**
Disarray, penetration, and attributes of spheres compare effectiveness   **12-10**
Overlay of objects permits comparison   **10-10**
Side-by-side representation permits comparison between types of object   **2-13**

compare position	Grid permits comparison of positions **13-12**, Figure B
compare scalar	Adjacent slice planes permit comparison of regions **9-10**
	Animated sequence permits comparison of scalars **5-7**
	Bar-chart permits comparison of numbers within groups **2-5**
	Colored surfaces permit comparison of areas **11-5**, Figure A
	Cost represented as distance permits comparison **13-11**
	Displaying time data as 2-D image permits temporal comparisons **2-2**
	Ordered layout of colored rectangles permits comparison **1-9**
	Ordered layout of shaded rectangles within a rectangle permits comparison **13-10**
	Representing density as opacity permits comparison of values **5-5**
	Sequential placement of image permits comparison of data over time **3-5**
	Side-by-side images permit comparison **1-1**
	Side-by-side representation permits comparison of amount **2-13**
	Stacked 1-D slices permit comparison of slices **3-7**
	Stacked colored surfaces permit comparison **2-6**
	Stacked images permit value comparison **2-2**
	Stacked, time-ordered 1-D slices permit comparison over time **3-3**
compare SERO	Ordered placement of successively magnified images permits comparison **7-9**
	Side-by-side images with a third image depicting the difference permit comparison **1-8**
	Superimposed wire frame permits comparison **13-3**
	Translucent surface superimposed on solid surface permits comparison **1-7**
compare shape	Multiple stacked images permit comparison of changes over time **5-5**
	Successive magnification permits comparison of overall image to detail **7-9**
compare structure	Diagonal arrangement and arrows permit sequential comparison **4-5**
correlate directions	Vector field of arrows correlates directions **6-4**
correlate nominal	White connectors facilitate correlation of objects **4-5**
correlate position and scalar	Reference object and colored isolines correlate position to value **7-7**
	Translucent object correlates position to internal colored vorticity **8-1**
correlate scalar and direction	Translucent isosurface and particle traces correlate scalar value with direction **5-9**
correlate scalar and nominal	Colored ribbons and translucent object correlate airspeed with object **6-1**
correlate scalar	2-D scalar field above 3-D scalar field correlates values **5-12**
	Color and texture correlate temperature and speed **5-4**
	Colored squares on an *x-y* plot correlate three values **3-2**
	Glyphs with similar patterns suggest correlation **13-10**
	Multiple plots permit correlation **2-9**
	Multiple-variable bar chart correlates values **1-3**

correlate scalar (continued)
Opacity, color, and filled or transparent isosurfaces correlate velocity and pressure **6-10**

Representing numbers as distance permits correlation **13-11**

Stacked images correlate variables **5-8**

correlate scalars and direction
Color and animated texture correlate value with direction **5-4**

Color, isolines, and glyph field correlate scalars with direction **6-2**

Vector field within a translucent isosurface correlates scalar with direction **6-6**

correlate SERO
Black lines from origin to magnified rectangle correlate images **5-3**

correlate shape
Stacked, outlined, transparent cubes correlate objects **8-11**

correlate structure and scalar
Colored slice planes correlate permeability structure with depth **8-5**

correlate structure and shape
Isolines and stylized model permit correlation of structure and shape **11-4**, Figure B

distinguish direction
Axis color and labels distinguish direction **6-2**

Color ranges distinguish direction **7-7**

Particle traces distinguish direction **5-9**

distinguish nominal
Color distinguishes type of object **2-12, 3-9, 4-7, 7-5, 7-8, 9-7**

Color of trace distinguishes properties **1-3**

Color, length, and rigidity distinguish type of object **10-10**

Colored lines and labels distinguish type of object **8-6**

Opacity distinguishes type of object **9-3**

Shading distinguishes activity **4-2**, Figure B

Texture distinguishes type of object **9-1**

distinguish position
Size of white region on map distinguishes position of objects **1-7**

distinguish scalar
Black distinguishes sign of value **4-6**

Bright lines and positioning distinguish relative importance of values **10-6**

Color ranges distinguish positive and negative values **7-6**

Colored lines plotted on top distinguish high values **4-4**

Colors distinguish areas of different densities **10-2**

Colors distinguish relative temperature **6-7**

Colors distinguish scalar ranges **7-7**

Colors distinguish values **3-6, 6-4**

Color distinguishes sign of field **9-2**

Dot color distinguishes magnitude of values **2-1**

Dotted lines distinguish negative values **11-4**, Figure B

Equal use of color distinguishes values **2-2**

Filled or transparent isosurfaces distinguish pressures **6-10**

distinguish SERO
Colored cubes among transparent cubes distinguish types **9-3**

Size of white region on map distinguishes regions **1-7**

distinguish shape   Colored outline distinguishes shape of polygon   **4-1**, Figures A and B
                     Small colored spheres distinguish internal and external shapes   **9-6**

distinguish structure   Dot color distinguishes structure   **2-1**
                         Small colored spheres distinguish internal and external structures   **9-6**

identify direction   Animated texture field identifies direction   **5-4**
                      Arrows identify direction   **6-4**, **13-12**, Figure A
                      Color identifies direction   **3-8**
                      Colored trace identifies path   **1-3**
                      Cometlike tail identifies direction   **6-6**
                      Context identifies direction   **12-6**
                      Light to dark color identifies direction   **5-3**
                      Lighted, shaded 3-D axis identifies direction   **13-2**
                      Line segments identify orientation   **6-8**
                      Pointed glyphs identify direction   **2-10**, **6-2**
                      Regularly spaced, equal-length arrows identify direction   **6-5**
                      Ribbons identify direction   **3-9**, **6-1**
                      Triangle identifies direction   **13-6**

identify nominal   Axis positions identify type   **2-13**
                    Bar color identifies type of group   **2-5**
                    Border colors identify heat sources and sinks   **9-5**
                    Bright, distinctly colored tetrahedrons identify event   **5-10**
                    Color and distortion identify temporal behavior   **5-6**
                    Color and pattern identify events   **3-1**
                    Color identifies type of object   **5-5**, **6-3**, **11-9**
                    Color identifies particulates   **5-1**
                    Color identifies properties   **2-13**
                    Geographic color conventions identify type of object   **7-8**
                    Labels identify objects   **13-11**
                    Letters identify substance   **2-13**
                    Lines joining rectangles identify communication path   **4-8**
                    Opacity and color identify area of interest   **11-12**
                    Polyhedrons identify objects   **13-5**
                    Smooth or flat shading identifies moving or stationary material   **2-10**
                    Spectral synthesis identifies objects   **12-3**
                    Stylized representation identifies object   **13-12**
                    Ternary color mapping identifies type of object   **2-6**, Figure A
                    Vertical parallel lines identify grouping as a matrix   **4-6**

identify position   3-D wire frame identifies position   **13-3**
                     Color of particle trace identifies height   **6-9**
                     Colored dot identifies location of measurements shown   **3-8**
                     Dots extending a line identify prior position   **13-12**, Figure A
                     Horizontal axis identifies longitude location   **3-3**
                     Line identifies positions over time   **5-8**
                     Point of pin identifies measurement location   **8-9**
                     Rectangle identifies location   **2-7**
                     Tip of line identifies position   **13-12**, Figure B

identify scalar   Axes labels identify scalar value **11-4**

Bar length identifies values **1-3**, **2-5**

Black bar identifies range of uncertainty **2-13**

Brightness identifies level of activity **5-10**

Circle identifies zero value **4-6**

Clock icon identifies time **5-7**

Color and height identify values **7-3**

Color and key identify values **2-9**

Color and line width identify volume **4-4**

Color and translucency identify value **3-6**

Color identifies amount of vorticity **7-7**, **8-1**

Color identifies brightness values **11-5**, Figure B

Color identifies density **3-7**

Color identifies depth **1-7**

Color identifies electron density **9-8**

Color identifies magnitude of vectors **6-5**

Color identifies pressure **8-4**

Color identifies probability **8-8**, Figure A

Color identifies saturation **2-6**, Figure A

Color identifies shear magnitude **6-2**

Color identifies speed **6-1**

Color identifies stress **8-2**

Color identifies temperature **5-3**

Color identifies utilization rate **8-3**

Color identifies velocity **7-6**

Color of text identifies relative amounts **2-12**

Color saturation identifies magnitude **1-4**

Distance between points identifies amount **13-11**

Distance between surface and slice identifies height **7-1**

Dot density identifies field strength **13-7**

Dot spacing identifies velocity **13-12**, Figure A

Glyph height identifies depth **2-10**

Glyph length identifies speed **2-10**

Grid size identifies relative population **1-7**

Height of pin identifies relative value **8-9**

Height of rectangle identifies value **4-6**

Intensity identifies amount **1-9**

Labeled isolines indexed to key identify scalar **11-4**, Figure B

Labeled, colored contour bands identify temperature **3-4**

Labels on circumference of world map identify time of day **3-4**

Labels on edge of map identify longitude and latitude **6-4**

Length of comet tail identifies velocity **6-6**

Length of rectangle identifies duration **4-8**, Figure A

Letter height identifies amount of substance **2-13**

Line length identifies degree of coherence **6-8**

Marker spacing identifies relative speed **5-3**

Opacity and color identify amount **11-12**

Opacity identifies density **5-5**

Opacity of isosurface identifies potential vorticity **5-9**

Polar, linear, and log plots identify values **13-1**

identify scalar (continued)
Dimension of rectangle identifies values **4-7**
Scale identifies height of isosurface **5-9**
Shadows on landscape identify time of day **1-6**
Size, color, and orientation of arrows and discs identify values **6-11**
Location of square identifies density and temperature **3-2**
Texture identifies velocity **5-4**
Thickness identifies velocity **5-11**
Tightness of spiral identifies turbulence **5-11**

identify SERO
Colored internal voxels identify object **10-9**
Colored, photorealistic image identifies object **10-8**
Colored, textured, lighted, and shaded sphere identifies object **10-7**
Exaggerated height identifies object **11-12**
Fractal scalar field identifies 3-D surface **12-2**
Lighted, perspective view identifies object **8-2**
Lighted, shaded terrain map identifies object **1-6**
Outlines on lighted sphere identify object **8-9**
Perspective and stochastic spectral synthesis identify object **12-3**
Ray-traced image identifies realistic room **11-5**, Figure A
Shaded, colored surface identifies object **11-9**
Shading, specular reflection, and color identify object **10-1**
Shadows, lighting, and transparency identify 3-D object **10-4**
Solid surface identifies object **1-7**
Stylized 3-D figure identifies object **1-3**
Stylized, interconnected components identify object **4-3**
Translucent surface identifies object **1-7**
U.S. map with outline of states identifies object **5-9**
White outline identifies object **3-4**
Wire frame identifies 3-D object **13-3**

identify shape
Black-and-white glyph plot identifies shape of object **13-9**, Figure A
Bright yellow, connected symbols identify border **7-8**
Color and opacity identify shape **5-5**
Color identifies shape **11-1**, Figure A
Colored haze identifies shape of region **9-2**
Colored isosurfaces identify shape **9-10**
Cross-hatched area identifies boundaries **11-4**
Diffusion density identifies shape **11-6**
Displaying voxels with equal value identifies object's shape **11-11**
GDM technique identifies shape **4-1**
Grayish, translucent isosurface identifies shape **2-3**
Isosurface and colored slice planes identify shape **8-7**
Isosurfaces identify shape **9-8**
Lighted and shaded isosurface identifies shape **9-1**
Lighted, shaded, isolined surface identifies shape **8-11**
Opaque surfaces identify shape **11-9**, Figure A
Perspective grid identifies boundary **6-10**
Polar plot identifies shape **13-1**
Shadows identify object's shape **8-3**
Slice planes and wire frame identify boundary shape **11-11**, Figure A

identify shape (continued)

Surface opacity identifies internal shape **9-4**

Translucent and highlighted single hue identifies shape **6-9**

Translucent surface with white isolines identifies surface shape **8-9**

Translucent surfaces identify internal shape **11-9**, Figure B

Translucent, colored spheres identify internal and external shape **9-6**

Wire frame identifies shape **2-4**

identify structure

3-D image with opaque portions identifies structure **11-8**

3-D mesh of cubes identifies connectivity of structure **9-9**

Arrangement of spheres identifies structure **10-11**

Ball-and-stick figure identifies structure **4-5**

Connected 2-D slice planes identify structure within 3-D region **8-6**

Contrasting colors identify structure **11-1**, Figure B

Coarse grayscale image identifies structure **13-4**

Cutaway of portion of 3-D object identifies internal structure **9-1**

Equal use of color identifies structure **11-3**

Lighted and shaded volume identifies object's structure **10-2**

Opaque, colored cube identifies external structure **11-10**

Parallel lines identify structure of solution space **2-1**

Small, translucent, colored spheres identify internal and external structure **9-6**

Sparsely spaced, colored cube surfaces identify internal and external structure **11-2**

Translucent, external surface identifies internal structure **11-11**, Figure D

Translucent, colored cube identifies internal structure **11-10**

locate direction

Colored particle traces locate direction **6-9**

locate nominal

Black dot locates reference **3-4**

Bright objects on a dark background locate objects **5-10**

Bright spot on black-and-white image locates object **13-9**, Figure A

Bright white symbol locates object **7-8**

Color locates different types of flow **7-4**

Colored rectangle locates object **1-9**

Convergence of objects locates point **5-11**

Distinct visual characteristics locate objects **10-10**

Glyph locates object **4-8**, Figure A

Gray isosurface locates object **5-7**

Gray regions represent likely location of source **8-8**

Highlighted 3-D object locates object **2-4**

Labeled, white vertical lines on slice plane locate object **8-5**

Rectangles locate reference **4-7**

Reference map locates objects **13-11**

Shadows on map locate position of particulate **5-1**

Sphere depicts location of object **5-8**

Translucent volume locates area of interest **11-12**

Vertical line connecting map to object locates object **13-12**, Figure B

White diamonds locate references **4-4**

White grids locate objects **1-7**

locate scalar   Bold isoline locates pressure of interest **6-2**
Color locates extremum **11-4**
Color locates maximum pressure **8-4**
Colored arrow points to location of maximum **2-4**
Dot density locates extremes **13-7**
Glyphs locate critical points **6-11**
Height locates maximum temperature **5-8**
Labeled grid lines locate coordinate values **7-2**
Opacity locates high values **2-6**, Figure A
Opacity locates maximum density **9-7**
Skewed color scale locates regions **2-6**, Figure B
Vertical, colored line on *x-y* plot marks current time **3-8**

locate SERO   Labeled white lines locate objects on map **8-5**
Stylized images locate one object with respect to another **12-6**
Superimposed images locate object with respect to map **5-9**
White coastlines on map locate region with respect to another **1-1**
White grid on colored elevation map locates one region with respect to another **1-7**

locates shape   Colored isosurface intersected by 2-D slice planes locates shape **9-10**

rank direction   Length of arrows on map ranks directions **6-4**
Length of tail on cometlike objects ranks directions **6-6**

rank nominal   Horizontal arrangement and arrow indicate order **4-6**
Zigzag line indicates approximate object order **2-12**

rank position   Color and height rank position with respect to amount **2-7**
Color ranks position with respect to amount **1-9**

rank scalar   Position of letter indicates order of relative amount **2-13**

rank SERO   Image size indicates relative importance **1-1**

rank shape   Sequential position ranks magnified shapes **7-9**

rank structure   Stepdown arrangement of images and arrow indicates order **4-5**

Appendix C
Major Visualization Goal of Image

We alphabetically list the major visualization goal of each image in Section II to provide a quick way to locate possible techniques if you have a similar goal for your data.

Analyzes feasibility **13-5**
Associates 3-D geometry and volume data **1-5**
Classifies results **13-6**
Compares effectiveness **12-10**
Compares images **1-2**
Compares scalar fields **1-4**
Compares scalars **1-1, 2-2**
Compares surfaces **1-7**
Compares variables **2-4**
Correlates 3-D and 2-D **5-12**
Correlates isosurface and flow path **5-9**
Correlates isosurface and vector field **6-6**
Correlates scalars **2-9, 6-1, 7-1, 13-1**
Correlates scalars and position **1-6**
Correlates scalars and shape **11-7**
Correlates variables **2-8, 2-10, 3-2, 5-4, 5-8, 6-4**
Correlates vector and scalar values **6-7**
Correlates vectors and scalars **6-2**
Creates natural scenes **12-2**
Depicts 3-D **12-4, 12-8**
Depicts behavior **4-3**
Depicts change **5-7**
Depicts concurrent processes **4-8**
Depicts context **10-3, 12-5**
Depicts flow **3-9, 5-11**
Depicts interaction **5-5, 6-3**
Depicts motion **3-8, 12-6**
Depicts organic objects **12-1**
Depicts patterns **2-13**
Depicts shape **8-3, 9-4, 9-5**

Depicts textures **13-13**
Depicts vector field **6-5**
Describes 3-D **12-9**
Describes vector field **6-11**
Determines shape **4-1**
Distinguishes classes **4-2, 7-4, 7-7, 7-8**
Distinguishes regions **7-5**
Enhances realism **10-4, 10-8**
Identifies classes of objects **11-9**
Identifies direction **4-5, 13-2**
Identifies periodic events **3-1**
Identifies relationships **13-10**
Identifies shape **10-7, 10-10, 11-6**
Illustrates algorithm dynamics **4-6**
Illustrates time history **3-7**
Locates class **9-3**
Locates cluster **1-9, 2-5, 2-7, 13-9**
Locates extremes **9-7, 11-4**
Locates extremum **8-4**
Locates maximum **8-2**
Locates path **6-9**
Locates regions **2-1, 2-6, 5-10, 8-1, 8-8**
Locates scalars **3-4, 5-1, 11-12**
Locates shape **9-10, 10-11**
Locates values **7-2, 13-7**

Models natural terrain **12-3**
Relates objects **5-3**
Relates position and scalars **1-3, 5-2**
Relates scalars and tensors **2-11**
Relates structure and shape **8-7**
Relates vector and scalar fields **6-10**
Reveals behavior **4-4, 4-7**
Reveals change **7-6**
Reveals differences **1-8, 7-10**
Reveals hidden information **12-7**
Reveals location **13-3**
Reveals orientation and coherence **6-8**
Reveals pattern **3-3, 5-6, 13-11**
Reveals shape **9-2, 9-8, 10-5, 10-9**
Reveals structure **3-5, 3-6, 7-3, 7-9, 8-5, 8-6, 9-1, 9-6, 9-9, 10-2, 10-6, 11-1, 11-2, 11-3, 11-8, 11-10, 11-11**
Reveals surface complexity **10-1**
Reveals surface values **8-9, 8-10, 8-11**
Shows 3-D position and velocity **13-12**
Shows multiple relationships **2-3**
Shows orientation **13-8**
Shows relationships **2-12**
Shows structure **13-4**
Shows surface values **11-5**

Appendix D
Number of Variables

Each image in Section II is listed here by the number of variables depicted. You can use this list as a quick reference to techniques that visualize data with the same number variables as you have in your data. Note that we claim artistic license for some of these variable counts. See footnote on page 36.

1 Dependent Variable, 1 Independent Variable **13-6**
1 Dependent Variable, 2 Independent Variables **1-1, 1-2, 1-6, 3-3, 3-4, 3-7, 7-1, 7-2, 7-3, 7-4, 7-5, 7-6, 7-7, 7-8, 7-9, 10-5, 11-1, 11-3, 11-4, 13-1, 13-7, 13-11**
1 Dependent Variable, 2–3 Independent Variables **4-1**
1 Dependent Variable, 3 Independent Variables **1-5, 1-8, 3-5, 3-6, 3-9, 5-1, 5-6, 5-7, 5-10, 6-11, 8-1, 8-2, 8-3, 8-4, 8-5, 8-6, 8-7, 8-8, 8-9, 8-10, 8-11, 9-1, 9-2, 9-3, 9-4, 9-5, 9-6, 9-7, 9-8, 9-10, 10-1, 10-2, 10-6, 10-7, 10-9, 11-2, 11-5, 11-6, 11-7, 11-8, 11-10, 11-11, 11-12**
1 Dependent Variable, 4 Independent Variables **4-4**
2-D Model **13-4**
2 Dependent Variables, 2 Independent Variables **1-4, 1-7, 1-9, 5-4, 6-4, 6-8, 13-9**
2 Dependent Variables, 3 Independent Variables **5-3, 5-5, 5-9, 5-12, 6-1, 6-5, 6-6, 6-7, 6-10**
2 Dependent Variables, 4 Independent Variables **4-7**
3-D Model **9-9, 10-3, 10-4, 10-8, 10-11, 11-9, 12-1, 12-2, 12-3, 12-4, 12-5, 12-6, 12-7, 12-8, 12-9, 12-10, 13-2, 13-3, 13-5, 13-8, 13-13**
3 Dependent Variables, 1 Independent Variable **2-2, 3-2, 3-8**
3 Dependent Variables, 2 Independent Variables **2-7, 7-10**
3 Dependent Variables, 3 Independent Variables **2-3, 5-8, 6-2, 10-10, 13-12**
3 Dependent Variables, 4 Independent Variables **6-9**
3 Variables **6-3**
4 Dependent Variables, 2 Independent Variables **2-10**
4 Dependent Variables, 3 Independent Variables **2-6, 2-9**
4 Variables **2-1, 2-5, 2-10**
5 Dependent Variables, 2 Independent Variables **2-8**
5 Dependent Variables, 3 Independent Variables **5-11**
6 Dependent Variables, 3 Independent Variables **2-4**

6 Variables **5-2**
7 Dependent Variables, 2 Independent Variables **2-11**
11 Variables **3-1**
12 Dependent Variables, 4 Independent Variables **13-10**
20 Dependent Variables, 1 Independent Variable **2-13**
21 Variables **1-3**

Appendix E
Discipline and Application

This list of techniques by discipline or application may help you identify a method for visualizing your data. Techniques employed by others in your discipline or by those dealing with similar applications may suggest new ways you can put your data into visual form.

3-D Reconstruction **11-9**
3-D Vector Fields **6-11**
Aerodynamics **8-4**
Agriculture **1-9**, **2-7**
Airflow **6-2**
Air Pollution **2-2**, **5-1**
Air-Quality Assessment **1-6**
Aircraft Navigation **13-12**
Aircraft Wing Design **6-1**
Algorithm Visualization **4-6**
Antenna Design **13-1**
Architecture **10-3**, **11-5**
Art **13-8**, **12-4**
Artistic Exploration **12-9**
Astronomy **3-5**, **5-5**, **11-1**
Astrophysics **7-6**
Atmospheric Science **1-1**, **3-3**, **3-4**, **5-4**, **5-12**, **6-4**, **7-5**
Biofluid Mechanics **6-9**, **8-1**
Biology **2-13**, **5-10**, **9-1**
Biomedical **11-9**
Building Illumination **11-5**
Business **3-1**, **4-2**, **13-11**
Business-System Analysis **4-2**
Cartography **13-11**
Chemical Vapor Deposition **2-9**, **5-3**, **6-7**
Chemistry **9-2**, **9-6**
Cockpit Display **13-12**
Combustion Engineering **11-10**
Commercial Art **12-7**, **12-8**

Compressible Mix Dynamics **3-7**
Computation of Chains **10-10**
Computational (Physical) Chemistry **9-8**
Computational Astrophysics **3-2, 3-5, 5-5, 11-1**
Computational Chemistry **1-5, 4-5, 8-7**
Computational Fluid Dynamics **1-4, 2-9, 5-3, 5-6, 6-1, 6-7, 6-10, 7-7, 8-4, 9-5, 11-8, 11-10**
Computational Materials Science **10-11**
Computational Physics **1-2, 1-4, 3-6, 3-7, 6-5, 7-6, 11-3, 11-4**
Computational Solid Mechanics **2-11**
Computer Art **12-1, 12-4, 12-5, 12-6, 12-7, 12-8, 12-9, 12-10, 13-8**
Computer Graphics **2-8, 5-11, 7-1, 7-3, 10-4, 10-5, 10-8, 11-2, 12-2, 12-3, 13-2, 13-13**
Computer Science **4-6, 4-8, 11-6**
Computer Vision **11-6**
Concurrent Software **4-8**
Data Visualization **7-10**
Design Analysis **13-5**
Dynamical Systems **7-9**
Electrical Discharge Modeling **10-6**
Electrical Engineering **2-3, 10-6, 13-1, 13-6, 13-7**
Electromagnetism **11-4**
Entertainment **12-1, 12-5, 12-6**
Entomology **1-9, 2-7**
Environmental Protection **11-12**
Experimental Physics **13-4, 13-10**
Feature Extraction **4-1, 6-8, 7-4**
Finite Element Analysis **9-4, 11-7**
Flow Visualization **6-8, 7-4**
Fluid Dynamics **13-4**
Fluid-Flow Visualization **3-9, 5-6, 5-11**
Fractal Aggregates **9-9**
Fracture Mechanics **2-11**
Fusion Engineering **13-5**
Fusion Reactor Design **13-10**
Genetics **2-12**
Geography **10-7**
Geology **1-7, 8-5, 8-6, 9-3, 9-10**
Geophysics **1-7, 3-8**
Global Climate Modeling **1-1, 3-3, 3-4, 5-4, 5-12, 6-4, 7-5**
Hand Strength **5-2**
Heat Convection **9-5**
Heat Transfer **7-2**
Human Genome **2-12**
Image Interpolation **1-8**
Incompressible Fluid Flow **6-10, 7-7**
Lasers **11-3**

Magnetic Fields **6-5**
Marine Science **8-8**
Material Mix Dynamics **1-2**
Mathematics **2-1, 7-9**
Mechanical Engineering **2-4, 2-10, 5-8, 7-2, 9-4, 11-7, 13-3**
Medical Imaging **8-3, 10-1, 10-2, 10-9, 11-11, 13-9**
Medicine **6-9, 8-1, 8-3, 10-1, 10-2, 10-9, 11-11, 13-9**
Meteorology **1-6, 2-2, 5-1, 5-7, 5-9, 6-6, 9-7**
Molecular Bonds **9-8**
Molecular Dynamics **10-11**
Molecular Modeling **1-5, 8-7, 9-6**
Molecule Visualization **9-2**
Multivariate Analysis **2-5**
Muscle Group Strength **1-3**
Network Analysis **4-4, 4-7**
Neurobiology **5-10**
Number Theory **2-1**
Ocean Pollution **11-12**
Oil Exploration **8-5, 8-6, 9-3, 9-10**
Ozone Pollution **5-7**
Particle Diffusion **7-8**
Performance Simulation **2-3**
Pharmaceutical Advertising **12-10**
Photorealism **10-4, 10-8, 13-13**
Physiometry **1-3, 5-2**
Picture Synthesis **12-2, 12-3**
Plasma Physics **3-2**
Plasma Turbulence **3-6**
Plastic Injection Molding **2-10**
Polymer Chemistry **10-10**
Process Control and Analysis **4-3**
Process Simulation **4-3**
Protein Patterns **2-13**
Reaction Modeling **4-5**
Reservoir Engineering **2-6**
Scattering and Coupling of Electromagnetic Energy **13-6, 13-7**
Seismology **3-8**
Site Modeling **10-3**
Solid State Physics **7-8, 9-9**
Steam Injection **2-6**
Stress Analysis **2-4, 8-2**
Strong Interaction Theory **6-3**
Structural Biology **9-1**
Structural Engineering **8-2**
Surface Modeling **10-5**
Surface-Value Visualization **8-9, 8-10, 8-11**
Telerobotics **13-3**
Terrain Visualization **10-7**

Theoretical High-Energy Physics **6-3**
Time Accounting **3-1**
Turbulent Fluid Flow **11-8**
Underwater-Source Localization **8-8**
Visualization **1-8, 2-5, 2-8, 3-9, 4-1, 4-4, 4-7, 6-2, 6-11,
    7-1, 7-3, 7-10, 8-9, 8-10, 8-11, 11-2, 13-2**
Weather Simulation **5-9, 6-6, 9-7**
Weld Simulation **5-8**

Appendix F
Hardware and Software

Here is the hardware and software that contributors indicated was used to produce the images in Section II. The list may help you determine how you might use the same or comparable hardware and software for your visualization needs. Although many images were generated using a supercomputer, just as many were created on less powerful machines. Expensive computer systems are not a necessity, though they are probably faster and better able to handle voluminous data.

4-D McIdas software **5-9, 6-6, 9-7**
300-dpi QMS laser printer **13-11**
Alliant VFX-80 **2-11**
Amiga 2000 **10-8**
ANSYS software by Swanson Analysis, Inc. **2-4**
apE visualization toolkit **10-9**
Apollo DN10000 **2-6, 6-2, 8-2**
Apple Macintosh II **3-2, 4-2, 7-6, 13-10**
AQUA **11-12**
Ardent Titan **1-8, 9-8**
AT&T Pixel Machine **9-6**
ATOMS **10-11**
AVS **3-8, 8-8**
CATIA, a 3-D CAD system by Dassault Systems **11-5**
CM Frame Buffer **13-9**
Cognivision, Inc. FOTO software package **2-6, 6-2, 8-2**
Computer Associates' DISSPLA graphics library **3-1, 13-1, 13-6, 13-7**
Computervision CADDS4X Solidesign software **13-8**
Control Data 205 **5-9**
Control Data 7600 **3-1, 13-5**
Control Data CYBER 170/855 mainframe **13-2**
Control Data's ICEM Solid Modeler software **13-2**
Cray 1 supercomputer **1-2, 1-4, 3-7, 11-4**
Cray 2 supercomputer **3-6, 8-4**
Cray rendering software **5-7, 7-1**
Cray supercomputer **1-7, 1-9, 2-1, 2-6, 2-7, 2-9, 2-10, 5-1, 5-3, 5-8, 5-10, 6-7,**
    10-11, 11-1

Cray X-MP supercomputer **1-8**, **3-4**, **6-4**, **6-6**, **7-7**, **9-5**, **9-7**, **11-3**

Cray Y-MP supercomputer **1-1**, **3-2**, **5-5**, **5-7**, **6-5**, **6-9**, **7-1**, **7-6**, **8-1**, **10-9**, **11-8**

Crystal Graphics' Crystal 3D software **12-4**, **12-7**, **12-8**, **12-9**, **12-10**

Datapix **13-10**

DEC 11/70 **13-12**

DECstation **4-3**

DECstation 5810 **7-2**

Design Futures' MEGACADD **10-3**

Dicomed film recorder **1-7**, **3-1**, **5-1**, **6-5**

DORÉ graphics package **1-8**, **5-10**, **9-1**, **9-8**

EDGE graphics library **5-11**, **10-4**

Evans and Sutherland PS II display device **13-12**

FAST **8-4**

GAS **6-9**, **8-1**

Gen-Lock board and real-time camera **13-3**

GGP **2-9**, **5-3**, **5-8**

Gould Image Processing system **8-3**, **10-1**

GRAFIC code **1-7**

Graphic Software's Big D **10-3**

HERESIM™ **8-5**, **8-6**, **9-3**, **9-10**

Hewlett-Packard HP 9000 series 300 workstation **1-6**

Hewlett-Packard HP 9000 series 370 TSRX workstation **5-11**, **10-4**

Hewlett-Packard HP 9000 series 370 workstation **4-6**

Hewlett-Packard HP 9000 series 375 workstation **11-12**

Hewlett-Packard's Starbase graphics package **1-6**

High-resolution CM display **13-9**

HITAC M-680H computer **12-3**

HOTFLO **9-5**

IBM 3090 **11-5**

IBM 3090 Processor Complex Model 500E **1-8**

IBM 4381 **5-9**, **6-6**, **9-7**

IBM Data Explorer **10-7**

IBM ES/3090 **6-1**

IBM Power Visualization System **10-7**

IBM RS6000 workstation **2-3**, **6-8**, **7-4**

Ikegami 80-inch stereo projector **4-8**

Ikonas frame buffers **12-1**

IMAGE **7-6**

I-nets **5-10**

Jack™ **1-3**, **5-2**

MacDraw II **4-2**

Mathematica's Tempra **10-3**

MESA package **6-7**, **7-3**

Micrografx Designer software **13-11**

Micronics 486 **12-4**, **12-9**

Motif **7-10**

Mrakevec **6-9**, **8-1**

NASA Ames PLOT3D **6-9**, **8-1**

NAV3D **6-1**

NCAR graphics package **1-1**, **3-4**, **6-4**

NCSA IMAGE **3-2**

NPA software **4-3**

PASTA2D code **5-8**

PC 386/25 **10-3**

PC compatible **12-7**, **12-8**, **12-10**

Pixar Image Computer **5-5**

Pixar's ChapVolumes software **5-5**

Polaroid CI-3000 film recorder **6-2**

Precision Visual's PV-WAVE **2-2**, **10-6**

PRESOLID **9-1**

Raster Technologies PHIGS+ software **4-1**

Raster Technology terminal **10-11**

REALS **11-5**

RELAP5 **4-3**

RENDACH **9-1**

ROSS **11-9**

SAMPP **13-5**

SCORE™ **9-10**

Silicon Graphics 4D 20 workstation **6-3**, **7-8**, **7-9**, **9-9**, **10-10**, **12-2**

Silicon Graphics 4D 25-GT workstation **6-1**

Silicon Graphics 4D 35 workstation **5-4**, **5-12**

Silicon Graphics 4D 220-GTX workstation **3-9**, **6-11**, **7-7**, **9-5**

Silicon Graphics 4D 320 workstation **8-9**, **8-10**, **8-11**, **11-2**, **11-10**

Silicon Graphics GL library **4-1**, **8-9**, **8-10**, **8-11**, **11-2**, **11-10**

Silicon Graphics IRIS 4D 210-VGX workstation **4-8**

Silicon Graphics IRIS 4D 320-VGX workstation **8-4**

Silicon Graphics IRIS 4D 370 workstation **10-5**

Silicon Graphics IRIS 4D workstation **13-13**

Silicon Graphics IRIS 4D-GT workstation **11-9**

Silicon Graphics IRIS 4D-GT70 workstation **13-3**

Silicon Graphics IRIS workstation **1-5**, **4-4**, **4-7**, **6-9**, **8-1**, **8-5**, **8-6**, **9-2**, **9-3**, **10-2**

Silicon Graphics workstation **1-3**, **1-9**, **2-7**, **2-8**, **2-10**, **5-2**, **9-10**, **11-1**

Sparcstation 1 **2-12**

Stardent computer **5-10**, **8-8**, **11-8**

Stardent Titan computer **3-8**, **9-1**

Sun Microsystems 4/370 workstation **3-5**

Sun Microsystems SPARCstation **12-5**

Sun Microsystems SPARCstation 1+ **12-6**, **13-8**
Sun Microsystems SPARCstation 1GX **2-5**
Sun Microsystems SPARCstation IPC **5-6**
Sun Microsystems voxvu software **3-5**
Sun Microsystems workstation **2-2**, **3-3**, **3-6**, **7-5**, **10-6**, **11-11**
SunVision **3-6**, **11-11**
SunVoxel software **11-11**
SURF **6-9**, **8-1**
SURMAP **9-8**
Targa 16 graphics card **10-3**
Targa graphics board **12-4**, **12-9**
Tektronix 4125 high-resolution color terminal **1-2**, **1-4**, **3-7**, **11-4**
Tektronix 4336 workstation **9-4**, **11-7**
Thinking Machine's Connection Machine **13-9**
Thinking Machine's Connection Machine (CM-2) **11-6**
Time Art's Lumena **12-7**, **12-8**, **12-10**

TRIDUAL simulator **7-7**
TRIVIEW **7-7**
UNIGRAPH 2000 **7-2**
VAX 11/785 **8-2**
VAX 780 **4-5**, **6-7**, **7-3**, **12-1**
VAX 8530 **8-3**, **10-1**, **10-5**
VAX 8600 **9-4**, **11-7**
VAX VMS system **13-1**, **13-6**, **13-7**
Versatec printer **11-3**
VISTApro **10-8**
VoxelView®/ULTRA **1-5**
Wavefront **12-6**
Wavefront Technologies' Data Visualizer **2-3**, **6-1**, **8-7**
Wavefront Technologies software **2-10**
X Window environment **1-8**, **4-6**, **7-10**
Zenith 386 IBM-compatible microcomputer **13-11**
Zeus application code **11-1**

Appendix G
Contributors

We list here all whose names were submitted as contributing to the images in Section II. We consider all the contributors to be among the leaders in the application of scientific visualization.

Mark Abrams **1-1**
Michael J. Allison **2-8, 5-4, 11-8**
Chris L. Anderson **3-6**
Paul N. Anderson **3-8**
Ken-ichi Anjyo **12-3**
Vincent Argio **1-5**
Linda Armijo **4-5**
Johnathon Arons **7-6**
Norman I. Badler **1-3, 5-2**
Scott Baldridge **1-7**
G. Bancroft **8-4**
M. I. Baskes **10-11**
Richard A. Becker **4-4, 4-7**
Jeff Beddow **13-10**
Antal K. Bejczy **13-3**
Chakib Bennis **8-5, 8-6, 9-3, 9-10**
Lee Bertram **5-8**
Jules Bloomenthal **12-1**
Edwin Boender **11-12**
Scott T. Brandon **11-4**
David E. Breen **4-1**
Van Bui-Tran **8-5, 8-6, 9-3, 9-10**
P. G. Buning **8-4**
Susan Bunker **5-1**
Ed Buturela **2-3**
Thomas S. Carman **3-7**
Daniel Carr **10-6**
Lee Carter **1-1, 3-4, 6-4**
Jean-Marc Chautru **8-6**
Hans Chen **9-1**
Rei Cheng **11-9**
Steven Chin **8-7**

I. T. Chiu **8-4**

Raymond C. Cochran **7-6**

Jean-François Colonna **6-3, 7-8, 7-9, 9-9, 10-10, 12-2**

John Compton **2-1**

Donna J. Cox **1-9, 2-7, 2-10, 11-1**

Cheryl Craig **1-1**

Roger A. Crawfis **2-8, 5-4, 5-12**

James A. Crotinger **3-6**

W. Patrick Crowley **3-7**

David de Young **5-5**

Fred Dech **9-6**

Borden D. Dent **13-11**

Bob Dickinson **3-4, 6-4**

Robert R. Dickinson **2-4**

Johan Dijkzeul **11-12**

Jesse W. Driver **5-10**

Tim Duke **12-5**

Kathleen M. Dyer **11-4**

David S. Ebert **5-11, 10-4**

Stephen G. Eick **4-4, 4-7**

Stephen R. Ellis **13-12**

Richard Ellson **2-10**

T. Todd Elvins **3-5, 5-5**

Greg Evans **5-3, 6-7**

M. D. Feit **11-3**

J. A. Fleck Jr. **11-3**

Thomas A. Foley **1-8, 8-9, 8-10, 8-11**

Ben Foster **3-4, 6-4**

Richard Franke **8-10, 8-11**

Verlan K. Gabrielson **2-9, 4-5, 5-3, 5-8, 6-7, 7-3, 10-11**

Catriona Gaeta **2-3, 6-1, 8-7**

Richard S. Gallagher **9-4, 11-7**

Edward Garelis **1-2**

Alexander Gelman **9-5**

Todd Gerhardt **11-7**

A. Globus **8-4**

Chris Gong **6-9, 8-1, 11-9**

Jean-François Gouyet **7-8**

Ned Greene **12-1**

Gary Griffin **1-5**

William H. Grush **4-3**

Dominique Guerillot **9-3, 9-10**

Robert B. Haber **2-11**

Hans Hagen **8-10, 8-11**

Charles A. Hall **7-7**

Bernd Hamann **8-10, 8-11, 11-2, 11-10**

Kenneth G. Hamilton **12-6, 13-8**

Lew Harstead **2-2, 10-6**

Paul Heckbert **12-1**

James L. Helman **3-9, 6-11**

Lambertus Hesselink **3-9, 6-11**

William L. Hibbard **5-9, 6-6, 9-7**

Andrea J. S. Hin **11-12**

Michitaka Hirose **4-8**

Michael Hoon **10-3**

John A. Horvath **13-5**

Ray Idaszak **1-9, 2-7, 2-10**

Hideaki Iwaida **11-5**

E. Ruth Johnson **11-11**

Anke Kamrath **5-5**

Brian C. Kaplan **3-8**

Margarida A. Karahalios **8-8**

Shinichi Kasahara **11-5**

R. J. Kee **4-5**

Stephan R. Keith **9-8**

P. Kelaita **8-4**

Thomas M. Kelleher **11-8**

Peter R. Keller **1-2, 1-4, 2-1, 3-2, 3-7, 7-6**

D. Kerlick **8-4**

Won S. Kim **13-3**

Cetin Kiris **6-9, 8-1**

S. J. Klein **6-10**

Richard I. Klein **7-6, 11-8**

Hyun M. Koh **2-11**

Alice E. Koniges **3-6**

Konstantinos Konstantinides **4-6**

Wolfgang Krueger **9-2, 10-2**

Dochan Kwak **6-9, 8-1**

Bob Lackman **1-1, 3-4, 6-4**

Claude Lallemand **8-5, 8-6, 9-3, 9-10**

David Lane **1-8, 8-9, 8-10, 8-11**

Olin Lathrop **2-6, 6-2, 8-2**

Hae Sung Lee **2-11**

Gisele Legendre **8-5, 8-6, 9-3, 9-10**

Pierre Lemouzy **9-3, 9-10**

Haim Levkowitz **7-10**

Gerald L. Lohse **4-2**

Marshall Long **11-10**

William E. Lorensen **4-1**

Gray Lorig **5-7**

Peter Lulleman **10-8**

Gregory MacNicol **12-4, 12-9**

Bill Mankin **1-1**

John Mareda **4-5**

Nelson Max **5-12**

Steven F. May **10-9**

R. McCabe **8-4**

Michael McCarthy **9-1**

Fred R. McClurg **7-2, 13-2**

Michael W. McGreevy **13-12**

Donna McMillan **11-11**
Gregory McRae **5-7, 7-1**
Fergus J. Merritt **6-10, 8-4**
George L. Mesina **7-7**
T. Mihalisin **2-5**
James V. Miller **4-1**
Eileen O. Miller **4-4, 4-7**
Alok Mitri **9-1**
Robert L. Mobley **3-3, 7-5**
Charles E. Mosher Jr. **11-11**
Vincent A. Mousseau **9-5**
Joop C. Nagtegaal **9-4, 11-7**
Julie Newdoll **9-1**
Hoa D. Nguyen **7-2**
Gregory M. Nielson **1-8, 8-9, 8-10, 8-11, 11-2, 11-10**
Michael Norman **11-1**
Christopher Nuuja **5-7, 7-1**
Robert M. O'Bara **4-1**
S. Obayashi **8-4**
Mark J. Oliver **7-7, 9-5**
David Onstad **1-9, 2-7**
Jean-Louis Pajon **8-5, 8-6, 9-3, 9-10**
Harry Partridge **9-8**
Theo Pavlidis **10-5**
Gary L. Pavlis **3-8**
David Payne **3-5**
Ronald M. Pickett **7-10**
T. Plessel **8-4**
Thomas A. Porsching **7-7**
Frits H. Post **11-12**
Melvin L. Prueitt **1-7, 5-1, 6-5**
John Prusinski **10-8**
Ramamani Ramaraj **8-9, 8-10, 8-11**
A. Ravishankar Rao **6-8, 7-4, 13-4**
Cicely Ridley **3-4, 6-4**
Y. M. Rizk **8-4**
S. K. Robinson **6-10**
Ray Roble **3-4, 6-4**
Stuart Rogers **6-9, 8-1**
Muriel D. Ross **11-9**
Michel Rosso **7-8**
Viviane C. Rupert **1-2**
Armistead Russel **5-7, 7-1**
L. Ted Ryder **1-6**
Daniel J. Sandin **9-6**
L. N. Sankar **6-1**
David A. Santek **5-9, 6-6**

Bernard Sapoval **7-8**
Lori L. Scarlatos **10-5**
Ronald F. Schmucker **13-1, 13-6, 13-7**
Thomas D. Schneider **2-13**
J. Schwegler **2-5**
Sudhanshu K. Semwal **1-6**
Keith Seyler **1-6**
Kerry Shetline **7-10**
Bob Shillito **12-5**
Mark Smith **8-2**
Stuart Smith **7-10, 13-9**
Dale M. Snider **4-3**
P. R. Spalart **6-10**
Tullia Redaelli Spreafico **12-7, 12-8, 12-10**
J. L. Steger **8-4**
Johan Stolk **5-6**
Don Stredney **10-9**
Yasuhito Suenaga **13-13**
A. Sugavanum **6-1**
J. Timlin **2-5**
Arthur W. Toga **8-3, 10-1**
Alade O. Tokuda **8-8**
Michael W. Torello **10-9**
Lloyd A. Treinish **10-7**
Milton Van Dyke **13-4**
Tjark van den Heuvel **11-12**
Theo van Walsum **11-12**
Jarke J. van Wijk **5-6**
Maggie Vancik **1-5**
Joseph Varelas **11-9**
Steven Venema **13-3**
Jack Versloot **11-12**
Donald Vickers **3-1**
James A. Viecelli **1-4**
Kurt L. Wagner **4-3**
Mark C. Wagner **2-12**
Richard A. Ward **3-2**
Yasuhiko Watanabe **13-13**
Susanna Wei **1-3, 5-2**
P. P. Weidhaas **11-3**
Allan R. Wilks **4-4, 4-7**
Dean N. Williams **3-3, 5-12, 7-5**
Mike Wilson **2-3, 6-1, 8-7**
Michael J. Wozny **4-1**
Yaser Yacoob **11-6**
Tetsuji Yamada **5-1**
Michael Stephen Zdepski **10-3**

Glossary

Just when we were getting comfortable with new graphics—that is, "plotting our dumps in color and seeing new and interesting things"— we learned that we were engaging in scientific visualization by rendering our data to an output device having a color gamut, which might cause the color-table implementation of our color scheme to be misrepresented. Adding to the wealth of terminology, scientific visualization not only is creating new words to describe new concepts, but has embraced other disciplines such as the movie industry, the film industry, computer graphics, imaging, CAD/CAM, computer vision, and signal processing, each with its own jargon. The encouraging interchange among experts is complicated by debates about precise meanings for these coinages. But such debate reflects growing pains in a new discipline. Our approach in this glossary is to provide definitions for words in *Visual Cues* and also for words you may encounter when discussing *Visual Cues* with others. Current dictionaries are catalogued at the end for readers who are interested in pursuing the jargon of the industry.

Definitions

A-buffer. A hidden surface algorithm that also addresses anti-aliasing.

Adaptive mesh. A computational mesh that adapts to the changing data values associated with a simulation. The coarseness of the mesh changes according to a predetermined accuracy that the computational algorithm needs in a region.

Algorithm. A procedure; set of rules, commands, instructions; or program instructing the computer to perform some task.

Alpha blend. The merging of two pixel images based on the translucency of the pixels. Can also be used to composite several slices of a volume for a quick volume rendering. The appearance of a resultant volume image is sometimes like looking through smoke to see the opaque pixels of interest. See **11-8** for an example of a volume rendered with the alpha blend.

Animation. A movie. A sequence of related images viewed in rapid succession to see and experience the apparent movement of objects. See also **Viewpoint animation**.

Anti-aliasing. Techniques that minimize the stair-stepping effect sometimes seen when straight lines are plotted. The stair-stepping patterns are sometimes called *jaggies*.

Application. A computer program specific to a scientific problem and generally specific to a discipline.

Application dependent. Describes hardware, procedures, techniques, algorithms, and so on that pertain to or are used specifically with one type of application.

Aspect ratio. The ratio of height to width of a rectangular shape; usually refers to the height and width of an image, such as 4:3.

Bicubic interpolation. Using two piecewise cubic functions to approximate values along a surface.

Bicubic surface. A surface resulting from a mathematical technique for approximating the shape of a surface.

Bounding box. The lines or surface that represent the bounds or physical limit of the data being viewed. See **2-3** or **11-12**.

Brightness. The apparent intensity of light.* Often a synonym for *intensity*. See **Intensity**.

Bump map. A visual technique for making a surface look textured by varying the shading applied to that surface rather than by distorting it.

CAD. Computer-aided design.

CAE. Computer-aided engineering.

CAM. Computer-aided manufacturing.

Cathode ray tube. See **CRT**.

Chroma. See **Saturation**.

Color bar. See **Color scale**. Also refers to the color calibration frame of vertical color bars used in television and video.

Color coding. Objects are colored according to some color scheme; for example, all hot objects are colored red, or a range of values is colored to the visible light spectrum (low values, blue; mid-values, green; high values, red). Also called *data mapping* and *color mapping*. The color representation of data is said to be *coded* if the colors are discrete and *mapped* if the colors are continuous.

Color-filled contours. The color coding to a single color of the range of data values between adjacent isolines. See **3-4**.

Color gamut. The physical constraints that limit the range of produceable colors from an output device.

Color key. A cue that establishes the correspondence between a value or range of values to a color. See **2-9** or **11-4**, Figure A, for examples of color keys. Also called *legend* or *color legend*.

Color lookup table. See **Color table**.

Color mapping. See **Color coding**.

---

* Color and the perception of color is complex and often misunderstood. We recommend *The Psychology of Visual Perception*, by Ralph Norman Haber and Maurice Hershenson (New York: Holt Rinehart and Winston, 1973), which provides a clear and detailed description of hue, saturation, value, brightness, lightness, and intensity.

Color palette. The precision of the color or the number of possible colors available on the hardware or software. Manufacturers often designate the precision of the color as a number of bits, such as 8-bit or 24-bit color. Often used as a synonym for *color table*.

Color scale. A color key represented as a rectangle, usually with smoothly varying color, and labeled tick marks indicating the value associated with the color. **7-6** or **11-2** effectively illustrate color scales.

Color scheme. An abstract concept generally useful to the graphic designer. Describes the predominant colors used in an image.

Color table. A computer's internal array of colors. This array is usually specially defined to accomplish a visual effect. The color table implements the color scheme for the image. See **11-1**, which illustrates the difference in visual appearance achieved by changing the color table. The color table is generally used to color code objects in the image. Often a synonym for *color palette*.

Computational grid. See **Computational mesh**.

Computational lattice. See **Computational mesh**.

Computational mesh. Name for the internal structure with which a computer program arranges and processes data. The computational mesh is usually associated with an application program.

Contextual cue. The element in an image that relates the data representation to the data values or the phenomenon studied. Contextual cues include lines to direct attention; colors to suggest meaning; object positioning to suggest relationships; and reference cues, such as axis labels, grid lines, models, and coastlines.

Contour (line). See **Isoline**.

Contour plot. An image generally consisting of more than one isoline. Often the isolines are labeled by their value or are indexed by letter or symbol associated with a table that identifies the values. See **11-4**, Figure B.

Contrast. The apparent color difference between objects. Black and white have great contrast and shades of gray have less. Saturated blue and yellow have great contrast and shades of green have less.

CRT. Cathode ray tube. Usually the appliance on which a visualization is first seen. Sometimes referred to as VDT. Also called display, screen, tube, monitor, or workstation (screen).

Cubic mesh. A computational mesh of cubes for representing volumetric data.

Cues. See **Contextual cue**.

Cutaway model. A visual method for showing the internal parts of a model, leaving external parts partially visible for reference. See **9-1**.

Cutting plane. A plane for locating and subsequently visualizing values at the intersection of the plane and a 3-D model or volume. The plane is said to cut or slice through the 3-D model or volume. See **2-9** or **9-10**.

Data mapping. See **Color coding**.

Data representation. The mapping of data values to visual symbols or discrete entities. Such symbols or entities can be lines, points, shapes, colored regions, and many others.

Depth cue. A cue for enhancing the illusion of depth. Cues indicating depth include attenuating the contrast, increasing the blurring, shrinking objects, and darkening objects.

Design element. Components of an image, such as line weight, font style, font size, hue, position, orientation, and intensity.

Dials. An interactive hardware or software tool for adjusting a value by turning a knob. The dial is usually calibrated. A common example is a temperature-setting dial for a home oven. Can also be an output mechanism for illustrating a value, such as an analog radio dial.

Diffuse surface. A surface that reflects light evenly in many directions.

Diffusion. The random dispersion of gas molecules.

Direct color. The method for selecting a color by directly setting the intensities of the primary colors on an output medium. Generally used when more than 256 colors are needed in the image. In contrast, see **Indexed color**.

Direction field. See **Vector field**.

Directional glyph. A pointed symbol. A glyph that indicates direction.

Display. See **CRT**. To display; see **Rendering**. Also, to draw directly on the CRT.

Distributed computing. A manner of organizing and executing a computer program so that different parts of the program execute on different computers. The distribution of program parts is meant to execute the parts on types of computers best able to execute each part, thus optimizing program execution.

Dominant visual code. A powerful, hard-to-miss cue.

Exploration. See **Visual exploration**.

Filled contours. See **Color-filled contours**.

Filter. A mathematical algorithm that takes signal or image data as input and then alters them in some prescribed manner. A filter may be used to smooth, enhance, identify edges, and so on, of the incoming data.

Flat-shaded. Shading a polygon with one color. Describes how a surface constructed of polygons is shaded. Flat-shading often reveals the underlying computational mesh. See **9-8**.

Flow path. See **Particle-stream lines**.

Flow ribbons. A ribbonlike object created by juxtaposing several particle-stream lines. The ribbon not only shows the flow path, but graphically exposes any twisting or vortexlike behavior. See **6-1**.

Fractal. A pattern or shape often seen in nature that exhibits self-similarity. Geometric objects described by mathematical rules that obey specified patterns and conditions. Ferns and the universe are claimed to exhibit a fractal pattern.

Gamut. See **Color gamut.**

Geometric model. The geometric description of the objects in the image.

Glyph. An object or symbol for representing data values. Glyphs are generally a way of representing many data values and are sometimes called icons. A common glyph is the arrow, often chosen to represent vector fields. The arrow depicts both speed and direction at a point. See **2-10** or **13-9**.

Gouraud shaded. Smoothly changing a color across a polygon to make the edges of the polygons less apparent. This technique contrasts with flat-shading, which allows the edges to show. See **9-4** and **10-8**.

Graphical representation. Commonly defined as a category of image, such as *x-y* plot, contour plot, and vector plot. See also **Data representation** and **Image**.

Graphics utility. A computer program that performs some general graphics function. An example is a program that creates a video movie from a collection of images. Graphics utilities are often discipline or application specific.

Grid lines. Position cues often used with orthogonal axis scales to more accurately determine position. See **7-2**.

Hidden surface (algorithm). An algorithm for computing at a specified viewpoint the visibility or occlusion of a graphic object by another object.

Hidden-surface removal. See **Hidden surface.**

Highlight. A technique that creates bright areas on surfaces. Also refers to the various cues that make an object stand out or appear more obvious. See also **Shading.**

Histogram equalization. A mathematical technique for grouping data values so that each group has approximately the same number of values. Often used together with a data color coding to color each group differently, especially when the data values cluster around a few values.

Hue. Names the phenomenon commonly called *color*. A narrow band of wavelengths of light gives rise to a specific sensation of hue. Color has three components: hue, saturation (or chroma), and value (or lightness).*

Image. The product of visualization, available for exploration, analysis, or presentation. The image may be represented on any medium, such as CRT, slide, video, or print. Also referred to as a picture, an output, or a plot. See also **Visualization.**

Image element. The visible objects in an image. A basic component of an image, such as an axis scale, a title, contouring lines, a vector field, grid lines, a color key, or fiducial marks.

Indexed color. The method for selecting predefined colors from a color table. The table is said to be referenced by index. In contrast, see **Direct color.**

Intensity (of color). The amount of measured light energy.* Often a synonym for *brightness*. See **Brightness.**

---

* See footnote in above discussion of **Brightness.**

Interactive. Describes behavior of the computer and program designed to respond to a user's request in a timely manner, generally a few seconds or milliseconds. *Interactive* generally implies use of a CRT and mouse or their equivalent.

Interpolation. A mathematical technique for approximating a point when one knows the value at adjacent points.

Intersecting. The placement of two geometric objects so that one passes through the other. The common points are called *points of intersection.*

Isolevel surface. See **Isosurface**.

Isoline. On a surface with data values, a line linking positions of equal value. Sometimes referred to as *contour line* or *isopleth*. Data-specific ways of referring to isolines include *isotherms,* which are equal-temperature lines, and *isobars*, which are equal-pressure lines.

Isosurface. A surface that lies in a volume so that all the values on the surface are equal to some constant value. Sometimes referred to as an *isolevel surface* or *3-D contour*. See **9-4** or **9-8**.

Lattice. See **Computational mesh**.

Lighting (model). Simulating the effect of shining light on 3-D objects. The lighting model includes the position of the light sources and the properties of the light. The definition also covers simulation of how the light reflects off objects.

Lightness (of color). See **Value**.

Logical cube. A volume that has six faces, but is not necessarily a cube.

Logically rectangular grid. A grid consisting of four-sided polygons, not necessarily rectangular. A polygon having four sides. So named because the computer software for accessing a four-sided polygon is logically the same as the software for accessing a rectangle.

Low-pass filter. A filter that smooths or blends large gradients. A low-pass filter tends to make a rough surface smooth.

Marching Cubes. An algorithm for creating a surface of triangles of value from a 3-D volume of values. **8-4** is a visualization made with this algorithm.

Marker particles. Small, discrete graphical objects such as dots used for indicating position or motion. The objects may be identified by color. See **5-1**. *Marker particle* is the experimentalist's name for a small particle released into a fluid to visualize the flow.

Massively parallel computers. Computers combining many (1000 or more) processing units. Expected to be the next generation of supercomputers.

Mesh. See **Computational mesh**.

Modeling. The process, often interactive, for developing a geometric model.

Monitor. See **CRT**.

Motion blur. A visualization technique for indicating motion in a single image. Motion blur mimics the blur registered on still-photograph film when the subject or the camera moves during exposure. See **6-3**.

NTSC. National Television System Committee. Refers to the electronic video-encoding technique.

NURB-based modeling. The NURB or nonuniform rational B-spline is a mathematical technique for approximating surfaces.

Opacity. Property of an object that determines the amount of light that can pass through it. Opacity determines the amount of translucency. An object through which no light can pass is *opaque*; an object through which some light passes is *translucent*.

Output medium. The tangible means for displaying the image. Familiar media include slides, video tape, transparencies, and the CRT screen.

Palette. See **Color palette**.

Pan. To move the camera up, down, right, or left. This panning in turn moves a displayed object down, up, left, or right. The expression is borrowed from the movie industry.

Particle-stream lines. The path taken by a marker particle and indicated by a continuous line. See **5-9**.

Particle trace. A collection of marker particles showing the path taken by the particles. See **5-3**.

Perspective. A visual technique that causes distant objects or parts of objects to look smaller.

Photorealism. The visual goal sought in making a CRT image look like a photograph. See **10-8**.

Picture. See **Image**.

Pixel. Derived from *picture element*. The smallest element or cell in an image; it is generally square. Sometimes refers to a position.

Plot. See **Image**. To plot, see **Render**.

Pseudocolor. False color. Arbitrary assignment and mapping of a color to a data value. Generally, many specially ordered colors are applied to a range of values. A pseudocolored image is often shown with its associated color scale. See **3-3** or **7-6**.

Radiograph. A photographic image recording intensity of x-radiation after it has passed through an object. The image is studied to find the object's relative density. Also called *x-ray*.

Radiosity. A rendering algorithm that handles the diffuse interreflection between the objects in the image. This technique is not fast, but provides a realistic image.

Raster. A 2-D rectangular array of pixels.

Raster point. See **Pixel**. Sometimes considered to be a physical location on a (raster) CRT or a location in the raster array.

Ray cast. A rendering algorithm based on the mathematics of geometric optics. Light rays are propagated from the point representing the eye through the pixel on the viewing plane through the geometric scene. The color of the pixel is determined by following the ray and accumulating light values until encountering an object or distance. Ray casting can be very slow and does not handle shadows caused by interobject reflections.

Ray tracing. A rendering algorithm based on the mathematics of geometric optics. Light rays are propagated through the geometric scene to the pixel on the viewing plane. These rays are used to compute the pixel color by the objects that are "seen" from the camera. Ray tracing can be very slow.

Rectilinear mesh. A computational mesh consisting of rectangles.

Reference axis. A labeled line, often with tick marks, that relates objects in the image to a number on the axis. See **7-2**.

Reflectance. A visual parameter that controls the appearance of objects by the amount of light it reflects.

Reflection. The light that bounces off or reflects from an object.

Render. See **Rendering**.

Rendering (algorithm). The final step that converts the computer's geometric representation of objects or data into an image that can be seen. Usually refers to application of the lighting model to the 3-D objects.

Resolution. The spacing between pixels and the ability to discern adjacent pixels. Sometimes refers to the number of pixels, such as 640 × 480; or dots per inch, such as 300 dpi.

Saturation (of color). Also called *chroma*. The amount of color in terms of its purity, richness, or vividness. A hue becomes less saturated as white light is added to it. Color has three components: hue, saturation (or chroma), and value (or lightness).*

Scalar field. A collection of scalars. A scalar is a quantity that is completely specified by a single number on an appropriate scale.

Scale. See **Reference axis**. Also a verb, meaning magnify or reduce.

Scanned. Describes the input technique of reading an image into the computer.

Scatterplot. Points (dots) plotted that represent the relationship among the values indicated on the axes.

Scientific visualization. An emerging discipline that studies, develops, and classifies ways of visually communicating meaning in data.

Screen. See **CRT**.

Self-similarity. The geometric property indicating that the magnified portion of an image is identical in shape to the original. Fractals have this property.

Semitranslucent. See **Translucent**.

Semitransparent. See **Translucent**.

---

* See footnote in above discussion of **Brightness**.

Shading. The procedure for determining the color of an object based on the object's defined color, surface characteristics, and lighting environment. Part of the rendering process.

Simulation. A computer program that mimics or calculates some scientific, economic, or other real process.

Slice plane. See **Cutting plane**.

Slider bars. An interactive hardware or software tool for adjusting a value by moving a cursor on a rectangular bar. The bar is usually calibrated. See **2-5**.

Smooth-shaded. Visual techniques for smoothly shading a surface. The Gouraud shading algorithm is an example.

Smoothing. Mathematical algorithms for fitting or approximating data points to curves and surfaces and removing wide variations in the data.

Solids. 3-D objects that are described by surfaces. A 3-D solid does not necessarily have its interior described; volumetric data, however, define each point of their interior.

Specular. The reflection of a shiny surface.

Spline. An interpolation technique for creating curves and surfaces that are collections of polynomial or other function segments.

Stereo pairs. Two images created so that when viewed, one by the left eye and the other by the right, the stereopsis depth cue is experienced.

Stereo viewer. Hardware for viewing stereo pairs.

Stereoscopy. Use of stereo to view images.

Still frame. A single image, such as one frame of a movie. The image displayed when the VCR pause is selected.

Surface geometry. The shape of a surface.

Surface normal. A mathematical concept referring to a vector perpendicular to a surface. Determines the orientation of the surface at the normal.

Technique. See **Visual technique**.

Texture. The appearance of a surface. Textures can be rough, smooth, irregular, and so on.

Texture mapped. The visual technique of drawing textures on the surface of objects. See **5-4**.

Three-dimensional contour. See **Isosurface**.

Time-history plot. Plot in which one of the axes is time.

Topological visualization. Visualization of structures. See **3-9** and **6-11**.

Translucent. Describes the property that allows light to partially pass through and partially reflect. Translucency has the effect of making the translucent area appear smoky or cloudlike, thus revealing objects behind. See **8-2** or **11-9**, Figure B.

Transparent. Describes the property of an object that allows light to pass through. Transparency has the effect of making the transparent object (or part of an object) invisible. Often a synonym for translucency. See **9-3**.

Value. The lightness or darkness of the hue (color). A hue is lighter or darker depending on the perceived brightness. Color has three components: hue, saturation (or chroma), and value (or lightness).*

VCR. Video cassette recorder.

VDT. A video display terminal. See **CRT**.

Vector field. Also called *direction-field*. A collection of vectors. Generally indicates flow. Usually represented as a field of arrows, as in **6-4**, but can be represented by other directional glyphs, including "paper planes" as in **6-2** or as "comet tails" in **6-6**.

Vertex. The points used to describe a polygon.

Vertical scale. A vertical reference axis.

VHS. Video home system. Refers to the video electronic encoding.

Viewpoint animation. An animation in which the object remains fixed and we view it from different positions; also called *flying around the object*.

Virtual reality. Creating a visual experience so realistic or captivating that the viewer treats it as real. See **4-8**. The "hand" that the viewer controls may also be a humanlike figure or cartoon character.

Visual. An image.

Visual exploration. The interactive adjustment of contextual cues and data representations of a data set. Usually involves visually scanning the data to identify relationships, abnormalities, and features.

Visual representation. See **Visualization**.

Visual (visualization) technique. Any rule, method, procedure, or algorithm used to construct an image. Techniques include data-representation algorithms, contextual cues, and data-conversion techniques.

Visualization. An image constructed to convey information about data. See also **Scientific visualization**.

Visualization goal. The meaning one hopes to derive from an image and, if appropriate, to communicate to others about data.

Volume. A closed 3-D space. A 3-D data set where all points of the volume have a defined value.

Volume rendering. See **Volume visualization**.

Volume visualization. Visual techniques for creating images from the data in a volume. Visual techniques for simultaneously seeing all the data in a volume.

Volumetric data. Data filling a volume. See **Volume**.

---

* See footnote in above discussion of **Brightness**.

Voxel. A volume element. The smallest element, cell, or cube of a three-dimensional volume. The name, an extension of *pixel*, also refers to a location within a volume.

VTR. Video tape recorder.

Wire-frame model. A model (shape) described by lines. The shape consisting of lines looks like a wire frame, hence the name.

Workstation (screen). See **CRT**.

X-ray. See **Radiograph**.

Z-buffer. A 3-D rendering technique that is very fast but does not easily handle translucency and reflections.

Zoom. A geometric transformation that enlarges or reduces the displayed object. *Magnify* or *zoom in* are other terms that denote enlargement; *zoom out* means to reduce; *scale* indicates a change in size.

References   Roy Latham, *The Dictionary of Computer Graphics Technology and Applications*; (New York: Springer-Verlag, 1991).

Robi Roncarelli, *The Computer Animation Dictionary*; (New York: Springer-Verlag, 1989).

John Vince, *The Language of Computer Graphics*; (New York: Van Nostrand Reinhold, 1990).

Index

To compile this simple, single-level index, we used Microsoft Word's Index Entry command to list selected words, phrases, and concepts in the text. The appendixes also provide page references to information in *Visual Cues*.

3-D block diagram   81
3-D glyphs   61, 62, 104
3-D projector   14
3-D reconstruction   74, 117, 136, 144
3-D reference (axis)   47, 70, 106, 117, 120, 121, 138, 153, 170
3-D vector 59, 96, 98, 104, 180

A

accretion   110
acetylcholine receptor protein structure   126
actions safe and unsafe   45
adaptive mesh   154
additive color   31
aesthetic rules   23
AIDS   131
air traffic   180
air-pollution   82
air-quality   53
airflow   95
airfoil   94
airline rate structure   179
algorithm dynamics   79
alpha-blend   154
altitude   49
ambient light   27, 32
amino acid   64
amplitude of motion   72
analysis graphics   7
angular position   169
animation   17, 18, 19
annotation   22
antiquarks   96
architectural design   138, 151
artificial heart   102, 115
aspect ratio   17
astrophysical jet   147
atmosphere   43, 68, 97, 132

atmospheric models   109
attenuating contrast   159
AZT   131

B

background   23, 27, 28, 32
background color   15
bar chart   45, 56, 64, 65
base grid   83
bathymetry   142
bicubic interpolation   129, 153
black and white   20, 21
blood cells   115
blood flow   102
Bloomenthal's method   111, 130
body posture   83
bounding box   99
bounding faces   60
boxcar averaging   141
brain   117, 136
brightness   50, 151
bulletin board   38
bump map   59, 85, 159
bump map isoline   59

C

callouts   76
carbon monoxide   48, 53
Cartesian plot   66
chaos   113
chemical reactions   78
chemical vapor deposition   78, 84, 100
chemical-bonds   47
climate   43, 85, 93, 109
clone   63
cloud cover   132
cloudiness   93
cloudlike features   47

clouds 93, 161
CMYK model 15, 27, 31
coherence 101
coherent structures 70
collision avoidance 180
color 20
color bands 30, 68, 73, 95, 97, 151
color differences 26
color discrimination 32
color encoding of the video 16
color formulation 26
color illusions 29
color key 48, 60, 121, 151
color scheme 27
color selection 26
color table 29, 110
color wheel 27, 29
color-filled polygons 76
color-output media 31
colored trace 45
complementary colors 29
complex image 23
composite image 78
compressive stress 55
computational fluid dynamic 86
computational mesh 54, 111
computed tomography (CT) 74, 114, 137, 157
computer availability 65
concurrent processes 81
concurrent software 81
conducting rings 98
conductors 98
connectivity 112, 134
context 162, 163, 165
contextual cues 6, 10, 11, 12
contour-banding 97
contrast 28, 29, 30, 31, 32
contrasting background 28
convey continuity 29
cool colors 28
corn borers 51, 58
cornfield 51
cortex 91
cosmic jet 69, 86
crack propagation 62
crisis event 90
critical angle 94
critical level 29
critical points 73, 104, 108
critical value 95, 107
CRT 15
cutaway 116, 126
cutting plane 135, 157
cycle 53, 65, 67
cyclic behavior 67
cyclical events 65
cyclone 90

D

data 4
data conversion 9
data format 8
data structure 8
data-conversion algorithms 8
data-representation 6, 10, 11
delineate shape 29
density 46, 48, 58, 66, 69, 71, 86, 92, 99, 126, 132, 133, 137, 147, 154, 157, 175
dependent variable 10
depth 96
depth cueing 87
design principles 23
determining complexity 24
difference 50
differential equations 108
diffuse 138
diffusion 112, 134, 152
dimensions 9
dimethyl sulfide 121
Diophantine equation 52
direct color 29
direction 61, 77, 84, 98, 99, 180
directional glyphs 95
discern edges 29
discharge 141
dislocation 146
dispersion 158
displacement 72
dissipation 103
distribution 48, 56, 64, 130, 135, 153
DNA 63
dominant visual codes 178
duration 65
dynamical systems 73, 104, 113

E

earth 85, 93, 142
earth movement 120
earthquake 39, 72, 77
eddies 111
El Niño 67
elastic wave pattern 62
electric field 54, 106, 169
electric-charge 47
electrical discharge 141
electromagnetic energy 174, 175
electromagnetic field 175
electron density 121, 131, 133
electron micrographs 155
electropotential field 54
electrostatic potential 150
engine cylinder head 153
epicenter 40
expansions 118
experiential cues 164
exploration graphics 7

F

faceted shading 61
fault line 120
fiducials 173
field effects 127
film 15
flame 156
flat shading 61
flight path 180
flow dynamics 87
flow field 87
flow patterns 147, 172
flow ribbons 94
flows 61, 73, 90, 94, 100, 101, 115, 118, 139
fluid flow 60, 61, 84, 92, 101, 103, 104, 108, 111, 119, 128, 135, 147, 154, 158
fluid motion 172
format conversion 8
fractal aggregate 134
fractal geometry 160
frequency 64, 65
fuzziness 96

G

gas 92
gas concentrations 57
gas flow 139
Gaussian elimination 79
geographic features 161
geomagnetic storm 68, 97
geometric model 74
geometrically deformed model (GDM) 74
geostatistical 128
global climate 43, 85
global heating 132
globins 64
glucose utilization rate 117
gluons 96
glyphs 61, 104, 177, 178
Gouraud shading 118, 129, 143, 166
gradients 59, 129, 150
grayscale 20
guide bracket 55

H

hair 181
hand movements 83
hand strength 83
haze 127, 159
HDTV 14
heat 85, 93
heat sink 130
heat source 130
heat transfer 60, 84, 100, 106
helium bubble 146
helium shell flash 66
hidden-surface 148
highlights 45, 83, 88, 90, 102, 104, 127, 132, 164, 168, 170

histogram 56
histogram equalization 53, 149
horizontal ground motion 72
HSV 27
hue 27, 46
hurricanes 85

I

I-nets 91
ice 109
icons 76
illumination 151
image components 20
image distortion 17
image-smoothing 141
imaging 8
incompressible fluid 111
independent variable 10
indexed color 29
information flow 75
inner ear 155
intensities 149
interactive analysis tool 63
intergalactic medium 86
Internet 38
interpolation 50
intersection 119, 135
interstellar cloud 154
ionized stellar plasma 66
iron protein molecule 127
irregular surface 124, 125
isodensity surfaces 127
isolines 43, 67, 68, 95, 109, 111, 123, 125, 133, 150
isoplot 89, 95, 105, 111, 149, 175
isosurface 88, 90, 99, 103, 121, 126, 127, 128, 131, 129, 130, 133, 135, 153

K

kinetic energy density 62

L

label 22
labeled bars 83
land 109
landscape 160, 161
laser 149
levels of presentation 45
light spectrum 30
lighting 59, 62, 73, 95, 98, 116, 126, 131, 133, 138, 143, 151, 165
line width 77
lines 21
lithofacies 120, 128
long-wave radiation 93
low-pass filter 96

M

macroscopic 113
magnetic field 69, 98
magnetic lines 98

magnetic resonance imaging (MRI)   74, 114, 136, 144, 177

magnetohydrodynamics   70, 147

magnitude   98

Mandelbrot set   113

marching cubes   118, 129, 130, 135, 153

marker particles   84, 100

Mars   143

material-mix   44

matrix   79

measured data   83

medical surgery   137

membrane density   126

memory aid   64

mesh plot   54

microelectronics processing   60, 84

microscopic   113

microsporidium   51, 58

mixture   57

mnemonic device   112

moiré   107

molding process   61

molecular bonds   133

molecular orbitals   131

molecule   47

Mollweide   40

motion   72

motion blur   96, 99

multimedia   14

multiparameter graytone   114

multiparameter image data   114

multivariate   56

multivariate data   10, 178

muscles   157

muscular dystrophy   63

N

narration   18

natural scenes   160, 161

Navier-Stokes   60, 94, 100, 103

negative space   23

nerve cells   126

nested bounding boxes   83

netnews   38

network   77, 80

network analysis   80

network diagram   75

network traffic   80

neural elements   155

neurons   91

neutron star   110

nickel   146

nimbus-7   43

nitrogen oxides   105

nodes   108

nuclear energy   66

numeric representation   11

nurb-based modeling   176

NutraSweet   47

O

ocean floor   142

oil platform   116

oil reservoir   57, 119, 120, 128

oil saturation   57

oil shale   82

oil wells   135

Omnimax   14

opacity   86, 92, 93

organics   105

orientation   24, 54, 61, 95, 101, 176

orientation field   101, 108

outgoing long-wave radiation   85

output media   14

ozone   43, 88, 105

P

Pacific Ocean   67

paper   15

particle plot   82

particle stream lines   94

particle traces   72, 84, 90, 102, 104

particulate density   82

path   45, 89, 102

patterns   107, 177, 179

peer graphics   7

perception of color   27

periodic event   53

permeability   119

personal graphics   7

perspective   45, 47, 59, 82, 83, 87, 88, 89, 90, 95, 96, 98, 99, 103, 116, 117, 120, 123, 132, 135, 136, 146, 162, 167

perspective translucent plane   78

perspective-bounding box   62

pest control   51, 58

phase portraits   108

phenomenon   6, 11

photorealism   143, 181

pixel values   44, 50

planar surface   117

plasma globe   141

plastic   61

plumes   158

point cloud   157

pollution   48, 158

polymer chains   145

population dynamics   51, 58

porous substance   134

position   45, 180

positron emission tomography (PET),   114

posture   45, 83

presentation graphics   7

pressure   87, 95, 103, 118

probability   122, 133

process   78

projecting color   32

properties   64

protein density   126

pseudocolor   44, 46, 47, 53, 54, 59, 67, 72, 88, 89, 93, 94, 97, 106, 107, 109, 110, 115, 116, 118, 119, 121, 122, 143, 147, 149, 150, 151, 157
psi-function   127
pulsar   110

Q

quarks   96

R

radiograph   44, 117
radiosity   91
ray casting   50, 69, 157
ray tracing   88, 105, 151
realism   136, 141, 151, 159, 160
recurring patterns   65
red-green color blindness   27
redundantly encoded   10
reference map   85, 88, 93
reflectances   138
reflection   78, 165, 167
relationships   75
relative altitude   180
relative data values   123
relative density   46
relative size   43
relative speed   84, 95, 100, 180
relative temperature   100
rendering   14
rendering images to film   16
rendering to a transparency   15
resolution   16, 18
RGB   15, 27, 31
ribbons   94
rigidity   145
robot   171

S

saddles   108
safe actions   45
sans-serif typefaces   22
saturated colors   27, 28, 46
scan-line algorithm   144
scan line A-buffer   139
scatterplot   52
Schrödinger equation   127, 133
scientific visualization   3
sea surface   67
seismic   39
seismic-wave   72
seismometers   72
self-focusing   149
self-shadowing   139
self-similarity   113
semi-globalized spectral synthesis   161
semiconductor   54
semitransparent   57
sequence logo   64
sequence of images   78
serif typefaces   22

shading   73, 75, 82, 90, 96, 117, 127, 132, 134, 136, 170
shadow   78, 82, 87, 117, 142, 164, 165, 168
Shannon information   64
shape   74, 127, 144, 150
shear magnitude   95
shear stress   115
shock   46, 71, 118, 154
shock-tube   71
shuttle   118
slice   54, 60, 69, 70, 118, 120, 121, 122
slice plane   60, 120, 121
slide projectors   32
slider bars   56
smooth shading   61, 155
sounds   18, 122
spatial behavior   87
spatial decay   127
specular reflection   117, 136, 138
speed   84, 87, 94, 99, 100
spherical projection   40
steam   139
stereo CRT   14
strain energy density   62
streak camera   71
stream tube   87
strength of vortex   92
stress   55, 67, 89, 116, 129
structure   107, 120, 121, 122, 133, 134, 137, 147, 148, 149, 154, 156, 157, 172
structure conversion   9
stylized model   174, 175
subtractive color   31
successive magnification   113
sulfur dioxide   53
summary station   39
surface charge   106
surface distortion   72
surface geometry   117
surface height   57, 59
surface normal   87
surface particles   87
surface plot   72, 105, 106, 140
surface stress   116
surface values   123, 124, 125
system behavior   76

T

table-based shadowing   139
technique   4
tectonic plates   40
telephone traffic   77, 80
temperature   53, 66, 67, 68, 84, 87, 89, 97, 106, 109, 130, 153
temporal behaviors   87
tensile stress   55
tensor   55
ternary color key   57
terrain   48, 90, 119, 132, 140
textile surfaces   181

texture   59, 85, 98, 138, 142, 159, 161, 181
thunderstorm   99
time chart   81
time comparison   88
time history   66, 67, 70, 71, 73, 74, 81, 84, 86
tissues   157
tokamak fusion reactor   70, 178
topography   49, 82, 142, 143
total ozone mapping spectrometer (TOMS)   43
traffic volume   80
translucency   47, 48, 54, 55, 88, 90, 93, 99, 103, 123, 124, 129, 132, 153, 156, 158
transparency   15, 32, 57, 70, 87, 102, 115, 116, 128, 130, 138
transport theory   127, 137
tumor   177
turbulence   46, 92, 103, 139
type styles   22
typeface   22

U

underwater sounds   122
unsafe actions   45
unstructured grid   54

V

value   27
vector bump   59
velocity   54, 59, 60, 61, 73, 85, 92, 95, 96, 97, 98, 99, 103, 110
vertical motion   72
video   14, 15
virtual cathode oscillator   150
virtual reality   14, 81

visible light spectrum   11
visualization   3
visualization goal   7
vivid colors   16
vortex fall-off power   92
vortices   92, 102, 103, 147, 172
vorticity   46, 70, 90, 111, 115
voxels   70

W

water saturation   135
water vapor   99
wave pattern   62
wax transfer   32
weight lifted   45
weld   89
welding tip   89
window in time   72
wire frame   55, 136, 157, 171
word recognition   22
word shape   22

X

x-y plot   72, 105, 174

Y

yield surface   89
Yin-Yang magnet   173

Z

Z-buffer   160, 161
zooming   52, 79, 113